THE DAILY GOD BOOK™
A YEAR WITH JESUS

THE DAILY GOD BOOK™

A YEAR WITH JESUS

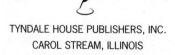

TYNDALE HOUSE PUBLISHERS, INC.
CAROL STREAM, ILLINOIS

Visit Tyndale's exciting Web site at www.tyndale.com.

TYNDALE and Tyndale's quill logo are registered trademarks of Tyndale House Publishers, Inc.

The Daily God Book is a trademark of Tyndale House Publishers, Inc.

The Daily God Book A Year with Jesus

Copyright © 2000 by The Livingstone Corporation. All rights reserved.

Cover marble texture copyright © by duncan1890/iStockphoto. All rights reserved.

Designed by Mark Anthony Lane II

Previously published as *One Year with Jesus* by Tyndale House Publishers, Inc., under ISBN 978-0-8423-3461-7.

The Daily God Book A Year with Jesus first published in 2010 by Tyndale House Publishers, Inc.

Notes are adapted from the *Life Application Bible*, copyright © 1988 by Tyndale House Publishers, Inc.

The Bible text used in *The Daily God Book A Year with Jesus* is taken from the *Holy Bible*, New Living Translation, copyright © 1996, 2004, 2007 by Tyndale House Foundation. Used by permission of Tyndale House Publishers, Inc., Carol Stream, Illinois 60188. All rights reserved.

Produced for Tyndale House Publishers with the assistance of The Livingstone Corporation. James C. Galvin, Linda Chaffee Taylor, David R. Veerman, project staff.

ISBN 978-1-4143-1930-8

Printed in the United States of America

16   15   14   13   12   11   10

7   6   5   4   3   2   1

INTRODUCTION

The Daily God Book A Year with Jesus has been prepared especially for those who want to learn more about Jesus and grow closer to him throughout the year. Each day contains a selection from the four Gospels, a Life Application note, and an informational note.

You can deepen your study by looking up parallel passages that are noted for certain readings. The Life Application notes provide insight and encouragement to take action. The informational notes provide interesting background and helpful explanations.

Although the daily readings begin January 1, you can easily start your reading with today's date. The structure of the daily format is not meant to confine you; it is simply there to help you if you enjoy the daily method. No matter how you approach your reading, *The Daily God Book A Year with Jesus* will help you learn more about Jesus and grow closer to him.

Luke's purpose in writing

Many people have set out to write accounts about the events that have been fulfilled among us. They used the eyewitness reports circulating among us from the early disciples. Having carefully investigated everything from the beginning, I also have decided to write a careful account for you, most honorable Theophilus, so you can be certain of the truth of everything you were taught.   LUKE 1:1-4

GOD'S TRUTH

As a medical doctor, Luke knew the importance of being thorough. He used his skills in observation and analysis to carefully investigate the stories about Jesus. His diagnosis? The gospel of Jesus Christ is true! You can read the accounts of Jesus' life with confidence that they are factual and reliable. Because the gospel is founded on historical truth, our spiritual growth must involve careful, disciplined, and thorough investigation of God's Word so that we can understand how God has acted in history. Christianity doesn't say, "Close your eyes and believe," but rather, "Check it out for yourself." The Bible encourages you to investigate its claims thoroughly (John 1:46; 21:24; Acts 17:11-12) because your conclusion about Jesus is a life-and-death matter. Check out the evidence.

The Gospel of Luke tells Jesus' story from Luke's unique perspective as a Gentile, a physician, and the first historian of the early church. Though not an eyewitness of Jesus' ministry, Luke nevertheless was concerned that eyewitness accounts be preserved accurately.

God became a human being

In the beginning the Word already existed. The Word was with God, and the Word was God. He existed in the beginning with God. God created everything through him, and nothing was created except through him. The Word gave life to everything that was created, and his life brought light to everyone. The light shines in the darkness, and the darkness can never extinguish it. JOHN 1:1-5

READ AND BELIEVE

What Jesus taught and what he did are tied inseparably to who he is. John shows Jesus as fully human and fully God. Although Jesus took upon himself full humanity and lived as a man, he never ceased to be the eternal God who has always existed, the Creator and Sustainer of all things, and the source of eternal life. This is the truth about Jesus and the foundation of all truth. If we cannot or do not believe this basic truth, we will not have enough faith to trust our eternal destiny to him. That is why John wrote this Gospel—to build faith and confidence in Jesus Christ so that we may believe that he truly was and is the Son of God (John 20:30-31). You can trust John, an eyewitness to what Jesus said and did. You can believe in Christ, God's Son.

Christ created the world, but the people he created didn't recognize him (John 1:10). Even the Jews rejected him, although they had been chosen by God to prepare the rest of the world for the Messiah (John 1:11) and although the entire Old Testament pointed to his coming.

God became a human being

God sent a man, John the Baptist, to tell about the light so that everyone might believe because of his testimony. John himself was not the light; he was simply a witness to tell about the light. The one who is the true light, who gives light to everyone, was coming into the world.

He came into the very world he created, but the world didn't recognize him. He came to his own people, and even they rejected him. But to all who believed him and accepted him, he gave the right to become children of God. They are reborn—not with a physical birth resulting from human passion or plan, but a birth that comes from God. JOHN 1:6-13

A NEW PERSON

All who welcome Jesus Christ as Lord of their lives are reborn spiritually, receiving new life from God. Through faith in Christ, we are changed from the inside out— as God helps us rearrange our attitudes, desires, and motives. Being born makes you physically alive and places you in your parents' family (John 1:13). Being born of God makes you spiritually alive and puts you in God's family (John 1:12). Have you asked Christ to make you a new person? This fresh start in life is available to all who believe in Christ.

John wrote to believers everywhere, both Jews and non-Jews (Gentiles). As one of Jesus' twelve disciples, John was an eyewitness to Jesus' ministry. His book is not a biography (as is the book of Luke); it is a thematic presentation of Jesus' life.

January 4

God became a human being

So the Word became human and made his home among us. He was full of unfailing love and faithfulness. And we have seen his glory, the glory of the Father's one and only Son.

John testified about him when he shouted to the crowds, "This is the one I was talking about when I said, 'Someone is coming after me who is far greater than I am, for he existed long before me.'"

From his abundance we have all received one gracious blessing after another. For the law was given through Moses, but God's unfailing love and faithfulness came through Jesus Christ. No one has ever seen God. But the unique One, who is himself God, is near to the Father's heart. He has revealed God to us.

JOHN 1:14-18

GOD AND MAN

When Christ "became human and made his home among us," he became (1) *the perfect teacher*—in Jesus' life we see how God thinks and therefore how we should think (Philippians 2:5-11); (2) *the perfect example*—as a model of what we are to become, he shows us how to live and gives us the power to live that way (1 Peter 2:21); and (3) *the perfect sacrifice*—Jesus came as a sacrifice for all sins, and his death satisfied God's requirements for the removal of sin (Colossians 1:15-23). Keep your focus on Christ.

When Christ was conceived and born, God became a man. He was not part man and part God; he was completely human and completely divine. Christ was the perfect expression of God in human form. The two most common errors people make about Jesus are to minimize his humanity or to minimize his divinity. Jesus is both God and man.

The ancestors of Jesus

Jesus was about thirty years old when he began his public ministry.

Jesus was known as the son of Joseph. Joseph was the son of Heli. Heli was the son of Matthat. Matthat was the son of Levi. Levi was the son of Melki. Melki was the son of Jannai. Jannai was the son of Joseph. Joseph was the son of Mattathias. Mattathias was the son of Amos. Amos was the son of Nahum. Nahum was the son of Esli. Esli was the son of Naggai. Naggai was the son of Maath. Maath was the son of Mattathias. Mattathias was the son of Semein. Semein was the son of Josech. Josech was the son of Joda. Joda was the son of Joanan. Joanan was the son of Rhesa. Rhesa was the son of Zerubbabel. Zerubbabel was the son of Shealtiel. Shealtiel was the son of Neri. Neri was the son of Melki. Melki was the son of Addi. Addi was the son of Cosam. Cosam was the son of Elmadam. Elmadam was the son of Er. Er was the son of Joshua. Joshua was the son of Eliezer. Eliezer was the son of Jorim. Jorim was the son of Matthat. Matthat was the son of Levi. Levi was the son of Simeon. Simeon was the son of Judah. Judah was the son of Joseph. Joseph was the son of Jonam. Jonam was the son of Eliakim. Eliakim was the son of Melea. Melea was the son of Menna. Menna was the son of Mattatha. Mattatha was the son of Nathan. Nathan was the son of David. David was the son of Jesse. Jesse was the son of Obed. Obed was the son of Boaz. Boaz was the son of Salmon. Salmon was the son of Nahshon. Nahshon was the son of Amminadab. Amminadab was the son of Admin. Admin was the son of Arni. Arni was the son of Hezron. Hezron was the son of Perez. Perez was the son of Judah. Judah was the son of Jacob. Jacob was the son of Isaac. Isaac was the son of Abraham. Abraham was the son of Terah. Terah was the son of Nahor. Nahor was the son of Serug. Serug was the son of Reu. Reu was the son of Peleg. Peleg was the son of Eber. Eber was the son of Shelah. Shelah was the son of Cainan. Cainan was the son of Arphaxad. Arphaxad was the son of Shem. Shem was the son of Noah. Noah was the son of Lamech. Lamech was the son of Methuselah. Methuselah was the son of Enoch. Enoch was the son of Jared. Jared was the son of Mahalalel. Mahalalel was the son of Kenan. Kenan was the son of Enosh. Enosh was the son of Seth. Seth was the son of Adam. Adam was the son of God.

LUKE 3:23-38 *(see also Matthew 1:1-17)*

GOD'S TIMING

Imagine the Savior of the world working in a small-town carpenter's shop until he was thirty years old! It seems incredible that Jesus would have been content to remain in Nazareth all that time, but he patiently trusted his heavenly Father's timing for his life and ministry. Priests began their ministry at thirty (Numbers 4:3), Joseph began serving the king of Egypt at thirty (Genesis 41:46), and David was thirty years old when he began to reign over Judah (2 Samuel 5:4). Age thirty, then, was a good time to begin an important task in the Jewish culture. Like Jesus, we need to resist the temptation to jump ahead of the Spirit's direction. Are you waiting and wondering what your next step should be? Don't jump ahead—trust God's timing.

Matthew's genealogy goes back to Abraham and shows that Jesus was related to all Jews. Luke's genealogy goes back to Adam, showing that Jesus is related to all human beings. This is consistent with Luke's picture of Jesus as the Savior of the whole world.

An angel promises the birth of John to Zechariah

When Herod was king of Judea, there was a Jewish priest named Zechariah. He was a member of the priestly order of Abijah, and his wife, Elizabeth, was also from the priestly line of Aaron. Zechariah and Elizabeth were righteous in God's eyes, careful to obey all of the Lord's commandments and regulations. They had no children because Elizabeth was unable to conceive, and they were both very old.

One day Zechariah was serving God in the Temple, for his order was on duty that week. As was the custom of the priests, he was chosen by lot to enter the sanctuary of the Lord and burn incense. While the incense was being burned, a great crowd stood outside, praying.

While Zechariah was in the sanctuary, an angel of the Lord appeared to him, standing to the right of the incense altar. Zechariah was shaken and overwhelmed with fear when he saw him. But the angel said, "Don't be afraid, Zechariah! God has heard your prayer. Your wife, Elizabeth, will give you a son, and you are to name him John. You will have great joy and gladness, and many will rejoice at his birth, for he will be great in the eyes of the Lord. He must never touch wine or other alcoholic drinks. He will be filled with the Holy Spirit, even before his birth. And he will turn many Israelites to the Lord their God. He will be a man with the spirit and power of Elijah. He will prepare the people for the coming of the Lord. He will turn the hearts of the fathers to their children, and he will cause those who are rebellious to accept the wisdom of the godly."

Zechariah said to the angel, "How can I be sure this will happen? I'm an old man now, and my wife is also well along in years."

Then the angel said, "I am Gabriel! I stand in the very presence of God. It was he who sent me to bring you this good news! But now, since you didn't believe what I said, you will be silent and unable to speak until the child is born. For my words will certainly be fulfilled at the proper time."   LUKE 1:5-20

LET GOD DO THE IMPOSSIBLE

While Zechariah was burning incense on the altar, he was also praying, perhaps for a son or for the coming of the Messiah. In either case, God answered his prayer. He would soon have a son, who would prepare the way for the Messiah. God answers prayer in his own way and in his own time. He worked in an "impossible" situation—Zechariah's wife was barren—to bring about the fulfillment of all the prophecies concerning the Messiah. If you want to have your prayers answered, you must be open to what God can do in impossible situations. And you must wait for God to work in his way, in his time.

An angel promises the birth of John to Zechariah

Meanwhile, the people were waiting for Zechariah to come out of the sanctuary, wondering why he was taking so long. When he finally did come out, he couldn't speak to them. Then they realized from his gestures and his silence that he must have seen a vision in the sanctuary.

When Zechariah's week of service in the Temple was over, he returned home. Soon afterward his wife, Elizabeth, became pregnant and went into seclusion for five months. "How kind the Lord is!" she exclaimed. "He has taken away my disgrace of having no children." LUKE 1:21-25

FAITHFULNESS

Zechariah and Elizabeth were faithful people, yet they were suffering. At that time some Jews did not believe in a bodily resurrection, so their hope of immortality rested on their children. In addition, children would care for their elderly parents, and they added to the family's financial security and social status. Children were considered a blessing, and childlessness was seen as a curse. Zechariah and Elizabeth had been childless for many years, and at this time they were too old to expect any change in their situation. They felt humiliated and hopeless. But God was waiting for the right time to encourage them and take away their disgrace. If you are facing difficult times, remain faithful to God. One day, in this world or in the world to come, God will take away your pain and replace it with his glory and peace!

The people were waiting outside for Zechariah to come out and pronounce the customary blessing (Numbers 6:24-26) upon them.

An angel promises the birth of Jesus to Mary

In the sixth month of Elizabeth's pregnancy, God sent the angel Gabriel to Nazareth, a village in Galilee, to a virgin named Mary. She was engaged to be married to a man named Joseph, a descendant of King David. Gabriel appeared to her and said, "Greetings, favored woman! The Lord is with you!"

Confused and disturbed, Mary tried to think what the angel could mean. "Don't be afraid, Mary," the angel told her, "for you have found favor with God! You will conceive and give birth to a son, and you will name him Jesus. He will be very great and will be called the Son of the Most High. The Lord God will give him the throne of his ancestor David. And he will reign over Israel forever; his Kingdom will never end!" LUKE 1:26-33

FEELING INADEQUATE
Mary was young, poor, female—all characteristics that, to the people of her day, would make her seem unusable by God for any major task. But God chose Mary for one of the most important acts of obedience he has ever demanded of anyone. You may feel that your ability, experience, or education makes you an unlikely candidate for God's service. Don't limit God's choices. He can use you if you trust him.

Nazareth, Joseph and Mary's hometown, was a long way from Jerusalem, the center of Jewish life and worship. Located near a major trade route, Nazareth may have been frequently visited by Gentile merchants and Roman soldiers. Jesus was born in Bethlehem but grew up in Nazareth. Nevertheless, the people of Nazareth would reject him as the Messiah (Luke 4:22-30).

An angel promises the birth of Jesus to Mary

Mary asked the angel, "But how can this happen? I am a virgin."

The angel replied, "The Holy Spirit will come upon you, and the power of the Most High will overshadow you. So the baby to be born will be holy, and he will be called the Son of God. What's more, your relative Elizabeth has become pregnant in her old age! People used to say she was barren, but she has conceived a son and is now in her sixth month. For nothing is impossible with God."

Mary responded, "I am the Lord's servant. May everything you have said about me come true." And then the angel left her. LUKE 1:34-38

WILLING OBEDIENCE

A young unmarried girl who became pregnant risked disaster. Unless the father of the child agreed to marry her, she would probably remain unmarried for life. If her own father rejected her, she could be forced into begging or prostitution in order to earn her living. Mary, with her story about being made pregnant by the Holy Spirit, also risked being considered crazy. Still Mary said, despite the possible risks, "May everything you have said about me come true." When Mary made that statement, she didn't know about the tremendous opportunity she would have. She knew only that God was asking her to serve him, and she willingly obeyed. Don't wait to see the bottom line before offering your life to God. Offer yourself willingly, even when the outcome seems difficult.

Jesus was born without the sin that had entered the world through Adam. He was born holy, just as Adam was created sinless. In contrast to Adam, who disobeyed God, Jesus obeyed God and was thus able to face sin's consequences in our place and make us acceptable to God (Romans 5:14-19).

Mary visits Elizabeth

A few days later Mary hurried to the hill country of Judea, to the town where Zechariah lived. She entered the house and greeted Elizabeth. At the sound of Mary's greeting, Elizabeth's child leaped within her, and Elizabeth was filled with the Holy Spirit.

Elizabeth gave a glad cry and exclaimed to Mary, "God has blessed you above all women, and your child is blessed. Why am I so honored, that the mother of my Lord should visit me? When I heard your greeting, the baby in my womb jumped for joy. You are blessed because you believed that the Lord would do what he said." LUKE 1:39-45

GOD DELIVERS

When told he would have a son, Zechariah doubted the angel's word. From a human perspective, his doubt is understandable—but with God, anything is possible. Although Zechariah and Elizabeth seemed long past the age of childbearing, God gave them a child! It is easy to doubt or misunderstand what God wants to do in our lives. Even God's people sometimes make the mistake of trusting their intellect or experience rather than God. When you are tempted to think that one of God's promises is impossible, remember his work throughout history. God's power is not confined by our narrow perspectives or bound by human limitations. Trust him completely.

***

Apparently the Holy Spirit had told Elizabeth that Mary's child was the Messiah because Elizabeth called her young relative "the mother of my Lord" as she greeted her. Elizabeth's greeting must have strengthened Mary's faith. Mary's pregnancy may have seemed impossible, but her wise relative believed in the Lord's faithfulness and rejoiced in Mary's blessed condition.

***

Mary visits Elizabeth

Mary responded, "Oh, how my soul praises the Lord. How my spirit rejoices in God my Savior! For he took notice of his lowly servant girl, and from now on all generations will call me blessed. For the Mighty One is holy, and he has done great things for me. He shows mercy from generation to generation to all who fear him. His mighty arm has done tremendous things! He has scattered the proud and haughty ones. He has brought down princes from their thrones and exalted the humble. He has filled the hungry with good things and sent the rich away with empty hands. He has helped his servant Israel and remembered to be merciful. For he made this promise to our ancestors, to Abraham and his children forever."

Mary stayed with Elizabeth about three months and then went back to her own home. LUKE 1:46-56

GOD'S GOOD GIFTS

When Mary said, "From now on all generations will call me blessed," was she being proud? No, she was recognizing and accepting the gift God had given her. If Mary had denied her incredible position, she would have been throwing God's blessing back at him. Pride is refusing to accept God's gifts or taking credit for what God has done; humility is accepting the gifts and using them to praise and serve God. Don't deny, belittle, or ignore your gifts. Thank God for them and use them to his glory.

This song is often called the Magnificat, the first word in the Latin translation of this passage. Mary's song has often been used as the basis for choral music and hymns. Like Hannah, the mother of Samuel (1 Samuel 2:1-10), Mary praised God in song for what he was going to do for the world through her.

John the Baptist is born

When it was time for Elizabeth's baby to be born, she gave birth to a son. And when her neighbors and relatives heard that the Lord had been very merciful to her, everyone rejoiced with her.

When the baby was eight days old, they all came for the circumcision ceremony. They wanted to name him Zechariah, after his father. But Elizabeth said, "No! His name is John!"

"What?" they exclaimed. "There is no one in all your family by that name." So they used gestures to ask the baby's father what he wanted to name him. He motioned for a writing tablet, and to everyone's surprise he wrote, "His name is John." Instantly Zechariah could speak again, and he began praising God.

Awe fell upon the whole neighborhood, and the news of what had happened spread throughout the Judean hills. Everyone who heard about it reflected on these events and asked, "What will this child turn out to be?" For the hand of the Lord was surely upon him in a special way.   LUKE 1:57-66

GOD'S FAMILY

The circumcision ceremony was an important event in the family of a Jewish baby boy. God commanded circumcision when he was beginning to form his holy nation (Genesis 17:4-14), and he reaffirmed it through Moses (Leviticus 12:1-3). This ceremony was a time of joy when friends and family members celebrated the baby's becoming part of God's covenant nation. Today there is also great joy when a baby is born, and some churches have special ceremonies to commemorate the blessed event. You were born into a human family, but to become a part of God's family, you must accept Jesus as your Savior. Are you a part of God's family?

Family lines and family names were important to the Jews. The people naturally assumed that the child would receive Zechariah's name, or at least a family name. Thus they were surprised that both Elizabeth and Zechariah wanted to name the boy John, as the angel had told them to do (Luke 1:13).

John the Baptist is born

Then his father, Zechariah, was filled with the Holy Spirit and gave this prophecy: "Praise the Lord, the God of Israel, because he has visited and redeemed his people. He has sent us a mighty Savior from the royal line of his servant David, just as he promised through his holy prophets long ago. Now we will be saved from our enemies and from all who hate us. He has been merciful to our ancestors by remembering his sacred covenant—the covenant he swore with an oath to our ancestor Abraham. We have been rescued from our enemies so we can serve God without fear, in holiness and righteousness for as long as we live.

"And you, my little son, will be called the prophet of the Most High, because you will prepare the way for the Lord. You will tell his people how to find salvation through forgiveness of their sins. Because of God's tender mercy, the morning light from heaven is about to break upon us, to give light to those who sit in darkness and in the shadow of death, and to guide us to the path of peace."

John grew up and became strong in spirit. And he lived in the wilderness until he began his public ministry to Israel. LUKE 1:67-80

GOD'S POWER AND FAITHFUL PEOPLE

Zechariah had just recalled hundreds of years of God's sovereign work in history, beginning with Abraham and going on into eternity. Then, in tender contrast, he personalized the story. His son had been chosen for a key role in the drama of the ages. Although God has unlimited power, he chooses to work through frail humans who begin as helpless babies. Don't minimize what God can do through those who are faithful to him. You may not feel as though you can do much for God, but all he requires is faith and a willing spirit. Let God do his work in and through you!

———————————◆◆———————————

Zechariah prophesied the coming of a Savior who would redeem his people, and he predicted that his son, John, would prepare the Messiah's way. All the Old Testament prophecies were coming true. The Jews were eagerly awaiting the Messiah, but they thought he would come to save them from the powerful Roman Empire. They were ready for a military Savior but not a peaceful Messiah who would conquer sin.

———————————◆◆———————————

An angel appears to Joseph

This is how Jesus the Messiah was born. His mother, Mary, was engaged to be married to Joseph. But before the marriage took place, while she was still a virgin, she became pregnant through the power of the Holy Spirit. Joseph, her fiancé, was a good man and did not want to disgrace her publicly, so he decided to break the engagement quietly.   MATTHEW 1:18-19

BORN OF A VIRGIN

Why is the Virgin Birth important to the Christian faith? Jesus Christ, God's Son, had to be free from the sinful nature passed on to all other human beings by Adam. Born of a woman, Jesus was a human being; as the Son of God, Jesus was born without any trace of human sin. Jesus is both fully human and fully divine.

Because Jesus lived as a man, we know that he fully understands our experiences and struggles (Hebrews 4:15-16). Because he is God, he has the power and authority to deliver us from sin (Colossians 2:13-15). We can tell Jesus all our thoughts, feelings, and needs. He has been where we are now, and he has the ability to help.

An engaged couple in our culture may call off a wedding at any time. But for the Jews, engagement was more permanent and could be broken only through death or divorce (even though sexual relations were not yet permitted). Because Mary and Joseph were engaged, Mary's apparent unfaithfulness carried a severe social stigma. According to Jewish civil law, Joseph had a right to divorce her, and the Jewish authorities could have had her stoned to death (Deuteronomy 22:23-24).

January 15

An angel appears to Joseph

As [Joseph] considered this, an angel of the Lord appeared to him in a dream. "Joseph, son of David," the angel said, "do not be afraid to take Mary as your wife. For the child within her was conceived by the Holy Spirit. And she will have a son, and you are to name him Jesus, for he will save his people from their sins."

All of this occurred to fulfill the Lord's message through his prophet: "Look! The virgin will conceive a child! She will give birth to a son, and they will call him Immanuel, which means 'God is with us.'"

When Joseph woke up, he did as the angel of the Lord commanded and took Mary as his wife. But he did not have sexual relations with her until her son was born. And Joseph named him Jesus. MATTHEW 1:20-25

A CHANGE OF PLANS

Perhaps Joseph thought he had only two options: divorce Mary quietly or have her stoned. But God had a third option—marry her. In view of the circumstances, this had not occurred to Joseph. God often shows us that there are more options available than we think. Joseph changed his plans quickly after learning that Mary had not been unfaithful to him. He obeyed God and proceeded with the marriage plans. Although others may have disapproved of his decision, Joseph went ahead with what he knew was right. Sometimes we avoid doing what is right because of what others might think. Like Joseph, we must choose to obey God rather than seek the approval of others.

***

The angel declared to Joseph that Mary's child was conceived by the Holy Spirit and would be a son. This reveals an important truth about Jesus—he is both God and human. The infinite, unlimited God took on the limitations of humanity so he could live and die for the salvation of all who would believe in him.

***

Jesus is born in Bethlehem

At that time the Roman emperor, Augustus, decreed that a census should be taken throughout the Roman Empire. (This was the first census taken when Quirinius was governor of Syria.) All returned to their own ancestral towns to register for this census. And because Joseph was a descendant of King David, he had to go to Bethlehem in Judea, David's ancient home. He traveled there from the village of Nazareth in Galilee. He took with him Mary, his fiancée, who was now obviously pregnant.   LUKE 2:1-5

GOD'S PLAN

The government forced Joseph to make a long trip just to pay his taxes. His fiancée, who had to go with him, was about to have a baby. Joseph and Mary were both descendants of David. (The Old Testament is filled with prophecies that the Messiah would be born in David's royal line [see, for example, Isaiah 11:1; Jeremiah 33:15; Hosea 3:5].) But when they arrived in Bethlehem, they couldn't find a place to stay. When we do God's will, we are not guaranteed a comfortable life. However, we are promised that everything, even our discomfort, has meaning in God's plan.

Augustus's decree went out in God's perfect timing and according to God's perfect plan to bring his Son into the world. God controls all history. By the decree of Emperor Augustus, Jesus was born in the very town prophesied for his birth (Micah 5:2), even though his parents did not live there.

January 17 READ LUKE 2:6-7

Jesus is born in Bethlehem

And while they were there, the time came for her baby to be born. She gave birth to her first child, a son. She wrapped him snugly in strips of cloth and laid him in a manger, because there was no lodging available for them. LUKE 2:6-7

MORE THAN A BABY

This mention of the manger is the basis for the traditional belief that Jesus was born in a stable. Stables were often caves with feeding troughs (mangers) carved into the rock walls. Although our first picture of Jesus is as a baby in a manger, it must not be our last. The Christ child in the manger has been made into a beautiful Christmas scene, but we cannot leave him there. This tiny, helpless baby lived an amazing life, died for us, rose from the dead, ascended to heaven, and will come back to this earth as King of kings. Christ will rule the world and judge all people according to their decisions about him. Do you still picture Jesus as a baby in a manger—or is he your Lord? Make sure you don't underestimate Jesus. Let him grow up in your life.

The blanket that Mary wrapped Jesus in actually was strips of cloth. These were used to keep a baby warm and give the baby a sense of security. The cloths were believed to protect the internal organs. The custom of wrapping infants this way continues to be practiced in many Mideastern countries.

Shepherds visit Jesus

That night there were shepherds staying in the fields nearby, guarding their flocks of sheep. Suddenly, an angel of the Lord appeared among them, and the radiance of the Lord's glory surrounded them. They were terrified, but the angel reassured them. "Don't be afraid!" he said. "I bring you good news that will bring great joy to all people. The Savior—yes, the Messiah, the Lord—has been born today in Bethlehem, the city of David! And you will recognize him by this sign: You will find a baby wrapped snugly in strips of cloth, lying in a manger."

Suddenly, the angel was joined by a vast host of others—the armies of heaven—praising God and saying, "Glory to God in highest heaven, and peace on earth to those with whom God is pleased." LUKE 2:8-14

GREAT NEWS!

What a birth announcement! The shepherds were terrified, but their fear turned to joy as the angels announced the Messiah's birth. First, the shepherds ran to see the baby; then, they spread the word. The good news about Jesus is that he comes to all, including the plain and the ordinary. He comes to anyone with a heart humble enough to accept him. Whoever you are, whatever you do, you can have Jesus in your life. Don't think you need extraordinary qualifications—he accepts you as you are. Jesus is *your* Messiah, *your* Savior. Do you look forward to meeting him in prayer and in his Word each day? Discover a Lord so wonderful that you can't help sharing your joy with your friends!

Some of the Jews were waiting for a savior to deliver them from Roman rule; others hoped the Christ (Messiah) would deliver them from physical ailments. But Jesus, while healing their illnesses and establishing a spiritual Kingdom, delivered them from sin. His work is more far-reaching than anyone could imagine. Christ paid the price for sin and opened the way to peace with God.

Shepherds visit Jesus

When the angels had returned to heaven, the shepherds said to each other, "Let's go to Bethlehem! Let's see this thing that has happened, which the Lord has told us about."

They hurried to the village and found Mary and Joseph. And there was the baby, lying in the manger. After seeing him, the shepherds told everyone what had happened and what the angel had said to them about this child. All who heard the shepherds' story were astonished, but Mary kept all these things in her heart and thought about them often. The shepherds went back to their flocks, glorifying and praising God for all they had heard and seen. It was just as the angel had told them.   LUKE 2:15-20

SHEPHERDS AND THE LAMB OF GOD

God continued to reveal his Son, but not to those we might expect. Luke wrote that Jesus' birth was announced to shepherds in the fields. These may have been the shepherds who supplied many of the lambs that were sacrificed in the Temple for the forgiveness of sin. The angels invited these shepherds to greet the Lamb of God (John 1:36), who would take away the sins of the whole world forever. Christ paid the price for sin and opened the way to peace with God. He offers us more than temporary political or physical changes—he offers us new hearts, which will last for eternity. God continues to invite men and women to discover the Savior. Have you found him?

The conception and birth of Jesus Christ are supernatural events beyond human logic or reasoning. Thus, God sent angels to help certain people understand the significance of what was happening (Luke 1:11, 26; 2:9, 13, 20). Angels are spiritual beings created by God who live in God's presence and help carry out his work on earth.

Mary and Joseph bring Jesus to the Temple

Eight days later, when the baby was circumcised, he was named Jesus, the name given him by the angel even before he was conceived.

Then it was time for their purification offering, as required by the law of Moses after the birth of a child; so his parents took him to Jerusalem to present him to the Lord. The law of the Lord says, "If a woman's first child is a boy, he must be dedicated to the LORD." So they offered the sacrifice required in the law of the Lord—"either a pair of turtledoves or two young pigeons." LUKE 2:21-24

A BABY'S BIRTH

Why did Joseph and Mary have to return to the Temple? For forty days after the birth of a son and eighty days after the birth of a daughter, the mother was ceremonially unclean and could not enter the Temple. At the end of her time of separation, the parents were to bring a lamb for a burnt offering and a dove or pigeon for a sin offering. The priest would sacrifice these animals and declare her to be clean. If a lamb was too expensive, the parents could bring a second dove or pigeon instead. This is what Mary and Joseph did. Jesus was God's Son, but his family carried out all the specified ceremonies according to God's law. Jesus was not above the law; instead, he fulfilled it perfectly. Mary and Joseph forthrightly obeyed God, fulfilling the requirements in the law. What has God told you to do? Be obedient, be faithful.

Jewish families went through several ceremonies soon after a baby's birth: (1) Circumcision. Every boy was circumcised and named on the eighth day after birth (Leviticus 12:3; Luke 1:59-60). (2) Redemption of the firstborn. A firstborn son was presented to God one month after birth (Exodus 13:2, 11-16; Numbers 18:15-16). (3) Purification of the mother (Leviticus 12:4-8).

Mary and Joseph bring Jesus to the Temple

At that time there was a man in Jerusalem named Simeon. He was righteous and devout and was eagerly waiting for the Messiah to come and rescue Israel. The Holy Spirit was upon him and had revealed to him that he would not die until he had seen the Lord's Messiah. That day the Spirit led him to the Temple. So when Mary and Joseph came to present the baby Jesus to the Lord as the law required, Simeon was there. He took the child in his arms and praised God, saying, "Sovereign Lord, now let your servant die in peace, as you have promised. I have seen your salvation, which you have prepared for all people. He is a light to reveal God to the nations, and he is the glory of your people Israel!"

Jesus' parents were amazed at what was being said about him. Then Simeon blessed them, and he said to Mary, the baby's mother, "This child is destined to cause many in Israel to fall, but he will be a joy to many others. He has been sent as a sign from God, but many will oppose him. As a result, the deepest thoughts of many hearts will be revealed. And a sword will pierce your very soul."

LUKE 2:25-35

ALL WHO BELIEVE

The Jews were well acquainted with the Old Testament prophecies that spoke of the Messiah's blessings to their nation. They did not always give equal attention to the prophecies saying that he would bring salvation to the entire world, not just the Jews (see, for example, Isaiah 49:6). In the days following the Ascension, many thought that Christ had come to save only his own people. Luke made sure his Greek audience understood that Christ had come to save *all* who believe, Gentiles as well as Jews. Simeon prophesied that Jesus would have a paradoxical effect on Israel. Some would fall because of him (Isaiah 8:14-15), while others would rise (Malachi 4:2). With Jesus there would be no neutral ground: People would either joyfully accept him or totally reject him. What have you done with Jesus?

When Mary and Joseph brought Jesus to the Temple to be consecrated to God, they met an old man who told them what their child would become. Simeon's song is often called the Nunc Dimittis because these are the first words of its Latin translation. Simeon could die in peace because he had seen the Messiah.

Mary and Joseph bring Jesus to the Temple

Anna, a prophet, was also there in the Temple. She was the daughter of Phanuel from the tribe of Asher, and she was very old. Her husband died when they had been married only seven years. Then she lived as a widow to the age of eighty-four. She never left the Temple but stayed there day and night, worshiping God with fasting and prayer. She came along just as Simeon was talking with Mary and Joseph, and she began praising God. She talked about the child to everyone who had been waiting expectantly for God to rescue Jerusalem.

When Jesus' parents had fulfilled all the requirements of the law of the Lord, they returned home to Nazareth in Galilee. There the child grew up healthy and strong. He was filled with wisdom, and God's favor was on him.   LUKE 2:36-40

NEVER TOO OLD

Although Simeon and Anna were very old, they had never lost their hope that they would see the Messiah. Led by the Holy Spirit, they were among the first to bear witness to Jesus. In the Jewish culture, elders were respected, so because of Simeon's and Anna's age, their prophecies carried extra weight. Our society, however, values youthfulness over wisdom, and potential contributions by the elderly are often ignored. As Christians, we should reverse those values whenever we can. Encourage older people to share their wisdom and experience. Listen carefully when they speak. Offer them your friendship and help them find ways to continue to serve God.

Did Mary and Joseph return immediately to Nazareth, or did they remain in Bethlehem for a time (as implied in Matthew 2)? Apparently there is a gap of several years between Luke 2:38 and 39—ample time for them to find a place to live in Bethlehem, flee to Egypt to escape Herod's wrath, and return to Nazareth when it was safe to do so.

Visitors arrive from eastern lands

Jesus was born in Bethlehem in Judea, during the reign of King Herod. About that time some wise men from eastern lands arrived in Jerusalem, asking, "Where is the newborn king of the Jews? We saw his star as it rose, and we have come to worship him."

King Herod was deeply disturbed when he heard this, as was everyone in Jerusalem. He called a meeting of the leading priests and teachers of religious law and asked, "Where is the Messiah supposed to be born?"

"In Bethlehem in Judea," they said, "for this is what the prophet wrote: 'And you, O Bethlehem in the land of Judah, are not least among the ruling cities of Judah, for a ruler will come from you who will be the shepherd for my people Israel.'"

Then Herod called for a private meeting with the wise men, and he learned from them the time when the star first appeared. Then he told them, "Go to Bethlehem and search carefully for the child. And when you find him, come back and tell me so that I can go and worship him, too!"   MATTHEW 2:1-8

WISE MEN

Not much is known about these astrologers (also known as wise men). We don't know where they came from or how many there were. Tradition says they were men of high position from Parthia, near the site of ancient Babylon. How did they know that the star represented the Messiah? (1) They could have been descendants of Jews who had remained in Babylon after the Exile and knew the Old Testament predictions of the Messiah's coming. (2) They may have been eastern astrologers who studied ancient manuscripts from around the world. Because of the Jewish exile centuries earlier, they would have had copies of the Old Testament. (3) They may have had a special message from God directing them to the Messiah. Some scholars say that each of these astrologers was from a different nation, representing the entire world bowing before Jesus. These men from faraway recognized Jesus as the Messiah even though most of God's chosen people in Israel did not. Matthew pictures Jesus as King over the whole world, not just Judea. These men traveled thousands of miles to see the King of the Jews. When they finally found him, they responded with joy, worship, and gifts. This is quite different from the approach people often take today. We expect God to come looking for us, to explain himself, prove who he is, and give *us* gifts. But those who are wise still seek and worship Jesus, not for what they can get, but for who he is.

Visitors arrive from eastern lands

After this interview the wise men went their way. And the star they had seen in the east guided them to Bethlehem. It went ahead of them and stopped over the place where the child was. When they saw the star, they were filled with joy! They entered the house and saw the child with his mother, Mary, and they bowed down and worshiped him. Then they opened their treasure chests and gave him gifts of gold, frankincense, and myrrh.

When it was time to leave, they returned to their own country by another route, for God had warned them in a dream not to return to Herod.

MATTHEW 2:9-12

TRUE WORSHIP

The astrologers gave these expensive gifts because they were worthy presents for a future king. Bible students have seen in the gifts symbols of Christ's identity and what he would accomplish. Gold was a gift for a king; frankincense, a gift for deity; myrrh was a medicine and was also used as a burial spice. The astrologers brought gifts and worshiped Jesus for who he is. This is the essence of true worship—honoring Christ for who he is and being willing to give him what is valuable to you. Worship God because he is the perfect, just, and almighty Creator of the universe, worthy of the best you have to give.

Jesus was probably one or two years old when the astrologers found him. By this time Mary and Joseph were married, living in a house, and intending to stay in Bethlehem for a while.

The escape to Egypt

After the wise men were gone, an angel of the Lord appeared to Joseph in a dream. "Get up! Flee to Egypt with the child and his mother," the angel said. "Stay there until I tell you to return, because Herod is going to search for the child to kill him."

That night Joseph left for Egypt with the child and Mary, his mother, and they stayed there until Herod's death. This fulfilled what the Lord had spoken through the prophet: "I called my Son out of Egypt." MATTHEW 2:13-15

FOLLOWING HIS LEAD

This was the second dream or vision that Joseph received from God. Joseph's first dream had revealed that Mary's child would be the Messiah (Matthew 1:20-21). His second dream told him how to protect the child's life. Although Joseph was not Jesus' natural father, he was Jesus' legal father and was responsible for his safety and well-being. Divine guidance comes only to prepared hearts. Joseph remained receptive to God's guidance. How willing are you to listen to God? When you know what God wants, are you willing to follow his instructions?

———————————————•◦•———————————————

Going to Egypt was not unusual because there were colonies of Jews in several major Egyptian cities. These colonies had developed during the time of the great captivity (see Jeremiah 43–44).

———————————————•◦•———————————————

The escape to Egypt

*Herod was furious when he realized that the wise men had outwitted him.
He sent soldiers to kill all the boys in and around Bethlehem who were
two years old and under, based on the wise men's report of the star's first
appearance. Herod's brutal action fulfilled what God had spoken through the
prophet Jeremiah: "A cry was heard in Ramah—weeping and great mourning.
Rachel weeps for her children, refusing to be comforted, for they are dead."*

MATTHEW 2:16-18

WHO'S ON THE THRONE?

Herod was afraid that this newborn King would one day take his throne. He completely misunderstood the reason for Christ's coming. Jesus didn't want Herod's
throne; he wanted to be king of Herod's life. Jesus wanted to give Herod eternal
life, not take away his present life. Today people are often afraid that Christ wants
to take things away, when in reality, he wants to give them real freedom, peace,
and joy. Don't fear Christ—give him the throne of your life.

*Herod, the king of the Jews, killed all the boys under two years of
age in an obsessive attempt to kill Jesus, the newborn King. He
stained his hands with blood, but he did not harm Jesus. Herod
was king by a human appointment; Jesus was King by a divine
appointment. No one can thwart God's plans.*

The return to Nazareth

When Herod died, an angel of the Lord appeared in a dream to Joseph in Egypt. "Get up!" the angel said. "Take the child and his mother back to the land of Israel, because those who were trying to kill the child are dead."

So Joseph got up and returned to the land of Israel with Jesus and his mother. But when he learned that the new ruler of Judea was Herod's son Archelaus, he was afraid to go there. Then, after being warned in a dream, he left for the region of Galilee. So the family went and lived in a town called Nazareth. This fulfilled what the prophets had said: "He will be called a Nazarene."

MATTHEW 2:19-23

ANYTHING GOOD?

Nazareth sat in the hilly area of southern Galilee near the crossroads of great caravan trade routes. The Roman garrison in charge of Galilee was housed in this small town. The people of Nazareth had constant contact with people from all over the world, so world news reached them quickly. These people had an attitude of independence that many of the Jews despised. This may have been why Nathanael commented, "Nazareth! . . . Can anything good come from Nazareth?" (John 1:46). Obviously, it was not wise for Nathanael to be prejudiced against the entire town, for someone truly good did live there: Jesus, the Messiah. Be careful not to make quick or prejudicial judgments because of where people live or originate.

Herod the Great died in 4 BC of an incurable disease. Rome trusted him but didn't trust his sons. Herod knew that Rome wouldn't give his successor as much power, so he divided his kingdom into three parts, one for each son. Archelaus received Judea, Samaria, and Idumea; Herod Antipas received Galilee and Perea; Herod Philip II received Traconitis.

Jesus speaks with the religious teachers

Every year Jesus' parents went to Jerusalem for the Passover festival. When Jesus was twelve years old, they attended the festival as usual. After the celebration was over, they started home to Nazareth, but Jesus stayed behind in Jerusalem. His parents didn't miss him at first, because they assumed he was among the other travelers. But when he didn't show up that evening, they started looking for him among their relatives and friends.

When they couldn't find him, they went back to Jerusalem to search for him there. Three days later they finally discovered him in the Temple, sitting among the religious teachers, listening to them and asking questions. All who heard him were amazed at his understanding and his answers.

His parents didn't know what to think. "Son," his mother said to him, "why have you done this to us? Your father and I have been frantic, searching for you everywhere."

"But why did you need to search?" he asked. "Didn't you know that I must be in my Father's house?" But they didn't understand what he meant.

LUKE 2:41-50

LETTING GO

Mary had to let go of her child and let him become a man. Fearful that she hadn't been careful enough with this God-given child, she searched frantically for him. But she was looking for a boy, not the young man who was in the Temple astounding the religious leaders with his questions. It is difficult to let go of people or projects that we have nurtured. It is both sweet and painful to see our children as adults, our students as teachers, our subordinates as managers, and our inspirations as institutions. But when the time comes to step back and let go, we must do so in spite of the hurt. Then our protégés can exercise their wings, take flight, and soar to the heights God intended for them.

***

According to God's law, every male was required to go to Jerusalem three times a year for the great festivals (Deuteronomy 16:16). In the spring the Passover was celebrated, followed immediately by the weeklong Festival of Unleavened Bread. Passover commemorated the night of the Jews' escape from Egypt when God had killed all the firstborn sons and firstborn male animals in Egypt but had passed over Israelite homes (Exodus 12:21-37). Passover was the most important of the three annual festivals.

***

January 29 READ LUKE 2:51-52

Jesus speaks with the religious teachers

Then he returned to Nazareth with them and was obedient to them. And his mother stored all these things in her heart.

Jesus grew in wisdom and in stature and in favor with God and all the people. LUKE 2:51-52

KEEPING IN BALANCE

The second chapter of Luke shows us that, although Jesus was unique, he had a normal childhood and adolescence. In terms of development, he went through the same progression that we do. He grew physically and mentally, he related to other people, and he was loved by God. A full human life is not unbalanced. It was important to Jesus—and it should be important to all believers—to develop fully and harmoniously in each of these key areas: physical, mental, social, and spiritual. Think about each area of your life. Work hard to stay physically fit, mentally sharp, socially adept, and spiritually in tune with God.

The Bible does not record any events of the next eighteen years of Jesus' life, but he undoubtedly was learning and maturing. As the oldest in a large family, he assisted Joseph in his carpentry work. Joseph may have died during this time, leaving Jesus to provide for the family. The normal routines of daily life gave Jesus a solid understanding of the Jewish people.

John the Baptist prepares the way for Jesus

This is the Good News about Jesus the Messiah, the Son of God. It began just as the prophet Isaiah had written: "Look, I am sending my messenger ahead of you, and he will prepare your way. He is a voice shouting in the wilderness, 'Prepare the way for the LORD's coming! Clear the road for him!'" This messenger was John the Baptist. He was in the wilderness and preached that people should be baptized to show that they had repented of their sins and turned to God to be forgiven. All of Judea, including all the people of Jerusalem, went out to see and hear John. And when they confessed their sins, he baptized them in the Jordan River. His clothes were woven from coarse camel hair, and he wore a leather belt around his waist. For food he ate locusts and wild honey.

MARK 1:1-6 *(see also Matthew 3:1-6; Luke 3:1-6)*

TIME FOR A CHANGE

John chose to live in the desert (1) to get away from distractions so he could hear God's instructions; (2) to capture the undivided attention of the people; (3) to symbolize a sharp break with the hypocrisy of the religious leaders who preferred their luxurious homes and positions of authority over doing God's work; and (4) to fulfill Old Testament prophecies that said John would be a voice calling in the wilderness to prepare the way for the Lord (Isaiah 40:3). The purpose of John's preaching was to prepare people to accept Jesus as God's Son. When John challenged the people to confess sin individually, he signaled the start of a new way to relate to God. Is change needed in your life before you can hear and understand Jesus' message? You have to admit that you need forgiveness before you can accept it. To prepare to receive Christ, repent. Denounce the world's dead-end attractions, sinful temptations, and harmful attitudes.

John's clothes were not the latest style of his day. He dressed much like the prophet Elijah (2 Kings 1:8) in order to distinguish himself from the religious leaders, whose long flowing robes reflected their great pride in their position. John's striking appearance reinforced his striking message.

January 31

John the Baptist prepares the way for Jesus

When the crowds came to John for baptism, he said, "You brood of snakes! Who warned you to flee God's coming wrath? Prove by the way you live that you have repented of your sins and turned to God. Don't just say to each other, 'We're safe, for we are descendants of Abraham.' That means nothing, for I tell you, God can create children of Abraham from these very stones. Even now the ax of God's judgment is poised, ready to sever the roots of the trees. Yes, every tree that does not produce good fruit will be chopped down and thrown into the fire."

The crowds asked, "What should we do?"

John replied, "If you have two shirts, give one to the poor. If you have food, share it with those who are hungry."

Even corrupt tax collectors came to be baptized and asked, "Teacher, what should we do?"

He replied, "Collect no more taxes than the government requires."

"What should we do?" asked some soldiers.

John replied, "Don't extort money or make false accusations. And be content with your pay." LUKE 3:7-14 *(see also Matthew 3:7-10)*

BEYOND WORDS

John's message demanded at least three specific responses: (1) Share what you have with those who need it; (2) whatever your job is, do it well and with fairness; and (3) be content with what you're earning. John had no time to address comforting messages to those who lived careless or selfish lives—he was calling the people to right living as he prepared the way for their Messiah. Just as a fruit tree is expected to bear fruit, God's people should produce a crop of good works.

Many of John's hearers were shocked when he said that being Abraham's descendants was not enough for God. The religious leaders relied more on their family lines than on their faith for their standing with God. For them, religion was inherited. But a personal relationship with God is not handed down from parents to children. Everyone has to commit to it on his or her own.

John baptizes Jesus

Jesus went from Galilee to the Jordan River to be baptized by John. But John tried to talk him out of it. "I am the one who needs to be baptized by you," he said, "so why are you coming to me?"

But Jesus said, "It should be done, for we must carry out all that God requires." So John agreed to baptize him.

After his baptism, as Jesus came up out of the water, the heavens were opened and he saw the Spirit of God descending like a dove and settling on him. And a voice from heaven said, "This is my dearly loved Son, who brings me great joy."

MATTHEW 3:13-17 *(see also Mark 1:9-11; Luke 3:21-22)*

LET GO OF EGO

Put yourself in John's situation. Your work is going well, people are taking notice. But you know that the purpose of your work is to prepare the people for Jesus (John 1:35-37). Then Jesus arrives, and his coming tests your integrity. Will you be able to turn your followers over to him? John passed the test by publicly baptizing Jesus. Soon he would say, "He must become greater and greater, and I must become less and less" (John 3:30). Can you, like John, put your ego and profitable work aside in order to point others to Jesus? Are you willing to lose some of your status so that everyone will benefit?

Why did Jesus ask to be baptized? It was not for repentance for sin, because Jesus never sinned. He was baptized because (1) he was confessing sin on behalf of the nation, as Nehemiah, Ezra, Moses, and Daniel had done; (2) he was showing support for what John was doing; (3) he was inaugurating his public ministry; and (4) he was identifying with the penitent people of God, not with the critical Pharisees who were only watching.

February 2 READ MATTHEW 4:1-4

Satan tempts Jesus in the wilderness

Then Jesus was led by the Spirit into the wilderness to be tempted there by the devil. For forty days and forty nights he fasted and became very hungry.

During that time the devil came and said to him, "If you are the Son of God, tell these stones to become loaves of bread."

But Jesus told him, "No! The Scriptures say, 'People do not live by bread alone, but by every word that comes from the mouth of God.'"

MATTHEW 4:1-4 *(see also Mark 1:12-13; Luke 4:1-4)*

TEMPTATION

The devil, also called Satan, tempted Eve in the Garden of Eden; here, he tempted Jesus in the wilderness. Satan is a fallen angel. He is *real*, not symbolic, and is constantly fighting against those who follow and obey God. Satan's temptations are strong, and he is always trying to get us to live his way or our way rather than God's way. One day Jesus will reign over all creation, but Satan tried to force Jesus' hand and get him to declare his kingship prematurely. The devil's temptations focused on three crucial areas: (1) physical needs and desires, (2) possessions and power, and (3) pride. If Jesus had given in, his mission on earth—to die for our sins and give us the opportunity to have eternal life—would have been lost. But Jesus did *not* give in! When temptations seem especially strong, or when you think you can rationalize giving in, consider whether Satan may be trying to block God's purposes for your life or for someone else's life.

Jesus was tempted by the devil, but he never sinned! Although we may feel dirty after being tempted, we should remember that temptation itself is not sin. We sin when we give in and disobey God. Remembering this will help us turn away from the temptation.

Satan tempts Jesus in the wilderness

Then the devil took him to the holy city, Jerusalem, to the highest point of the Temple, and said, "If you are the Son of God, jump off! For the Scriptures say, 'He will order his angels to protect you. And they will hold you up with their hands so you won't even hurt your foot on a stone.'"

Jesus responded, "The Scriptures also say, 'You must not test the LORD your God.'"   MATTHEW 4:5-7 *(see also Luke 4:9-13)*

THE WHOLE TRUTH

Satan used Scripture to try to convince Jesus to sin! Sometimes friends or associates will present attractive and convincing reasons why you should do something you know is wrong. They may even find Bible verses that *seem* to support their viewpoints. Study the Bible carefully, especially the broader contexts of specific verses, so that you understand God's principles for living and what he wants for your life. Only if you really understand what the *whole* Bible says will you be able to recognize errors of interpretation when people take verses out of context and twist them to say what people want them to say. Jesus was able to resist all of the devil's temptations because not only did he know Scripture, he also obeyed it. Ephesians 6:17 says that God's Word is a sword to use in spiritual combat. Knowing Bible verses is an important step in helping us resist the devil's attacks, but we must also obey the Bible. Even though Satan had memorized Scripture, he failed to submit to it. Knowing and obeying the Bible help us follow God's desires rather than the devil's.

The Temple was the religious center of the Jewish nation and the place where the people expected the Messiah to arrive (Malachi 3:1). The Temple was the tallest building in the area, and its highest point was actually a pinnacle on the corner wall that jutted out of the hillside, overlooking the valley below. From this spot, Jesus could see all Jerusalem behind him and the country for miles in front of him.

February 4 READ MATTHEW 4:8-11

Satan tempts Jesus in the wilderness

Next the devil took him to the peak of a very high mountain and showed him all the kingdoms of the world and their glory. "I will give it all to you," he said, "if you will kneel down and worship me."

"Get out of here, Satan," Jesus told him. "For the Scriptures say, 'You must worship the LORD your God and serve only him.'"

Then the devil went away, and angels came and took care of Jesus.

MATTHEW 4:8-11 (see also Luke 4:5-8)

THE TEST

This time of testing showed that Jesus really was the Son of God, able to overcome the devil and his temptations. A person has not shown true obedience if he or she has never had an opportunity to disobey. We read in Deuteronomy 8:2 that God led the Israelites into the wilderness to humble and test them. God wanted to see whether or not his people would really obey him. We, too, will be tested. Because we know that testing will come, we should be alert and ready for it. Remember, your convictions are strong only if they hold up under pressure!

Did the devil have the power to give Jesus the kingdoms of the world? Satan may have been lying about his implied power, or he may have based his offer on his temporary control and free rein over the earth because of humanity's sinfulness.

John the Baptist declares his mission

This was John's testimony when the Jewish leaders sent priests and Temple assistants from Jerusalem to ask John, "Who are you?" He came right out and said, "I am not the Messiah."

"Well then, who are you?" they asked. "Are you Elijah?"

"No," he replied.

"Are you the Prophet we are expecting?"

"No."

"Then who are you? We need an answer for those who sent us. What do you have to say about yourself?"

John replied in the words of the prophet Isaiah: "I am a voice shouting in the wilderness, 'Clear the way for the LORD's coming!'"   JOHN 1:19-23

WHO WAS JOHN THE BAPTIST?

In the Pharisees' minds, there were four options regarding John the Baptist's identity: He was (1) the prophet foretold by Moses (Deuteronomy 18:15), (2) Elijah (Malachi 4:5), (3) the Prophet (the Messiah), or (4) a false prophet. John denied being any of the first three. Instead he called himself, in the words of the Old Testament prophet Isaiah, "the voice of someone shouting, 'Clear the way through the wilderness for the LORD!'" (Isaiah 40:3). The leaders kept pressing John to say who he was because people were expecting the Messiah to come (Luke 3:15). But John emphasized only *why* he had come—to prepare the way for the Messiah. The Pharisees missed the point. They wanted to know who John was, but John wanted to point them to Jesus. Believers need to be like John, preparing the way for the Savior. What can you do to point people to Christ?

The priests and Temple assistants were respected religious leaders in Jerusalem. Priests served in the Temple. These leaders that came to see John were Pharisees. Many of them outwardly obeyed God's laws to look pious, while inwardly their hearts were filled with pride and greed. They believed that their own oral traditions were just as important as God's inspired Word.

John the Baptist declares his mission

Then the Pharisees who had been sent asked him, "If you aren't the Messiah or Elijah or the Prophet, what right do you have to baptize?"

John told them, "I baptize with water, but right here in the crowd is someone you do not recognize. Though his ministry follows mine, I'm not even worthy to be his slave and untie the straps of his sandal."

This encounter took place in Bethany, an area east of the Jordan River, where John was baptizing. JOHN 1:24-28

TO FORGIVE SINS

John was baptizing Jews. The Essenes (a strict, monastic sect of Judaism) practiced baptism for purification, but normally only non-Jews (Gentiles) were baptized, when they converted to Judaism. When the Pharisees questioned John's authority to baptize, they were asking who gave John the right to treat God's chosen people like Gentiles. John said, "I baptize with water"—he was helping the people perform a symbolic act of repentance. But soon one would come who would truly *forgive* sins, something only the Son of God—the Messiah—could do. Jesus can forgive your sins, no matter how big or small they may be. Have you accepted his forgiveness? Confess to Christ.

John the Baptist said he was not worthy even to be Christ's slave. But according to Luke 7:28, Jesus said that John was the greatest of all prophets. If such a great person felt inadequate even to be Christ's slave, how much more should we lay aside our pride to serve Christ!

John the Baptist proclaims Jesus as the Messiah

The next day John saw Jesus coming toward him and said, "Look! The Lamb of God who takes away the sin of the world! He is the one I was talking about when I said, 'A man is coming after me who is far greater than I am, for he existed long before me.' I did not recognize him as the Messiah, but I have been baptizing with water so that he might be revealed to Israel."

Then John testified, "I saw the Holy Spirit descending like a dove from heaven and resting upon him. I didn't know he was the one, but when God sent me to baptize with water, he told me, 'The one on whom you see the Spirit descend and rest is the one who will baptize with the Holy Spirit.' I saw this happen to Jesus, so I testify that he is the Chosen One of God." JOHN 1:29-34

THE LAMB OF GOD

Every morning and evening, a lamb was sacrificed in the Temple for the sins of the people (Exodus 29:38-42). Isaiah 53:7 prophesied that the Messiah, God's servant, would be led to the slaughter like a lamb. To pay the penalty for sin, a life had to be given—and God chose to provide the sacrifice himself. The sins of the world were removed when Jesus died as the perfect sacrifice. This is the way our sins are forgiven (1 Corinthians 5:7). The "sin of the world" means everyone's sin, the sin of each individual. Jesus paid the price for *your* sin by his death. You can receive forgiveness by confessing your sin to him and asking for his forgiveness.

John the Baptist's baptism with water was preparatory, because it was for repentance and it symbolized the washing away of sins. Jesus, by contrast, would baptize with the Holy Spirit. He would send the Holy Spirit upon all believers, empowering them to live and to teach the message of salvation. This outpouring of the Spirit came after Jesus had risen from the dead and ascended into heaven (John 20:22; Acts 2).

February 8

The first disciples follow Jesus

The following day John was again standing with two of his disciples. As Jesus walked by, John looked at him and declared, "Look! There is the Lamb of God!" When John's two disciples heard this, they followed Jesus.

Jesus looked around and saw them following. "What do you want?" he asked them.

They replied, "Rabbi" (which means "Teacher"), "where are you staying?"

"Come and see," he said. It was about four o'clock in the afternoon when they went with him to the place where he was staying, and they remained with him the rest of the day.

Andrew, Simon Peter's brother, was one of these men who heard what John said and then followed Jesus. Andrew went to find his brother, Simon, and told him, "We have found the Messiah" (which means "Christ").

Then Andrew brought Simon to meet Jesus. Looking intently at Simon, Jesus said, "Your name is Simon, son of John—but you will be called Cephas" (which means "Peter"). JOHN 1:35-42

NAMES OF JESUS

These new disciples used several names for Jesus: Lamb of God (John 1:36), Messiah (John 1:41), Son of God (John 1:49), and King of Israel (John 1:49). As they got to know Jesus, their appreciation for him grew. The more time we spend getting to know Christ, the more we will understand and appreciate who he is. We may be drawn to him for his teaching, but we will come to know him as the Son of God. Although these disciples made this verbal shift in a few days, they would not fully understand Jesus until three years later (Acts 2). What they so easily professed had to be worked out in experience. We may find that words of faith come easily, but deep appreciation for Christ comes with living by faith.

One of the two disciples was Andrew (John 1:40). The other was probably John, the writer of this book. These were Jesus' first disciples, along with Peter (John 1:42) and Nathanael (John 1:45).

The first disciples follow Jesus

The next day Jesus decided to go to Galilee. He found Philip and said to him, "Come, follow me." Philip was from Bethsaida, Andrew and Peter's hometown.

Philip went to look for Nathanael and told him, "We have found the very person Moses and the prophets wrote about! His name is Jesus, the son of Joseph from Nazareth."

"Nazareth!" exclaimed Nathanael. "Can anything good come from Nazareth?"

"Come and see for yourself," Philip replied.

As they approached, Jesus said, "Now here is a genuine son of Israel—a man of complete integrity."

"How do you know about me?" Nathanael asked.

Jesus replied, "I could see you under the fig tree before Philip found you."

Then Nathanael exclaimed, "Rabbi, you are the Son of God—the King of Israel!"

Jesus asked him, "Do you believe this just because I told you I had seen you under the fig tree? You will see greater things than this." Then he said, "I tell you the truth, you will all see heaven open and the angels of God going up and down on the Son of Man, the one who is the stairway between heaven and earth."

JOHN 1:43-51

DON'T MISS JESUS

When Nathanael heard that the Messiah was from Nazareth, he was surprised. Philip responded, "Come and see for yourself." Fortunately for Nathanael, he went to meet Jesus and became a disciple. If he had stuck to his prejudice without investigating further, he would have missed the Messiah! Don't let people's stereotypes about Christ keep them from his power and love. Invite them to come and see the real Jesus.

Nazareth was despised by the Jews because a Roman army garrison was located near there, in Capernaum. Some have speculated that an aloof attitude or a poor reputation in morals and religion on the part of the people of Nazareth led to Nathanael's harsh comment. Nathanael's hometown was Cana, about four miles from Nazareth.

February 10

READ JOHN 2:1-12

Jesus turns water into wine

The next day there was a wedding celebration in the village of Cana in Galilee. Jesus' mother was there, and Jesus and his disciples were also invited to the celebration. The wine supply ran out during the festivities, so Jesus' mother told him, "They have no more wine."

"Dear woman, that's not our problem," Jesus replied. "My time has not yet come."

But his mother told the servants, "Do whatever he tells you."

Standing nearby were six stone water jars, used for Jewish ceremonial washing. Each could hold twenty to thirty gallons. Jesus told the servants, "Fill the jars with water." When the jars had been filled, he said, "Now dip some out, and take it to the master of ceremonies." So the servants followed his instructions.

When the master of ceremonies tasted the water that was now wine, not knowing where it had come from (though, of course, the servants knew), he called the bridegroom over. "A host always serves the best wine first," he said. "Then, when everyone has had a lot to drink, he brings out the less expensive wine. But you have kept the best until now!"

This miraculous sign at Cana in Galilee was the first time Jesus revealed his glory. And his disciples believed in him.

After the wedding he went to Capernaum for a few days with his mother, his brothers, and his disciples.   JOHN 2:1-12

GOD'S WAY

Mary was perhaps not asking Jesus to do a miracle; she was simply hoping that her son would help solve this major problem and find some wine. Tradition says that Joseph, Mary's husband, was dead, so she probably was used to asking for her eldest son's help in certain situations. Jesus' answer to Mary is difficult to understand, but maybe that is the point. Although Mary did not know what Jesus was going to do, she trusted him to do what was right. Those who believe in Jesus but encounter situations they cannot understand must continue to trust that he will work in the best way. Mary submitted to Jesus' way of doing things. She recognized that he was more than her human son—he was the Son of God. When we bring our problems to Christ, we may think we know how he should take care of them. But he may have a completely different plan. Like Mary, we should submit and allow Christ to deal with our problems as he sees fit.

Jesus clears the Temple

It was nearly time for the Jewish Passover celebration, so Jesus went to Jerusalem. In the Temple area he saw merchants selling cattle, sheep, and doves for sacrifices; he also saw dealers at tables exchanging foreign money. Jesus made a whip from some ropes and chased them all out of the Temple. He drove out the sheep and cattle, scattered the money changers' coins over the floor, and turned over their tables. Then, going over to the people who sold doves, he told them, "Get these things out of here. Stop turning my Father's house into a marketplace!"

Then his disciples remembered this prophecy from the Scriptures: "Passion for God's house will consume me." JOHN 2:13-17

RIGHTEOUS ANGER

The Temple area was always crowded during Passover with thousands of out-of-town visitors. The religious leaders crowded it even further by allowing money changers and merchants to set up booths in the Court of the Gentiles. They rationalized this practice as a convenience for the worshipers and as a way to make money for Temple upkeep. The religious leaders did not seem to care that the Court of the Gentiles was so full of merchants that foreigners found it difficult to worship. But worship was the main purpose for visiting the Temple. No wonder Jesus was angry at the merchants who exploited those worshipers. There is a difference between uncontrolled rage and righteous indignation—yet both are called anger. We must be very careful how we use the powerful emotion of anger. It is right to be angry about injustice and sin; it is wrong to be angry over trivial personal offenses.

The Passover celebration took place yearly at the Temple in Jerusalem. Every Jewish male was expected to make a pilgrimage to Jerusalem during this time (Deuteronomy 16:16).

February 12 READ JOHN 2:18-25

Jesus clears the Temple

But the Jewish leaders demanded, "What are you doing? If God gave you authority to do this, show us a miraculous sign to prove it."

"All right," Jesus replied. "Destroy this temple, and in three days I will raise it up."

"What!" they exclaimed. "It has taken forty-six years to build this Temple, and you can rebuild it in three days?" But when Jesus said "this temple," he meant his own body. After he was raised from the dead, his disciples remembered he had said this, and they believed both the Scriptures and what Jesus had said.

Because of the miraculous signs Jesus did in Jerusalem at the Passover celebration, many began to trust in him. But Jesus didn't trust them, because he knew human nature. No one needed to tell him what mankind is really like.

JOHN 2:18-25

STRONG PROOF

The Jews understood Jesus to mean the Temple out of which he had just driven the merchants and money changers. This was the Temple that Zerubbabel had built more than five hundred years earlier and that Herod the Great had begun remodeling, making it much larger and far more beautiful. It had been forty-six years since this remodeling was started (20 BC), and it still was not completely finished. The Jews understood Jesus' words to mean that this imposing building could be torn down and rebuilt in three days, and they were startled. However, Jesus was not talking about the Temple made of stones, but about his body. His listeners didn't realize it, but Jesus was greater than the Temple (Matthew 12:6). His words would take on meaning for his disciples after his resurrection. That Christ so perfectly fulfilled this prediction became the strongest proof for his claims to be God. If you ever have doubts about Jesus' divinity, remember that he fulfilled his promise to rise from the dead. You worship a *living* Savior.

The Son of God knows all about human nature. Jesus was well aware of the truth of Jeremiah 17:9, which states, "The human heart is the most deceitful of all things, and desperately wicked. Who really knows how bad it is?" Jesus was discerning, and he knew that the faith of some followers was superficial. Some of the same people claiming to believe in Jesus at this time would later yell, "Crucify him!"

Nicodemus visits Jesus at night

There was a man named Nicodemus, a Jewish religious leader who was a Pharisee. After dark one evening, he came to speak with Jesus. "Rabbi," he said, "we all know that God has sent you to teach us. Your miraculous signs are evidence that God is with you."

Jesus replied, "I tell you the truth, unless you are born again, you cannot see the Kingdom of God."

"What do you mean?" exclaimed Nicodemus. "How can an old man go back into his mother's womb and be born again?"

Jesus replied, "I assure you, no one can enter the Kingdom of God without being born of water and the Spirit. Humans can reproduce only human life, but the Holy Spirit gives birth to spiritual life. So don't be surprised when I say, 'You must be born again.' The wind blows wherever it wants. Just as you can hear the wind but can't tell where it comes from or where it is going, so you can't explain how people are born of the Spirit." JOHN 3:1-8

A NIGHT MEETING

Nicodemus was a Pharisee and a member of the ruling council called the Sanhedrin. The Pharisees were a group of religious leaders whom Jesus and John the Baptist often criticized for being hypocrites. Most Pharisees were intensely jealous of Jesus because he undermined their authority and challenged their views. But Nicodemus was searching for truth, and he believed that Jesus had some answers. A learned teacher himself, he came to Jesus to be taught. Nicodemus came to Jesus personally, although he could have sent one of his assistants. He wanted to examine Jesus for himself in order to separate fact from rumor. Perhaps Nicodemus was afraid of what his peers, the Pharisees, would say about his visit, so he came after dark. Later, when he understood that Jesus was truly the Messiah, he spoke up boldly in Jesus' defense (John 7:50-51). Like Nicodemus, we must examine Jesus for ourselves—others cannot do it for us. If we believe he is who he says, we will want to speak up for him.

What did Nicodemus know about the Kingdom? From the Bible he knew it would be ruled by God, it would be restored on earth, and it would incorporate God's people. Jesus revealed to this devout Pharisee that the Kingdom would come to the whole world (John 3:16), not just the Jews, and that Nicodemus wouldn't be a part of it unless he was personally born again (John 3:5).

Nicodemus visits Jesus at night

"How are these things possible?" Nicodemus asked.

Jesus replied, "You are a respected Jewish teacher, and yet you don't understand these things? I assure you, we tell you what we know and have seen, and yet you won't believe our testimony. But if you don't believe me when I tell you about earthly things, how can you possibly believe if I tell you about heavenly things? No one has ever gone to heaven and returned. But the Son of Man has come down from heaven. And as Moses lifted up the bronze snake on a pole in the wilderness, so the Son of Man must be lifted up, so that everyone who believes in him will have eternal life.

"For God loved the world so much that he gave his one and only Son, so that everyone who believes in him will not perish but have eternal life. God sent his Son into the world not to judge the world, but to save the world through him."

JOHN 3:9-17

THE GOSPEL

The entire gospel comes to a focus in John 3:16. God's love is not static or self-centered; it reaches out and draws others in. Here God sets the pattern of true love, the basis for all love relationships—when you love someone dearly, you are willing to give freely to the point of self-sacrifice. God paid with the life of his Son, the highest price he could pay. Jesus accepted our punishment, paid the price for our sins, and then offered us the new life that he had bought for us. When we share the gospel with others, our love must be like Jesus'—willing to give up our own comfort and security so that others might join us in receiving God's love. To "believe" is more than intellectual agreement that Jesus is God. It means to put our trust and confidence in him alone to save us. It is to put Christ in charge of our present plans and eternal destiny. Believing is both trusting his words as reliable and relying on him for the power to change. If you have never trusted Christ, let this promise of everlasting life be yours—and believe.

When the Israelites were wandering in the wilderness, God sent a plague of serpents to punish them for their rebellious attitude. Those doomed to die from snakebite could be healed by obeying God's command to look up at the elevated bronze snake and by believing that God would heal them if they did.

Nicodemus visits Jesus at night

"There is no judgment against anyone who believes in him. But anyone who does not believe in him has already been judged for not believing in God's one and only Son. And the judgment is based on this fact: God's light came into the world, but people loved the darkness more than the light, for their actions were evil. All who do evil hate the light and refuse to go near it for fear their sins will be exposed. But those who do what is right come to the light so others can see that they are doing what God wants." JOHN 3:18-21

LIVING IN THE LIGHT

Many people don't want their lives exposed to God's light because they are afraid of what will be revealed. They don't want to be changed. Don't be surprised when these same people are threatened by your desire to obey God and do what is right, because they are afraid that the light in you may expose some of the darkness in their lives. Rather than giving in to discouragement, keep praying that they will come to see how much better it is to live in light than in darkness.

People often try to protect themselves from their fears by putting their faith in something they do or have: good works, skill or intelligence, money or possessions. But only God can save us from the one thing that we really need to fear—eternal condemnation.

February 16 READ JOHN 3:22-30

John the Baptist tells more about Jesus

Then Jesus and his disciples left Jerusalem and went into the Judean countryside. Jesus spent some time with them there, baptizing people.

At this time John the Baptist was baptizing at Aenon, near Salim, because there was plenty of water there; and people kept coming to him for baptism. (This was before John was thrown into prison.) A debate broke out between John's disciples and a certain Jew over ceremonial cleansing. So John's disciples came to him and said, "Rabbi, the man you met on the other side of the Jordan River, the one you identified as the Messiah, is also baptizing people. And everybody is going to him instead of coming to us."

John replied, "No one can receive anything unless God gives it from heaven. You yourselves know how plainly I told you, 'I am not the Messiah. I am only here to prepare the way for him.' It is the bridegroom who marries the bride, and the best man is simply glad to stand with him and hear his vows. Therefore, I am filled with joy at his success. He must become greater and greater, and I must become less and less." JOHN 3:22-30

FOLLOWING GOD'S CALL

Why did John the Baptist continue to baptize after Jesus came onto the scene? Why didn't he become a disciple too? John explained that because God had given him his work, he had to continue it until God called him to do something else. John's main purpose was to point people to Christ. Even with Jesus beginning his own ministry, John could still turn people to Jesus. Although John was the first genuine prophet in four hundred years, Jesus the Messiah would be infinitely greater than he was. What John began, Jesus finished. What John prepared, Jesus fulfilled. Yet John willingly did the task to which he had been called. We must do the same, serving where we are called and doing the tasks set before us to the best of our ability. While others may get the glory and we may feel jealous of others or wish we had their gifts or positions, we must remember that our goal is to glorify Christ and complete his work on earth.

John's willingness to decrease in importance shows unusual humility. Pastors and other Christian leaders can be tempted to focus more on the success of their ministries than on Christ. Beware of those who put more emphasis on their own achievements than on God's Kingdom.

John the Baptist tells more about Jesus

"He has come from above and is greater than anyone else. We are of the earth, and we speak of earthly things, but he has come from heaven and is greater than anyone else. He testifies about what he has seen and heard, but how few believe what he tells them! Anyone who accepts his testimony can affirm that God is true. For he is sent by God. He speaks God's words, for God gives him the Spirit without limit. The Father loves his Son and has put everything into his hands. And anyone who believes in God's Son has eternal life. Anyone who doesn't obey the Son will never experience eternal life but remains under God's angry judgment." JOHN 3:31-36

THE CHOICE

Jesus' testimony was trustworthy because he had come from heaven and was speaking of what he had seen there. His words were the very words of God. Your whole spiritual life depends on your answer to one question: Who is Jesus Christ? If you accept Jesus as only a prophet or a teacher, you have to reject his teaching, for he claimed to be God's Son, even God himself. The heartbeat of John's Gospel is the dynamic truth that Jesus Christ is God's Son, the Messiah, the Savior who was from the beginning and will continue to live forever. This same Jesus has invited us to accept him and live with him eternally. When we understand who Jesus is, we are compelled to believe what he said. We are responsible to decide today whom we will obey (Joshua 24:15), and God wants us to choose him and life (Deuteronomy 30:15-20). The wrath of God is his final judgment and rejection of the sinner. To put off the choice is to choose not to follow Christ. Indecision is a fatal decision.

Jesus said that those who believe in him have (not will have) everlasting life. To receive eternal life is to join in God's life, which by nature is eternal. Thus, eternal life begins at the moment of spiritual rebirth.

February 18

Herod puts John in prison

John also publicly criticized Herod Antipas, the ruler of Galilee, for marrying Herodias, his brother's wife, and for many other wrongs he had done. So Herod put John in prison, adding this sin to his many others. LUKE 3:19-20

THROWING AWAY THE KEY

John the Baptist spoke out against Herod's adultery. This was Herod Antipas, tetrarch of Galilee and Perea. He had married Herodias, who was previously married to his brother, Herod Philip I. Besides being his brother's wife, Herodias was also his niece. Rather than accept John's rebuke, Herod moved to silence John. People hate to be confronted with their sin. We should not be surprised when the world tries to silence Christians today. Yet we should have the courage of John the Baptist and speak the truth in love, regardless of the consequences.

The Herods were a murderous and deceitful family. Rebuking a tyrannical Roman official who could imprison and execute him was extremely dangerous, yet that is what John did. He fearlessly risked his life to speak out against sin.

Jesus talks to a woman at the well

Jesus knew the Pharisees had heard that he was baptizing and making more disciples than John (though Jesus himself didn't baptize them—his disciples did). So he left Judea and returned to Galilee.

He had to go through Samaria on the way. Eventually he came to the Samaritan village of Sychar, near the field that Jacob gave to his son Joseph. Jacob's well was there; and Jesus, tired from the long walk, sat wearily beside the well about noontime. Soon a Samaritan woman came to draw water, and Jesus said to her, "Please give me a drink." He was alone at the time because his disciples had gone into the village to buy some food.

The woman was surprised, for Jews refuse to have anything to do with Samaritans. She said to Jesus, "You are a Jew, and I am a Samaritan woman. Why are you asking me for a drink?"

Jesus replied, "If you only knew the gift God has for you and who you are speaking to, you would ask me, and I would give you living water."

"But sir, you don't have a rope or a bucket," she said, "and this well is very deep. Where would you get this living water? And besides, do you think you're greater than our ancestor Jacob, who gave us this well? How can you offer better water than he and his sons and his animals enjoyed?"

Jesus replied, "Anyone who drinks this water will soon become thirsty again. But those who drink the water I give will never be thirsty again. It becomes a fresh, bubbling spring within them, giving them eternal life."

"Please, sir," the woman said, "give me this water! Then I'll never be thirsty again, and I won't have to come here to get water." JOHN 4:1-15

THIRST QUENCHER

Many spiritual functions parallel physical functions. As our bodies hunger and thirst, so do our souls. But our souls need *spiritual* food and water. The woman confused the two kinds of water, perhaps because no one had ever talked with her about her spiritual hunger and thirst before. We would not think of depriving our bodies of food and water when they hunger or thirst. Why then should we deprive our souls? The living Word, Jesus Christ, and the written Word, the Bible, can satisfy our hungry and thirsty souls. The woman mistakenly believed that if she received the water Jesus offered, she would not have to return to the well each day. She was interested in Jesus' message because she thought it could make her life easier. But if that were always the case, people would accept Christ's message for the wrong reasons. Christ did not come to take away challenges but to change us on the inside, helping us see our problems from God's perspective and empowering us to deal with them. Jesus wants to help you, too. Let him change you from the inside out.

Jesus talks to a woman at the well

"Go and get your husband," Jesus told her.

"I don't have a husband," the woman replied.

Jesus said, "You're right! You don't have a husband—for you have had five husbands, and you aren't even married to the man you're living with now. You certainly spoke the truth!"

"Sir," the woman said, "you must be a prophet. So tell me, why is it that you Jews insist that Jerusalem is the only place of worship, while we Samaritans claim it is here at Mount Gerizim, where our ancestors worshiped?"

Jesus replied, "Believe me, dear woman, the time is coming when it will no longer matter whether you worship the Father on this mountain or in Jerusalem. You Samaritans know very little about the one you worship, while we Jews know all about him, for salvation comes through the Jews. But the time is coming— indeed it's here now—when true worshipers will worship the Father in spirit and in truth. The Father is looking for those who will worship him that way. For God is Spirit, so those who worship him must worship in spirit and in truth."

The woman said, "I know the Messiah is coming—the one who is called Christ. When he comes, he will explain everything to us."

Then Jesus told her, "I AM the Messiah!"   JOHN 4:16-26

THE HOLY SPIRIT'S HELP

"God is Spirit" means he is not a physical being, limited to one place. He is present everywhere, and he can be worshiped anywhere, at any time. It is not *where* we worship that counts, but *how* we worship. Is your worship genuine and true? Do you have the Holy Spirit's help? How does the Holy Spirit help us worship? The Holy Spirit prays for us (Romans 8:26), teaches us the words of Christ (John 14:26), and tells us we are loved (Romans 5:5). Focus your worship on who God is and what he has done for you. Ask for the Holy Spirit's help.

The woman brought up a popular theological issue—the correct place to worship. But her question was a diversion to keep Jesus away from her deepest need. Jesus directed the conversation to a much more important point: The location of worship is not nearly as important as the attitude of the worshipers.

Jesus tells about the spiritual harvest

Just then his disciples came back. They were shocked to find him talking to a woman, but none of them had the nerve to ask, "What do you want with her?" or "Why are you talking to her?" The woman left her water jar beside the well and ran back to the village, telling everyone, "Come and see a man who told me everything I ever did! Could he possibly be the Messiah?" So the people came streaming from the village to see him.

Meanwhile, the disciples were urging Jesus, "Rabbi, eat something."

But Jesus replied, "I have a kind of food you know nothing about."

"Did someone bring him food while we were gone?" the disciples asked each other.

Then Jesus explained: "My nourishment comes from doing the will of God, who sent me, and from finishing his work. You know the saying, 'Four months between planting and harvest.' But I say, wake up and look around. The fields are already ripe for harvest. The harvesters are paid good wages, and the fruit they harvest is people brought to eternal life. What joy awaits both the planter and the harvester alike! You know the saying, 'One plants and another harvests.' And it's true. I sent you to harvest where you didn't plant; others had already done the work, and now you will get to gather the harvest." JOHN 4:27-38

WAGES OF JOY

The wages Jesus offers are the joys of working for him and seeing the harvest of believers. These wages come to sower and reaper alike because both find joy in seeing new believers come into Christ's Kingdom. The phrase "others had already done the work" (John 4:38) may refer to the Old Testament prophets and to John the Baptist, who paved the way for the gospel. Sometimes Christians excuse themselves from witnessing by saying that their families or friends aren't ready to believe. Jesus makes it clear, however, that around us a continual harvest waits to be reaped. Don't let Jesus find you making excuses. Look around. You will find people ready to hear God's Word.

The "food" about which Jesus was speaking was spiritual nourishment. It includes more than Bible study, prayer, and attending church. Spiritual nourishment also comes from doing God's will and helping to bring his work of salvation to completion. We are nourished not only by what we take in but also by what we give out for God.

February 22 READ JOHN 4:39-42

Many Samaritans believe in Jesus

Many Samaritans from the village believed in Jesus because the woman had said, "He told me everything I ever did!" When they came out to see him, they begged him to stay in their village. So he stayed for two days, long enough for many more to hear his message and believe. Then they said to the woman, "Now we believe, not just because of what you told us, but because we have heard him ourselves. Now we know that he is indeed the Savior of the world."

JOHN 4:39-42

BREAKING THE BARRIERS

After the northern kingdom, with its capital at Samaria, fell to the Assyrians, many Jews were deported to Assyria, and foreigners were brought in to settle the land and help keep the peace (2 Kings 17:24). The intermarriage between those foreigners and the remaining Jews resulted in a mixed race, impure in the opinion of Jews who lived in the southern kingdom. Thus, the pure Jews hated this mixed race, called Samaritans, because they felt that their fellow Jews who had intermarried had betrayed their people and nation. The Samaritans had set up an alternate center for worship on Mount Gerizim (referred to in John 4:20) to parallel the Temple at Jerusalem, but it had been destroyed 150 years earlier. The Jews did everything they could to avoid traveling through Samaria. But Jesus had no reason to live by such cultural restrictions. The route through Samaria was shorter, so that was the route he took. As a result, many Samaritans became believers. Never let cultural or social prejudices keep you from sharing the gospel.

The Samaritan woman immediately shared her experience with others. Despite her reputation, many took her invitation and came out to meet Jesus. Perhaps there are sins in our past of which we're ashamed. But Christ changes us. As people see these changes, they become curious. We share these opportunities to introduce people to Christ.

Jesus preaches in Galilee

When Jesus heard that John had been arrested, he left Judea and returned to Galilee. He went first to Nazareth, then left there and moved to Capernaum, beside the Sea of Galilee, in the region of Zebulun and Naphtali. This fulfilled what God said through the prophet Isaiah: "In the land of Zebulun and of Naphtali, beside the sea, beyond the Jordan River, in Galilee where so many Gentiles live, the people who sat in darkness have seen a great light. And for those who lived in the land where death casts its shadow, a light has shined."

From then on Jesus began to preach, "Repent of your sins and turn to God, for the Kingdom of Heaven is near."

MATTHEW 4:12-17 *(see also Mark 1:14-15; Luke 4:14-15; John 4:43-45)*

THE KINGDOM

The "Kingdom of Heaven" has the same meaning as the "Kingdom of God" in Mark and Luke. Matthew used this phrase because the Jews, out of intense reverence and respect, did not pronounce God's name. The Kingdom of Heaven began when God himself entered human history as a man. Today Jesus Christ reigns in the hearts of believers, but the Kingdom of Heaven will not be fully realized until all evil in the world is judged and removed. Christ came to earth first as a suffering Servant; he will come again as King and Judge to rule victoriously over all the earth. Still, the Kingdom of Heaven is near today because it has arrived in our hearts. When you feel overwhelmed by life and destroyed by circumstances, remember that this world isn't all there is. Jesus will return—the Kingdom of Heaven is near.

Jesus moved from Nazareth, his hometown, to Capernaum, about twenty miles farther north. Capernaum became Jesus' home base during his ministry in Galilee. Capernaum was a thriving city with great wealth as well as great decadence. Because it was the headquarters for many Roman troops, word about Jesus could spread all over the Roman Empire. Jesus' move fulfilled the prophecy of Isaiah 9:1-2, which stated that the Messiah would be a light to the land of Zebulun and Naphtali, the region of Galilee where Capernaum was located. Zebulun and Naphtali were two of the original twelve tribes of Israel.

Jesus heals a government official's son

As he traveled through Galilee, he came to Cana, where he had turned the water into wine. There was a government official in nearby Capernaum whose son was very sick. When he heard that Jesus had come from Judea to Galilee, he went and begged Jesus to come to Capernaum to heal his son, who was about to die.

Jesus asked, "Will you never believe in me unless you see miraculous signs and wonders?"

The official pleaded, "Lord, please come now before my little boy dies."

Then Jesus told him, "Go back home. Your son will live!" And the man believed what Jesus said and started home.

While the man was on his way, some of his servants met him with the news that his son was alive and well. He asked them when the boy had begun to get better, and they replied, "Yesterday afternoon at one o'clock his fever suddenly disappeared!" Then the father realized that that was the very time Jesus had told him, "Your son will live." And he and his entire household believed in Jesus. This was the second miraculous sign Jesus did in Galilee after coming from Judea.　JOHN 4:46-54

FAITH IN ACTION

This government official was probably in Herod's service. He had walked twenty miles to see Jesus and addressed him as "Lord," putting himself under Jesus even though he had legal authority over Jesus. Not only did this official believe Jesus could heal, he also obeyed Jesus by returning home, thus demonstrating his faith. It isn't enough for us to say we believe that Jesus can take care of our problems. We need to act out that faith. When you pray about a need or problem, live in a way that shows you believe Jesus can do what he says. Notice how the official's faith grew. First, he believed enough to ask Jesus to help his son. Second, he believed Jesus' assurance that his son would live, and he acted on it. Third, he and his whole household believed in Jesus. Faith is a gift that grows as we use it.

Jesus' miracles were not mere illusions, the product of wishful thinking. Although the official's son was twenty miles away, he was healed when Jesus spoke the word. Distance was no problem because Christ has mastery over space. We can never put so much space between ourselves and Christ that he can no longer help us.

Jesus is rejected at Nazareth

When [Jesus] came to the village of Nazareth, his boyhood home, he went as usual to the synagogue on the Sabbath and stood up to read the Scriptures. The scroll of Isaiah the prophet was handed to him. He unrolled the scroll and found the place where this was written: "The Spirit of the LORD is upon me, for he has anointed me to bring Good News to the poor. He has sent me to proclaim that captives will be released, that the blind will see, that the oppressed will be set free, and that the time of the LORD's favor has come."

He rolled up the scroll, handed it back to the attendant, and sat down. All eyes in the synagogue looked at him intently. Then he began to speak to them. "The Scripture you've just heard has been fulfilled this very day!"

Everyone spoke well of him and was amazed by the gracious words that came from his lips. "How can this be?" they asked. "Isn't this Joseph's son?"

Then he said, "You will undoubtedly quote me this proverb: 'Physician, heal yourself'—meaning, 'Do miracles here in your hometown like those you did in Capernaum.' But I tell you the truth, no prophet is accepted in his own hometown.

"Certainly there were many needy widows in Israel in Elijah's time, when the heavens were closed for three and a half years, and a severe famine devastated the land. Yet Elijah was not sent to any of them. He was sent instead to a foreigner—a widow of Zarephath in the land of Sidon. And there were many lepers in Israel in the time of the prophet Elisha, but the only one healed was Naaman, a Syrian."

When they heard this, the people in the synagogue were furious. Jumping up, they mobbed him and forced him to the edge of the hill on which the town was built. They intended to push him over the cliff, but he passed right through the crowd and went on his way. LUKE 4:16-30

GOOD NEWS

Jesus was quoting from Isaiah 61:1-2. Isaiah had pictured the deliverance of Israel from exile in Babylon as a Year of Jubilee, in which all debts are canceled, all slaves are freed, and all property is returned to original owners (Leviticus 25). But the release from Babylonian exile had not brought the fulfillment the people had expected; they were still a conquered and oppressed people. So Isaiah must have been referring to a future messianic age. Jesus boldly announced, "The Scripture you've just heard has been fulfilled this very day!" Jesus was proclaiming himself as the one who would bring this good news to pass, but in a way that the people would not yet be able to grasp. Jesus was not accepted as a prophet in his hometown. Many people have a similar attitude—an expert is anyone who carries a briefcase and comes from more than two hundred miles away. Don't be surprised when your Christian life and faith are not easily understood or accepted by those who know you well.

Jesus' remarks filled the people of Nazareth with rage because he was saying that God sometimes chooses to reach Gentiles rather than Jews. Jesus implied that his hearers were as unbelieving as the citizens of the northern kingdom of Israel in the days of Elijah and Elisha, a time notorious for its great wickedness.

Four fishermen follow Jesus

One day as Jesus was walking along the shore of the Sea of Galilee, he saw Simon and his brother Andrew throwing a net into the water, for they fished for a living. Jesus called out to them, "Come, follow me, and I will show you how to fish for people!" And they left their nets at once and followed him.

A little farther up the shore Jesus saw Zebedee's sons, James and John, in a boat repairing their nets. He called them at once, and they also followed him, leaving their father, Zebedee, in the boat with the hired men.

MARK 1:16-20 *(see also Matthew 4:18-22)*

TRUE FOLLOWERS

We often assume that Jesus' disciples were great men of faith from the first time they met Jesus. But they had to grow in their faith just as all believers do (Mark 14:48-50, 66-72; John 14:1-9; John 20:26-29). This is apparently not the only time Jesus called Peter (Simon), James, and John to follow him (see Luke 5:1-11 and John 1:35-42 for two other times). Although it took a while for Jesus' call and his message to get through, the disciples still *followed*. In the same way, we may question and falter, but we must never stop following Jesus.

Fishing was a major industry around the Sea of Galilee. Fishing with nets was the most common method. Capernaum, the largest of the more than thirty fishing towns around the lake at that time, became Jesus' new home (Matthew 4:12-13).

Jesus teaches with great authority

Jesus went to Capernaum, a town in Galilee, and taught there in the synagogue every Sabbath day. There, too, the people were amazed at his teaching, for he spoke with authority.

Once when he was in the synagogue, a man possessed by a demon—an evil spirit—began shouting at Jesus, "Go away! Why are you interfering with us, Jesus of Nazareth? Have you come to destroy us? I know who you are—the Holy One sent from God!"

Jesus cut him short. "Be quiet! Come out of the man," he ordered. At that, the demon threw the man to the floor as the crowd watched; then it came out of him without hurting him further.

Amazed, the people exclaimed, "What authority and power this man's words possess! Even evil spirits obey him, and they flee at his command!" The news about Jesus spread through every village in the entire region.

LUKE 4:31-37 *(see also Mark 1:21-28)*

JESUS VS. SATAN

A man possessed by a demon was in the synagogue where Jesus was teaching. This man made his way into the place of worship and verbally abused Jesus. The people were amazed at Jesus' authority to drive out demons—evil (unclean) spirits ruled by Satan and sent to harass people and tempt them to sin. Demons are fallen angels who have joined Satan in rebellion against God. Demons can cause a person to become mute, deaf, blind, or insane. Jesus faced many demons during his time on earth, and he always exerted authority over them. Not only did the evil spirit leave this man, but Luke records that the man was not even injured. Evil permeates our world, and it is no wonder that people are often fearful. Jesus' power, however, is far greater than Satan's. The first step toward conquering fear of evil is to recognize Jesus' authority and power. He has overcome all evil, including Satan himself.

Why was Jesus allowed to teach in the synagogues? Jesus was taking advantage of the policy of allowing visitors to teach. Itinerant rabbis were always welcome to speak to those gathered each Sabbath in the synagogues. The apostle Paul also profited from this practice (see Acts 13:5; 14:1).

Jesus heals Peter's mother-in-law and many others

After leaving the synagogue that day, Jesus went to Simon's home, where he found Simon's mother-in-law very sick with a high fever. "Please heal her," everyone begged. Standing at her bedside, he rebuked the fever, and it left her. And she got up at once and prepared a meal for them.

As the sun went down that evening, people throughout the village brought sick family members to Jesus. No matter what their diseases were, the touch of his hand healed every one. Many were possessed by demons; and the demons came out at his command, shouting, "You are the Son of God!" But because they knew he was the Messiah, he rebuked them and refused to let them speak.

LUKE 4:38-41 *(see also Matthew 8:14-17; Mark 1:29-34)*

READY TO SERVE

Jesus healed Simon's (Peter's) mother-in-law so completely that not only did the fever leave, but her strength was restored, and she immediately got up and prepared a meal for her guests. Peter's mother-in-law gives us a beautiful example to follow. Her response to Jesus' touch was to wait on Jesus and his disciples— immediately. Has God ever helped you through a dangerous or difficult situation? If so, you should ask yourself, *How can I express my gratitude to him?* Because God has promised us all the rewards of his Kingdom, we should look for ways to serve him and his followers now. God gives us health so that we may serve others.

Why didn't Jesus want the demons to reveal who he was? (1) By commanding the demons to remain silent, Jesus proved his authority and power over them. (2) Jesus wanted the people to believe he was the Messiah because of what he said and did, not because of the demons' words. (3) Jesus wanted to reveal his identity as the Messiah according to his timetable, not according to Satan's timetable. Satan wanted the people to follow Jesus around for what they could get out of him, not because he was the Son of God who could truly set them free from sin's guilt and power.

March 1 READ MARK 1:35-39

Jesus preaches throughout Galilee

Before daybreak the next morning, Jesus got up and went out to an isolated place to pray. Later Simon and the others went out to find him. When they found him, they said, "Everyone is looking for you."

But Jesus replied, "We must go on to other towns as well, and I will preach to them, too. That is why I came." So he traveled throughout the region of Galilee, preaching in the synagogues and casting out demons.

MARK 1:35-39 *(see also Matthew 4:23-25; Luke 4:42-44)*

TIME TO PRAY

Jesus took time to pray. Finding time to pray is not easy, but prayer is the vital link between us and God. Like Jesus, we must break away from others to talk with God, even if we have to get up early in the morning to do it! If Jesus needed solitude for prayer and refreshment, how much more is this true for us? Don't become so busy that life turns into a flurry of activity, leaving no room for quiet fellowship alone with God. No matter how much you have to do, you should always have time for prayer.

The Romans divided the land of Israel into three separate regions: Galilee, Samaria, and Judea. Galilee was the northernmost region, an area about sixty miles long and thirty miles wide. Jesus did much of his ministry in this area, an ideal place for him to teach because there were more than 250 towns concentrated there, with many synagogues.

Jesus provides a miraculous catch of fish

One day as Jesus was preaching on the shore of the Sea of Galilee, great crowds pressed in on him to listen to the word of God. He noticed two empty boats at the water's edge, for the fishermen had left them and were washing their nets. Stepping into one of the boats, Jesus asked Simon, its owner, to push it out into the water. So he sat in the boat and taught the crowds from there.

When he had finished speaking, he said to Simon, "Now go out where it is deeper, and let down your nets to catch some fish."

"Master," Simon replied, "we worked hard all last night and didn't catch a thing. But if you say so, I'll let the nets down again." And this time their nets were so full of fish they began to tear! A shout for help brought their partners in the other boat, and soon both boats were filled with fish and on the verge of sinking.

When Simon Peter realized what had happened, he fell to his knees before Jesus and said, "Oh, Lord, please leave me—I'm too much of a sinner to be around you." For he was awestruck by the number of fish they had caught, as were the others with him. His partners, James and John, the sons of Zebedee, were also amazed.

Jesus replied to Simon, "Don't be afraid! From now on you'll be fishing for people!" And as soon as they landed, they left everything and followed Jesus.

LUKE 5:1-11

DAY TO DAY WITH JESUS

This was the disciples' second call. After the first call (Matthew 4:18-22; Mark 1:16-20), Peter, Andrew, James, and John had gone back to fishing. They continued to watch Jesus, however, as he established his authority in the synagogue, healed the sick, and drove out demons. Here he also established his authority in their lives—he met them on their level and helped them in their work. Simon Peter was awestruck at this miracle, and his first response was to feel his own insignificance in comparison to this man's greatness. Peter knew that Jesus had healed the sick and driven out demons, but he was amazed that Jesus cared about his day-to-day routine and understood his needs. God is interested not only in saving us but also in helping us in our daily activities. From this point on, these disciples left their nets and remained with Jesus. For us, following Jesus means more than just acknowledging him as Savior. We must leave our past behind and commit our future to him.

March 3

Jesus heals a man with leprosy

A man with leprosy came and knelt in front of Jesus, begging to be healed. "If you are willing, you can heal me and make me clean," he said.

Moved with compassion, Jesus reached out and touched him. "I am willing," he said. "Be healed!" Instantly the leprosy disappeared, and the man was healed. Then Jesus sent him on his way with a stern warning: "Don't tell anyone about this. Instead, go to the priest and let him examine you. Take along the offering required in the law of Moses for those who have been healed of leprosy. This will be a public testimony that you have been cleansed."

But the man went and spread the word, proclaiming to everyone what had happened. As a result, large crowds soon surrounded Jesus, and he couldn't publicly enter a town anywhere. He had to stay out in the secluded places, but people from everywhere kept coming to him.

MARK 1:40-45 *(see also Matthew 8:1-4; Luke 5:12-16)*

THE HEALING TOUCH

Leprosy was a feared disease because it had no known cure, and some forms of it were highly contagious. Leprosy had an emotional impact and terror associated with it, just as AIDS does today. (Sometimes called Hansen's disease, leprosy still exists in a less contagious form that can be treated.) The priests monitored the disease, banishing lepers who were in a contagious stage to prevent the spread of infection and readmitting lepers whose disease was in remission. Because leprosy destroys the nerve endings, lepers often would unknowingly damage their fingers, toes, and noses. This man with leprosy had an advanced case, so he undoubtedly had lost much bodily tissue. Lepers were considered untouchable because people feared contracting their disease. Yet Jesus reached out and touched the leper to heal him.

The real value of a person is inside, not outside. Although a person's body may be diseased or deformed, the person inside is no less valuable to God. No person is too disgusting for God's touch. In a sense, we are all people with leprosy because we have all been deformed by the ugliness of sin. But by sending his Son, Jesus, God has touched us, giving us the opportunity to be healed. When you feel repulsed by someone, remember how God feels about that person—and about you.

Jesus heals a paralyzed man

When Jesus returned to Capernaum several days later, the news spread quickly that he was back home. Soon the house where he was staying was so packed with visitors that there was no more room, even outside the door. While he was preaching God's word to them, four men arrived carrying a paralyzed man on a mat. They couldn't bring him to Jesus because of the crowd, so they dug a hole through the roof above his head. Then they lowered the man on his mat, right down in front of Jesus. Seeing their faith, Jesus said to the paralyzed man, "My child, your sins are forgiven."

But some of the teachers of religious law who were sitting there thought to themselves, "What is he saying? This is blasphemy! Only God can forgive sins!"

Jesus knew immediately what they were thinking, so he asked them, "Why do you question this in your hearts? Is it easier to say to the paralyzed man 'Your sins are forgiven,' or 'Stand up, pick up your mat, and walk'? So I will prove to you that the Son of Man has the authority on earth to forgive sins." Then Jesus turned to the paralyzed man and said, "Stand up, pick up your mat, and go home!"

And the man jumped up, grabbed his mat, and walked out through the stunned onlookers. They were all amazed and praised God, exclaiming, "We've never seen anything like this before!"

MARK 2:1-12 *(see also Matthew 9:1-8; Luke 5:17-26)*

MOVED TO ACTION

It wasn't the paralyzed man's faith that impressed Jesus, but the faith of his friends. The paralyzed man's need moved his friends to action, and they brought him to Jesus. Jesus responded to their faith and healed the man. For better or worse, our faith affects others. When you recognize someone's need, do you act? Many people have physical and spiritual needs you can meet, either by yourself or with others who are also concerned. Human need moved these four men; let it also move you to compassionate action. We cannot make another person a Christian, but we can do much through our words, actions, and love to give him or her a chance to respond. Look for opportunities to bring your friends to the living Christ.

Houses in Bible times were built of stone. They had flat roofs made of mud mixed with straw. Outside stairways led to the roofs. These friends may have carried the paralyzed man up the outside stairs to the roof. They then could easily have taken apart the mud and straw mixture to make a hole through which to lower their friend to Jesus.

Jesus eats with sinners at Matthew's house

As Jesus was walking along, he saw a man named Matthew sitting at his tax collector's booth. "Follow me and be my disciple," Jesus said to him. So Matthew got up and followed him.

Later, Matthew invited Jesus and his disciples to his home as dinner guests, along with many tax collectors and other disreputable sinners. But when the Pharisees saw this, they asked his disciples, "Why does your teacher eat with such scum?"

When Jesus heard this, he said, "Healthy people don't need a doctor—sick people do." Then he added, "Now go and learn the meaning of this Scripture: 'I want you to show mercy, not offer sacrifices.' For I have come to call not those who think they are righteous, but those who know they are sinners."

MATTHEW 9:9-13 *(see also Mark 2:13-17; Luke 5:27-32)*

LEAVE IT BEHIND!

Matthew was a Jew who was appointed by the Romans to be the area's tax collector. He collected taxes from the citizens as well as from merchants passing through town. Tax collectors were expected to take a commission on the taxes they collected, but most of them overcharged and kept the profits. Thus, tax collectors were hated by the Jews because of their reputation for cheating and because of their support of Rome. When Jesus called Matthew to be one of his disciples, Matthew got up and followed, leaving a lucrative career. When God calls you to follow or obey him, do you do it with as much abandon as Matthew? Sometimes the decision to follow Christ requires difficult or painful choices. Like Matthew, we must decide to leave behind those things that would keep us from following Christ.

The Pharisees constantly tried to trap Jesus, and they thought his association with these "lowlifes" was the perfect opportunity. They were more concerned with their own appearance of holiness than with helping people, with criticism than with encouragement, with outward respectability than with practical help.

Religious leaders ask Jesus about fasting

One day some people said to Jesus, "John the Baptist's disciples fast and pray regularly, and so do the disciples of the Pharisees. Why are your disciples always eating and drinking?"

Jesus responded, "Do wedding guests fast while celebrating with the groom? Of course not. But someday the groom will be taken away from them, and then they will fast."

Then Jesus gave them this illustration: "No one tears a piece of cloth from a new garment and uses it to patch an old garment. For then the new garment would be ruined, and the new patch wouldn't even match the old garment.

"And no one puts new wine into old wineskins. For the new wine would burst the wineskins, spilling the wine and ruining the skins. New wine must be stored in new wineskins. But no one who drinks the old wine seems to want the new wine. 'The old is just fine,' they say."

LUKE 5:33-39 *(see also Matthew 9:14-17; Mark 2:18-22)*

SOFT HEARTS

Wineskins were goatskins sewed together at the edges to form watertight bags. Because new wine expands as it ages, it had to be put in new, pliable wineskins. A used skin, having become more rigid, would burst and spill the wine. Like old wineskins, the Pharisees were too rigid to accept Jesus, who could not be contained within the confines of their traditions or rules. Christianity required new approaches, new traditions, new structures. Our church programs and ministries should not be so structured that they have no room for a fresh touch of the Spirit, a new method, or a new idea. We, too, must be careful that our hearts do not become so hard that they prevent us from accepting the new way of thinking that Christ brings. We need to keep our hearts pliable so we can accept Jesus' life-changing message.

John's disciples fasted (went without food) as a sign of mourning for sin and to prepare for the Messiah's coming. Jesus' disciples did not need to fast because he is the Messiah and was with them! Jesus did not condemn fasting—he himself fasted (Luke 4:1-2). He emphasized that fasting must be done for the right reasons.

Jesus heals a lame man by a pool

Jesus returned to Jerusalem for one of the Jewish holy days. Inside the city, near the Sheep Gate, was the pool of Bethesda, with five covered porches. Crowds of sick people—blind, lame, or paralyzed—lay on the porches. One of the men lying there had been sick for thirty-eight years. When Jesus saw him and knew he had been ill for a long time, he asked him, "Would you like to get well?"

"I can't, sir," the sick man said, "for I have no one to put me into the pool when the water bubbles up. Someone else always gets there ahead of me."

Jesus told him, "Stand up, pick up your mat, and walk!"

Instantly, the man was healed! He rolled up his sleeping mat and began walking! JOHN 5:1-9

GOD MEETS NEEDS

Jesus appropriately asked, "Would you like to get well?" After thirty-eight years, this man's problem had become a way of life. No one had ever helped him. He had no hope of ever being healed and no desire to help himself. The man's situation looked hopeless. But no matter how trapped you feel in your infirmities, God can minister to your deepest needs. Don't let a problem or hardship cause you to lose hope. God may have special work for you to do in spite of your condition, or even because of it. Many have ministered effectively to hurting people because they have triumphed over their own hurts.

Some ancient manuscripts include an additional verse (verse 4, which is not in the better manuscripts) that refers to an angel of the Lord who came from time to time and stirred up the waters. Whether or not this occurred, Jesus healed the man who had been waiting for years to be healed.

Jesus heals a lame man by a pool

Jesus told him, "Stand up, pick up your mat, and walk!"

Instantly, the man was healed! He rolled up his sleeping mat and began walking! But this miracle happened on the Sabbath, so the Jewish leaders objected. They said to the man who was cured, "You can't work on the Sabbath! The law doesn't allow you to carry that sleeping mat!"

But he replied, "The man who healed me told me, 'Pick up your mat and walk.'"

"Who said such a thing as that?" they demanded.

The man didn't know, for Jesus had disappeared into the crowd. But afterward Jesus found him in the Temple and told him, "Now you are well; so stop sinning, or something even worse may happen to you." Then the man went and told the Jewish leaders that it was Jesus who had healed him.   JOHN 5:8-15

THE GREATEST MIRACLE

This man had been lame or paralyzed, and suddenly he could walk. This was a great miracle. But he needed an even greater miracle—to have his sins forgiven. The man was delighted to be physically healed, but he had to turn from his sins and seek God's forgiveness to be spiritually healed. God's forgiveness is the greatest gift you will ever receive. Don't neglect his gracious offer.

According to the Pharisees, carrying one's bed (a mat) on the Sabbath was work and was therefore unlawful. It did not break an Old Testament law, but merely the Pharisees' interpretation of God's command to "remember to observe the Sabbath day by keeping it holy" (Exodus 20:8). This was just one of hundreds of rules they had added to the Old Testament law.

Jesus claims to be God's Son

So the Jewish leaders began harassing Jesus for breaking the Sabbath rules. But Jesus replied, "My Father is always working, and so am I." So the Jewish leaders tried all the harder to find a way to kill him. For he not only broke the Sabbath, he called God his Father, thereby making himself equal with God.

So Jesus explained, "I tell you the truth, the Son can do nothing by himself. He does only what he sees the Father doing. Whatever the Father does, the Son also does. For the Father loves the Son and shows him everything he is doing. In fact, the Father will show him how to do even greater works than healing this man. Then you will truly be astonished. For just as the Father gives life to those he raises from the dead, so the Son gives life to anyone he wants. In addition, the Father judges no one. Instead, he has given the Son absolute authority to judge, so that everyone will honor the Son, just as they honor the Father. Anyone who does not honor the Son is certainly not honoring the Father who sent him."

JOHN 5:16-23

LIVING FOR JESUS

Jesus was identifying himself with God, his Father. There could be no doubt as to his claim to be God. Jesus does not leave us the option to believe in God while ignoring God's Son. Because of his unity with God, Jesus lived as God wanted him to live. Because of our identification with Jesus, we must honor him and live as he wants us to live. The questions "What would Jesus do?" and "What would Jesus have me do?" may help you make the right choices.

If God stopped every kind of work on the Sabbath, nature would fall into chaos, and sin would overrun the world. Genesis 2:2 says that God rested on the seventh day, but this doesn't mean that he stopped doing good. Jesus was teaching that when the opportunity to do good presents itself, we should act, even on the Sabbath.

Jesus claims to be God's Son

"I tell you the truth, those who listen to my message and believe in God who sent me have eternal life. They will never be condemned for their sins, but they have already passed from death into life.

"And I assure you that the time is coming, indeed it's here now, when the dead will hear my voice—the voice of the Son of God. And those who listen will live. The Father has life in himself, and he has granted that same life-giving power to his Son. And he has given him authority to judge everyone because he is the Son of Man. Don't be so surprised! Indeed, the time is coming when all the dead in their graves will hear the voice of God's Son, and they will rise again. Those who have done good will rise to experience eternal life, and those who have continued in evil will rise to experience judgment. I can do nothing on my own. I judge as God tells me. Therefore, my judgment is just, because I carry out the will of the one who sent me, not my own will." JOHN 5:24-30

TO LIVE FOREVER

When he said that the dead will hear his voice, Jesus was talking about the spiritually dead who hear, understand, and accept him. Those who accept Jesus, the Word, will have eternal life. Jesus was also talking about the physically dead. He raised several dead people while he was on earth, and at his second coming, "Christians who have died will rise from their graves" (1 Thessalonians 4:16). "Eternal life"—living forever with God—begins when you accept Jesus Christ as Savior. At that moment new life begins in you (2 Corinthians 5:17). It is a completed transaction. You still will face physical death, but when Christ returns, your body will be resurrected to live forever with him (1 Corinthians 15). Those who have rebelled against Christ, who have ignored God and lived only for themselves, will find that death does not end it all. There is a judgment to face. They will be resurrected, too, but will stand before God's throne and be sentenced to an eternity apart from him. You can help people be saved from eternal death by telling them the good news about Christ's eternal life.

God is the Source and Creator of life. Because Jesus is eternally existent with God, the Creator, he, too, is "the life" (John 14:6) through whom we may live eternally (see 1 John 5:11).

Jesus supports his claim

"If I were to testify on my own behalf, my testimony would not be valid. But someone else is also testifying about me, and I assure you that everything he says about me is true. In fact, you sent investigators to listen to John the Baptist, and his testimony about me was true. Of course, I have no need of human witnesses, but I say these things so you might be saved. John was like a burning and shining lamp, and you were excited for a while about his message. But I have a greater witness than John—my teachings and my miracles. The Father gave me these works to accomplish, and they prove that he sent me. And the Father who sent me has testified about me himself. You have never heard his voice or seen him face to face, and you do not have his message in your hearts, because you do not believe me—the one he sent to you.

"You search the Scriptures because you think they give you eternal life. But the Scriptures point to me! Yet you refuse to come to me to receive this life."

JOHN 5:31-40

MISSING THE SAVIOR

The religious leaders knew what the Bible said but failed to apply its words to their lives. They knew the teachings of the Scriptures but failed to see the Messiah to whom the Scriptures pointed. They knew the rules but missed the Savior. Entrenched in their own religious system, they refused to let the Son of God change their lives. Don't become so involved in "religion" that you miss Christ.

Jesus claimed to be equal with God (John 5:18), to give everlasting life (John 5:24), to be the source of life (John 5:26), and to judge sin (John 5:27). These statements make it clear that Jesus was claiming to be divine—an almost unbelievable claim, but one that was supported by another witness, John the Baptist.

Jesus supports his claim

"Your approval means nothing to me, because I know you don't have God's love within you. For I have come to you in my Father's name, and you have rejected me. Yet if others come in their own name, you gladly welcome them. No wonder you can't believe! For you gladly honor each other, but you don't care about the honor that comes from the one who alone is God.

"Yet it isn't I who will accuse you before the Father. Moses will accuse you! Yes, Moses, in whom you put your hopes. If you really believed Moses, you would believe me, because he wrote about me. But since you don't believe what he wrote, how will you believe what I say?"   JOHN 5:41-47

PRAISE SEEKERS

Whose praise do you seek? The religious leaders enjoyed great prestige in Israel, but their stamp of approval meant nothing to Jesus. He was concerned about God's approval. This is a good principle for us. If even the highest officials in the world approve of our actions and God does not, we should be concerned. But if God approves, even though others don't, we should be content.

The Pharisees prided themselves on being the true followers of their ancestor Moses. They were trying to follow every one of his laws to the letter. Jesus' warning that Moses would accuse them stung them to fury. Moses wrote about Jesus (Genesis 3:15; Numbers 24:17; Deuteronomy 18:15), yet the religious leaders refused to believe Jesus when he came.

March 13

The disciples pick wheat on the Sabbath

Jesus was walking through some grainfields on the Sabbath. His disciples were hungry, so they began breaking off some heads of grain and eating them. But some Pharisees saw them do it and protested, "Look, your disciples are breaking the law by harvesting grain on the Sabbath."

Jesus said to them, "Haven't you read in the Scriptures what David did when he and his companions were hungry? He went into the house of God, and he and his companions broke the law by eating the sacred loaves of bread that only the priests are allowed to eat. And haven't you read in the law of Moses that the priests on duty in the Temple may work on the Sabbath? I tell you, there is one here who is even greater than the Temple! But you would not have condemned my innocent disciples if you knew the meaning of this Scripture: 'I want you to show mercy, not offer sacrifices.' For the Son of Man is Lord, even over the Sabbath!"

MATTHEW 12:1-8 *(see also Mark 2:23-28; Luke 6:1-5)*

REMEMBERING THE SABBATH

The Pharisees had established thirty-nine categories of actions forbidden on the Sabbath, based on interpretations of God's law and on Jewish custom. Harvesting was one of those forbidden actions. By picking wheat and rubbing it in their hands, the disciples were technically harvesting, according to the religious leaders. Jesus and the disciples were picking grain because they were hungry, not because they wanted to harvest it. They were not working on the Sabbath. The Pharisees, however, could not (and did not want to) see beyond their laws' technicalities.

Many of the Pharisees were so caught up in their man-made laws and traditions that they lost sight of what was good and right. The Ten Commandments prohibit work on the Sabbath (Exodus 20:8-11). That was the *letter* of the law. But because the *purpose* of the Sabbath is to rest and to worship God, the priests were allowed to work by performing sacrifices and conducting worship services. This "work" was serving and worshiping God. Jesus always emphasized the intent of the law, the meaning behind the letter. God is far more important than the created instruments of worship. If we become more concerned with the means of worship than with the one we worship, we will miss God even as we think we are worshiping him.

Jesus heals a man's hand on the Sabbath

Jesus went into the synagogue again and noticed a man with a deformed hand. Since it was the Sabbath, Jesus' enemies watched him closely. If he healed the man's hand, they planned to accuse him of working on the Sabbath.

Jesus said to the man with the deformed hand, "Come and stand in front of everyone." Then he turned to his critics and asked, "Does the law permit good deeds on the Sabbath, or is it a day for doing evil? Is this a day to save life or to destroy it?" But they wouldn't answer him.

He looked around at them angrily and was deeply saddened by their hard hearts. Then he said to the man, "Hold out your hand." So the man held out his hand, and it was restored! At once the Pharisees went away and met with the supporters of Herod to plot how to kill Jesus.

MARK 3:1-6 *(see also Matthew 12:9-14; Luke 6:6-11)*

WHEN THERE IS A NEED . . .

As the Pharisees watched the man with the deformed hand, they wondered if Jesus would heal him, thereby breaking the Sabbath. Their Sabbath rules said that people could be helped on the Sabbath only if their lives were in danger. Jesus had healed on the Sabbath several times, and none of those healings was in response to an emergency. If Jesus waited until another day, he would be submitting to the Pharisees' authority, showing that their petty rules were equal to God's law. If he healed the man on the Sabbath, the Pharisees could claim that because Jesus broke their rules, his power was not from God. But Jesus made it clear how ridiculous and petty their rules were. God is more concerned about people than rules. The best time to reach out to someone is when he or she needs help. The Pharisees placed their laws above human need. They were so concerned about Jesus breaking one of their rules that they did not care about the man's deformed hand. What is your attitude toward others? If your convictions don't allow you to help certain people, those convictions are not in tune with God's Word. Don't allow dogma to blind you to human need.

The Pharisees plotted Jesus' death because they were outraged (Luke 6:11). Jesus had overruled their authority and had exposed their evil attitudes in front of the entire crowd in the synagogue. Jesus had shown that the Pharisees were more loyal to their religious system than to God.

Large crowds follow Jesus

Jesus went out to the lake with his disciples, and a large crowd followed him. They came from all over Galilee, Judea, Jerusalem, Idumea, from east of the Jordan River, and even from as far north as Tyre and Sidon. The news about his miracles had spread far and wide, and vast numbers of people came to see him.

Jesus instructed his disciples to have a boat ready so the crowd would not crush him. He had healed many people that day, so all the sick people eagerly pushed forward to touch him. And whenever those possessed by evil spirits caught sight of him, the spirits would throw them to the ground in front of him shrieking, "You are the Son of God!" But Jesus sternly commanded the spirits not to reveal who he was. MARK 3:7-12 *(see also Matthew 12:15-21)*

THE TRUE MESSIAH

Jesus warned the demons not to reveal his identity because he did not want them to reinforce a popular misconception. The huge crowds were looking for a political and military leader who would free them from Rome's control, and they thought that the Messiah predicted by the Old Testament prophets would be this kind of man. Jesus wanted to teach the people about the kind of Messiah he was— one who was far different from their expectations. Christ's Kingdom is spiritual. It begins not with the overthrow of governments but with the overthrow of sin in people's hearts. The demons knew that Jesus was the Son of God, but they refused to turn from their evil purposes. Knowing about Jesus, or even believing that he is God's Son, does not guarantee salvation. You must also want to follow and obey him (James 2:17). Have you allowed Christ to reign in your heart?

While Jesus was drawing fire from the religious leaders, he was gaining great popularity among the people. Some were curious, some sought healing, some wanted evidence to use against him, and others wanted to know if Jesus truly was the Messiah. Most of the leaders could only dimly guess at the real meaning of what was happening among them.

Large crowds follow Jesus

Jesus knew what they were planning. So he left that area, and many people followed him. He healed all the sick among them, but he warned them not to reveal who he was. This fulfilled the prophecy of Isaiah concerning him: "Look at my Servant, whom I have chosen. He is my Beloved, who pleases me. I will put my Spirit upon him, and he will proclaim justice to the nations. He will not fight or shout or raise his voice in public. He will not crush the weakest reed or put out a flickering candle. Finally he will cause justice to be victorious. And his name will be the hope of all the world." MATTHEW 12:15-21 *(see also Mark 3:7-12)*

THE SERVANT KING

The people expected the Messiah to be a king. This quotation from Isaiah's prophecy (Isaiah 42:1-4) showed that the Messiah was indeed a king, but it illustrated what *kind* of king—a quiet, gentle ruler who brings justice to the nations. His final victory puts the cross before a crown, brings justice without courtly pomp, and yields victory without an army. As a servant, he brings hope. He brings life by offering his own. Like the crowd in Jesus' day, we may want Christ to rule as a king and bring great and visible victories in our lives. But often Christ's work is quiet, and it happens according to *his* perfect timing, not ours. Take time to reflect on Christ's quiet work in your life. Thank him for what he has done, and continue to stay close to him.

Jesus did not want those he healed to tell others about his miracles because he didn't want the people coming to him for the wrong reasons. That would hinder his teaching ministry and arouse false hopes about an earthly kingdom. But the news of Jesus' miracles spread, and many came to see for themselves.

March 17 READ MARK 3:13-19

Jesus selects the twelve disciples

Afterward Jesus went up on a mountain and called out the ones he wanted to go with him. And they came to him. Then he appointed twelve of them and called them his apostles. They were to accompany him, and he would send them out to preach, giving them authority to cast out demons. These are the twelve he chose: Simon (whom he named Peter), James and John (the sons of Zebedee, but Jesus nicknamed them "Sons of Thunder"), Andrew, Philip, Bartholomew, Matthew, Thomas, James (son of Alphaeus), Thaddaeus, Simon (the zealot), Judas Iscariot (who later betrayed him). MARK 3:13-19 *(see also Luke 6:12-16)*

WILLING DISCIPLES

From the hundreds of people who followed him from place to place, Jesus chose twelve men and "called them his apostles," to be sent out to preach and to cast out demons. He did not choose these twelve to be his companions because of their faith; their faith often faltered. He didn't choose them because of their talent and ability; no one stood out with unusual ability. The disciples represented a wide range of backgrounds and life experiences, but apparently they had no more leadership potential than those who were not chosen. The one characteristic they all shared was their willingness to obey Jesus. After Jesus' ascension, they were filled with the Holy Spirit and empowered to carry out special roles in the growth of the early church. We should not disqualify ourselves from service to Christ because we do not have the expected credentials. Being a good disciple is simply a matter of following Jesus with a willing heart.

Why did Jesus choose twelve men? The number twelve corresponds to the twelve tribes of Israel (Matthew 19:28), showing the continuity between the old religious system and the new one based on Jesus' message. Many people followed Jesus, but these twelve received the most intense training. We see the impact of these men throughout the rest of the New Testament.

Jesus gives the Beatitudes

One day as he saw the crowds gathering, Jesus went up on the mountainside and sat down. His disciples gathered around him, and he began to teach them.
MATTHEW 5:1-2 *(see also Luke 6:17-19)*

WHAT A DISCIPLE CAN EXPECT

Enormous crowds were following Jesus—he was the talk of the town, and everyone wanted to see him. The disciples, who were the closest associates of this popular man, were certainly tempted to feel important, proud, and possessive. Being with Jesus gave them not only prestige but also opportunity for receiving money and power.

The crowds were gathering once again. But before speaking to them, Jesus pulled his disciples aside and warned them about the temptations they would face as his associates. Don't expect fame and fortune, Jesus was saying; instead, expect mourning, hunger, and persecution. Nevertheless, Jesus assured his disciples, they would be rewarded—but perhaps not in this life. There may be times when following Jesus will bring us great popularity. If we don't live by Jesus' words in this sermon, we will find ourselves using God's message only to promote our personal interests.

Matthew 5–7 is called the Sermon on the Mount because Jesus gave it on a hillside near Capernaum. This "sermon" probably covered several days of preaching. The Sermon on the Mount challenged the proud and legalistic religious leaders of the day. It called them back to the messages of the Old Testament prophets who, like Jesus, taught that heartfelt obedience is more important than legalistic observance.

March 19 READ MATTHEW 5:2-3

Jesus gives the Beatitudes

[Jesus] began to teach them. "God blesses those who are poor and realize their need for him, for the Kingdom of Heaven is theirs."

MATTHEW 5:2-3 *(see also Luke 6:20)*

REWARDS OF HUMILITY

With Jesus' announcement that the Kingdom was near (Matthew 4:17), people were naturally asking, "How do I qualify to be in God's Kingdom?" Jesus said that God's Kingdom is organized differently from worldly kingdoms. In the Kingdom of Heaven, wealth and power and authority are unimportant. Kingdom people seek different blessings and benefits, and they have different attitudes. They desire humility rather than chasing after the things of the world, which lead to pride. Are your attitudes a carbon copy of the world's selfishness, pride, and lust for power, or do they reflect the humility and self-sacrifice of Jesus, your King?

The blessings of the Beatitudes aren't a promise of laughter, pleasure, or earthly prosperity. To Jesus, "blessed" means the experience of hope and joy, independent of outward circumstances. To find hope and joy, the deepest form of happiness, follow Jesus no matter what the cost.

Jesus gives the Beatitudes

"God blesses those who mourn, for they will be comforted." MATTHEW 5:4

FORTUNATE MOURNERS

Jesus' words seem to contradict one another. How can people who mourn be blessed? But God's way of living usually contradicts the world's. If you want to live for God, you must be ready to say and do what seems strange to the world. You must be willing to give when others take, to love when others hate, to help when others abuse. By giving up your own rights in order to serve others, you will one day receive everything God has in store for you.

———————————————

The Greek word for "mourn" is the strongest word in that language to designate it—thus it refers to mourning for the dead. People who mourn loved ones know there is no other hope but in the Savior. They experience the reality of the comfort brought by the certainty of eternal life.

———————————————

Jesus gives the Beatitudes

"God blesses those who are humble, for they will inherit the whole earth."

MATTHEW 5:5

MEEK, NOT WEAK

Gentle people are not wimps. Rather, they have tenderhearted spirits that allow them to truly enjoy life. Because they are humble, willing to learn, willing to forgive and be forgiven, willing to take life in stride, it is true that "they will inherit the whole earth." Too often it seems that the movers, pushers, and shakers are the ones who own everything. But how much can they appreciate, really? Instead, it is the people who have learned balance in life and genuine humility who can enjoy all that God has given them. How much of "the whole earth" have you accepted by God's grace? Can you set aside pride and earthly desires in order to be one of God's gentle and lowly ones?

***

Being gentle and lowly (humble) means having a true perspective on ourselves. It does not mean that we should put ourselves down. We see that we are sinners, saved only by God's grace; but we are saved and, therefore, have great worth in God's Kingdom. We should place ourselves in his hands to be used as he wants in order to spread his Word and share his love with others.

***

Jesus gives the Beatitudes

"God blesses those who hunger and thirst for justice, for they will be satisfied."

MATTHEW 5:6 *(see also Luke 6:21)*

THE JUST AND GOOD

The reference in Luke reads, "God blesses you who are hungry now, for you will be satisfied." Some believe that the hunger about which Jesus was speaking is a hunger for righteousness, a desire for "justice," as here in Matthew's verse. Others say this is physical hunger. In any case, in a nation where riches were seen as a sign of God's favor, Jesus startled his hearers by pronouncing blessings on those who hunger. In doing so, however, he was in line with an ancient tradition. The Old Testament is filled with texts proclaiming God's concern for the poor and needy. See, for example, 1 Samuel 2:5; Psalm 146:7; and Isaiah 58:6-7, as well as Jesus' own mother's prayer in Luke 1:53. This promise gives hope to all who are hungry and poor. When you experience loss and are struggling financially, remember God's covenant and look for God's blessings in the midst of poverty.

Only God is truly just and good; we should long to be like him.

Jesus gives the Beatitudes

"God blesses those who are merciful, for they will be shown mercy."

MATTHEW 5:7

THE KIND AND MERCIFUL

Kindness and mercy go hand in hand. Mercy is often used to describe God—the mercy we receive from him allows us to be saved. It is God's mercy alone that brought Jesus to the cross for undeserving sinners. Precisely because of this incredible mercy, believers ought to demonstrate that quality toward others. If we withhold mercy from others after having received it from God, we show that we don't understand or appreciate God's mercy toward us. Showing mercy means we don't criticize hastily; we don't set down demands and expectations of others; we show great patience; and we treat others with the same kindness, generosity, compassion, and understanding that God shows to us every day.

James wrote, "If you have been merciful, God will be merciful when he judges you" (James 2:13). In other words, showing mercy places us under God's mercy as well. Merciful actions are evidence of a vital relationship with Christ.

Jesus gives the Beatitudes

"God blesses those whose hearts are pure, for they will see God."   MATTHEW 5:8

PURE HAPPINESS

A follower of Christ becomes pure and holy through believing and obeying the Word of God (Hebrews 4:12). He or she has already accepted forgiveness through Christ's sacrificial death (Hebrews 7:26-27). But daily application of God's Word purifies our minds and hearts. Scripture points out sin, motivates us to confess, renews our relationship with Christ, and guides us back to the right path. Continue to read, study, and apply God's Word, allowing it to purify your life.

———————————◆◆◆———————————

The word for "pure" means "unmixed, without alloy, as with a pure metal." Pure people are transparent with unmixed motives. Their integrity shines through without question. Their only goal is to do God's will.

———————————◆◆◆———————————

March 25 READ MATTHEW 5:9

Jesus gives the Beatitudes

"God blesses those who work for peace, for they will be called the children of God." MATTHEW 5:9

WORKING FOR PEACE

Many barriers can divide us from other Christians: age, appearance, intelligence, political persuasion, economic status, race, theological perspective. One of the best ways to stifle Christ's love is to be friendly with only those people we like. Fortunately, Christ has knocked down the barriers and unified all believers in one family through his death on the cross. The Holy Spirit helps us look beyond the barriers to the unity we are called to enjoy. People who want peace allow the Holy Spirit to work in their lives and strive to live at peace with everyone (Romans 12:18). Because conflict with the world and its authorities is sometimes inevitable for a Christian (John 15:18 and Acts 5:29), there will be situations where you cannot obey both God and man. At those times you must obey God rather than man.

Because of Christ's death, we have peace with God and peace with one another. We are no longer foreigners or aliens to God, and we are all being built into a holy temple with Christ as our chief cornerstone (1 Peter 2:4).

Jesus gives the Beatitudes

"God blesses those who are persecuted for doing right, for the Kingdom of Heaven is theirs." MATTHEW 5:10

TOUGH HAPPINESS

Jesus said that people persecuted for their faith are blessed! Persecution can be good because (1) it takes our eyes off earthly rewards, (2) it strips away superficial belief, (3) it strengthens the faith of those who endure, and (4) it serves as an example to others who follow. The fact that we are being persecuted proves that we have been faithful; faithless people would not be noticed. Later, two of the disciples, Peter and John, would be imprisoned for their faith (Acts 5:17-41). Yet because they knew how Jesus had suffered, they praised God that he allowed them to be persecuted as their Lord had been. If you are mocked or persecuted for your faith, it isn't because you're doing something wrong but because God has counted you "worthy to suffer disgrace for the name of Jesus" (Acts 5:41). You can then be happy in the middle of persecution, for you have understood what it means to have the Kingdom of Heaven within you.

Notice the progression in the Beatitudes. People who live differently from the way society lives—exposing its evil values by their humility, kindness, gentleness, and peacemaking—will find themselves at odds and persecuted for their beliefs and lifestyle. Jesus would later warn his disciples, "Since [people of the world] persecuted me, naturally they will persecute you" (John 15:20).

Jesus gives the Beatitudes

"God blesses you when people mock you and persecute you and lie about you and say all sorts of evil things against you because you are my followers."

MATTHEW 5:11 *(see also Luke 6:22)*

REJOICING IN PERSECUTION

All believers face trials when they live for Christ in a hostile world. We must accept trials as part of the refining process that burns away impurities and prepares us to meet Christ. Trials teach us patience and help us grow to be the kind of people God wants us to be. Those who stand for Christ will be persecuted because the world is ruled by Christ's greatest enemy. But just as the small group of early believers stood against persecution, so we must be willing to stand for our faith with patience, endurance, and courage.

The early Christians were misunderstood, harassed, tortured, and even put to death. Persecution from Rome came for several reasons: (1) Christians refused to worship the emperor as a god and thus were viewed as atheists and traitors. (2) Christians refused to worship at heathen temples, so business for these moneymaking enterprises dropped wherever Christianity took hold. (3) Christians didn't support the Roman ideals of self, power, and conquest; and Romans scorned the Christian ideal of self-sacrificing service. (4) Christians exposed and rejected the immorality of heathen culture.

Jesus gives the Beatitudes

"Be happy about it! Be very glad! For a great reward awaits you in heaven. And remember, the ancient prophets were persecuted in the same way."

MATTHEW 5:12 *(see also Luke 6:23)*

FUTURE REWARDS

Persecution would become a harsh reality for many early Christians. At the time the apostle John wrote Revelation, the Roman government had stepped up its persecution of Christians, causing John to wonder whether the church could survive and stand against the opposition. But Jesus appeared to John in glory and splendor, reassuring him that he and his fellow believers had access to God's strength to face these trials (Revelation 1:17-18) and that tremendous rewards awaited them. If you are facing difficult problems, remember that the power available to John and the early church is also available to you. In the end, all believers will be with God in heaven. All who have been faithful through the ages will sing before God's throne (Revelation 7:14-17). Their tribulations and sorrows will be over: There will be no more tears for sin, for all sins will have been forgiven; no more tears for suffering, for all suffering will be over; no more tears for death, for all believers will have been resurrected, to die no more.

We can be comforted to know that God's greatest prophets were persecuted. Read about Jeremiah (Jeremiah 38:1-6); Isaiah (tradition says he was killed by King Manasseh—2 Kings 21:16); Amos (Amos 7:10-13); Zechariah (2 Chronicles 24:20-22); and Elijah (1 Kings 19:2).

Jesus gives the Beatitudes

"What sorrow awaits you who are rich, for you have your only happiness now. What sorrow awaits you who are fat and prosperous now, for a time of awful hunger awaits you. What sorrow awaits you who laugh now, for your laughing will turn to mourning and sorrow. What sorrow awaits you who are praised by the crowds, for their ancestors also praised false prophets." LUKE 6:24-26

THE POOR RICH

Despite overwhelming evidence to the contrary, most people still believe that money brings happiness. Rich people craving greater riches can be caught in a cycle that ends only in ruin and destruction. How can you keep away from the love of money? (1) Realize that one day riches will all be gone. (2) Be content with what you have. (3) Monitor what you are willing to do to get more money. (4) Love people more than money. (5) Love God's work more than money. (6) Freely share what you have with others.

There were many false prophets in Old Testament times. They were praised by kings and crowds because their predictions— prosperity and victory in war—were exactly what the people wanted to hear. But popularity is no guarantee of truth, and human flattery does not bring God's approval. Sadness lies ahead for those who chase after the crowd's praise rather than God's truth.

Jesus teaches about salt and light

"You are the salt of the earth. But what good is salt if it has lost its flavor? Can you make it salty again? It will be thrown out and trampled underfoot as worthless." MATTHEW 5:13

GOOD TASTE

If a seasoning has lost its flavor, it has no value. If we Christians make no effort to affect the world around us, we are of little value to God's Kingdom. If we are too much like the world, we are ineffective. Christians should not blend in with everyone else. Instead, we should affect others positively, just as seasoning brings out the best flavor in food. God wants to be active in your life, bringing out the best in you as well. Let him become part of you, penetrating every aspect of your life, preserving you from the evil all around, and healing you of your sins and shortcomings.

In Leviticus 2:13 we read that offerings were seasoned with salt as a reminder of the people's covenant (contract) with God. Salt is a good symbol of God's activity in a person's life because it penetrates, preserves, and aids in healing.

March 31 READ MATTHEW 5:14-16

Jesus teaches about salt and light

*"You are the light of the world—like a city on a hilltop that cannot be hidden.
No one lights a lamp and then puts it under a basket. Instead, a lamp is placed
on a stand, where it gives light to everyone in the house. In the same way,
let your good deeds shine out for all to see, so that everyone will praise your
heavenly Father."* MATTHEW 5:14-16

GOOD LIGHT

Can you hide a city that is sitting on top of a hill? At night, its light can be seen for
miles. If we live for Christ, we will glow like lights, showing others what Christ is
like. We hide our light by (1) being quiet when we should speak, (2) going along
with the crowd, (3) denying the light, (4) letting sin dim our light, (5) not explaining our light to others, or (6) ignoring the needs of others. If we want to have a
relationship with God, we must put aside our sinful ways of living. To claim that
we belong to God but then to go out and live for ourselves is hypocrisy. Be a
beacon of truth—don't shut your light off from the rest of the world.

Light represents what is good, pure, true, holy, and reliable.
Darkness represents what is sinful and evil. Light is also related
to truth in that light exposes whatever exists, whether it is good
or bad. In the dark, good and evil look alike; in the light, they can
be clearly distinguished. Just as darkness cannot exist in the
presence of light, sin cannot exist in the presence of a holy God.

Jesus teaches about the law

"Don't misunderstand why I have come. I did not come to abolish the law of Moses or the writings of the prophets. No, I came to accomplish their purpose. I tell you the truth, until heaven and earth disappear, not even the smallest detail of God's law will disappear until its purpose is achieved. So if you ignore the least commandment and teach others to do the same, you will be called the least in the Kingdom of Heaven. But anyone who obeys God's laws and teaches them will be called great in the Kingdom of Heaven.

"But I warn you—unless your righteousness is better than the righteousness of the teachers of religious law and the Pharisees, you will never enter the Kingdom of Heaven!" MATTHEW 5:17-20

GREATER RIGHTEOUSNESS

The Pharisees were exacting and scrupulous in their attempts to follow their laws. So how can Jesus reasonably call us to a greater righteousness than theirs? The Pharisees' weakness was that they were content to obey the laws outwardly without allowing God to change their hearts or attitudes. Jesus was saying, therefore, that the *quality* of our goodness should be greater than that of the Pharisees. They looked pious, but they were far from the Kingdom of God. God judges our hearts as well as our works, for it is in the heart that our real allegiance lies. Jesus was saying that his listeners needed a different kind of righteousness altogether (love and obedience), not just a more intense version of the Pharisees' righteousness (legal compliance). Our righteousness must (1) come from what God does in us, not what we can do by ourselves; (2) be God-centered, not self-centered; (3) be based on reverence for God, not approval from people; and (4) go beyond keeping the law to living by the principles behind the law.

If Jesus did not come to destroy the law, does that mean all the Old Testament laws still apply to us today? In the Old Testament, there were three categories of law: ceremonial, civil, and moral. The ceremonial law related specifically to Israel's worship. Its primary purpose was to point forward to Jesus Christ. The civil law applied to daily living in Israel. The moral law (such as the Ten Commandments) is the direct command of God, and it still requires strict obedience from God's people.

Jesus teaches about anger

"You have heard that our ancestors were told, 'You must not murder. If you commit murder, you are subject to judgment.' But I say, if you are even angry with someone, you are subject to judgment! If you call someone an idiot, you are in danger of being brought before the court. And if you curse someone, you are in danger of the fires of hell."   MATTHEW 5:21-22

THOUGHT CONTROL

Killing is a terrible sin, but *anger* is a great sin, too, because it also violates God's command to love. Anger in this case refers to a seething, brooding bitterness against someone. It is a dangerous emotion that always threatens to leap out of control, leading to violence, emotional hurt, increased mental stress, and spiritual damage. Anger keeps us from developing a spirit pleasing to God. Have you ever been proud that you didn't strike out and say what was really on your mind? Self-control is good, but Christ wants us to practice thought control as well. Jesus said that we will be held accountable even for our attitudes.

Jesus was not doing away with the law or adding his own beliefs. Rather, he was giving a fuller understanding of why God made the specific laws in the first place.

Jesus teaches about anger

"So if you are presenting a sacrifice at the altar in the Temple and you suddenly remember that someone has something against you, leave your sacrifice there at the altar. Go and be reconciled to that person. Then come and offer your sacrifice to God.

"When you are on the way to court with your adversary, settle your differences quickly. Otherwise, your accuser may hand you over to the judge, who will hand you over to an officer, and you will be thrown into prison. And if that happens, you surely won't be free again until you have paid the last penny."

MATTHEW 5:23-26

GET THINGS RIGHT

Broken relationships can hinder our relationship with God. If we have a problem or grievance with a friend, we should resolve the problem as soon as possible. We are hypocrites if we claim to love God while we hate others. A person's attitude toward others reflects his or her relationship with God. A disagreement may or may not take us to court, but even small conflicts mend more easily if we try to make peace right away. In a broader sense, these verses advise us to get things right with our brothers and sisters before we have to stand before God.

In Jesus' day, people who couldn't pay a debt were thrown into prison until their debt was paid. It is practical advice to resolve our differences with our enemies before their anger causes more trouble (Proverbs 25:8-10).

Jesus teaches about lust

"You have heard the commandment that says, 'You must not commit adultery.' But I say, anyone who even looks at a woman with lust has already committed adultery with her in his heart. So if your eye—even your good eye—causes you to lust, gouge it out and throw it away. It is better for you to lose one part of your body than for your whole body to be thrown into hell. And if your hand—even your stronger hand—causes you to sin, cut it off and throw it away. It is better for you to lose one part of your body than for your whole body to be thrown into hell." MATTHEW 5:27-30

DESIRES

The Old Testament law said that it is wrong for a person to have sex with someone other than his or her spouse (Exodus 20:14). But Jesus said that the *desire* to have sex with someone other than one's spouse is mental adultery and, thus, sin. Jesus emphasized that if the *act* is wrong, then so is the *intention*. To be faithful to your spouse with your body but not your mind is to break the trust so vital to a strong marriage. Jesus is not condemning natural interest in the opposite sex or even healthy sexual desire, but rather the deliberate and repeated filling of one's mind with fantasies that would be evil if acted out. Sinful desires can be just as damaging as sinful actions. Left unchecked, wrong desires will result in wrong actions and turn people away from God. Guard your thoughts—don't give sin a foothold through lust.

When Jesus said to get rid of your hand or your eye, he was speaking figuratively. He didn't mean literally to gouge out your eye, because even a blind person can lust. We sometimes tolerate sins in our lives that, left unchecked, could eventually destroy us. It is better to experience the pain of removal (getting rid of a bad habit or something we treasure too much, for instance) than to allow the sin to bring judgment and condemnation.

Jesus teaches about divorce

"You have heard the law that says, 'A man can divorce his wife by merely giving her a written notice of divorce.' But I say that a man who divorces his wife, unless she has been unfaithful, causes her to commit adultery. And anyone who marries a divorced woman also commits adultery." MATTHEW 5:31-32

A LIFETIME COMMITMENT

Divorce is as hurtful and destructive today as it was in Jesus' day. God intends marriage to be a lifetime commitment (Genesis 2:24). When entering into marriage, people should never consider divorce as an option for solving problems or a way out of a relationship that seems dead. In these verses, Jesus is also attacking those who purposefully abuse the marriage contract, using divorce to satisfy their lustful desire to marry someone else. Are your actions today helping your marriage grow stronger, or are you tearing it apart?

Jesus said that divorce is not permissible except for unfaithfulness. This does not mean that divorce should automatically occur when a spouse commits adultery. "Fornication" implies a sexually immoral lifestyle, not a confessed and repented act of adultery. Those who discover that their partners have been unfaithful should first make every effort to forgive, reconcile, and restore those relationships.

Jesus teaches about vows

"You have also heard that our ancestors were told, 'You must not break your vows; you must carry out the vows you make to the LORD.' But I say, do not make any vows! Do not say, 'By heaven!' because heaven is God's throne. And do not say, 'By the earth!' because the earth is his footstool. And do not say, 'By Jerusalem!' for Jerusalem is the city of the great King. Do not even say, 'By my head!' for you can't turn one hair white or black. Just say a simple, 'Yes, I will,' or 'No, I won't.' Anything beyond this is from the evil one." MATTHEW 5:33-37

PROMISES, PROMISES

Jesus was emphasizing the importance of telling the truth. People were breaking promises and using sacred language casually and carelessly. Keeping oaths and promises is important; it builds trust and makes committed human relationships possible. Are you known as a person of your word? Truthfulness seems so rare that we feel we must end our statements with "I promise." If we tell the truth all the time, we will have less pressure to back up our words with an oath or a promise.

The Bible condemns making vows or taking oaths casually, giving your word while knowing that you won't keep it, or swearing falsely in God's name (Exodus 20:7; Leviticus 19:12; Numbers 30:1-2; Deuteronomy 19:16-20). Oaths are needed in certain situations only because we live in a sinful society that breeds distrust.

Jesus teaches about retaliation

*"You have heard the law that says the punishment must match the injury:
'An eye for an eye, and a tooth for a tooth.' But I say, do not resist an evil person!
If someone slaps you on the right cheek, offer the other cheek also. If you are
sued in court and your shirt is taken from you, give your coat, too. If a soldier
demands that you carry his gear for a mile, carry it two miles. Give to those
who ask, and don't turn away from those who want to borrow."*

MATTHEW 5:38-42

GETTING EVEN

When we are wronged, often our first reaction is to get even. Jesus said, however,
that we should do *good* to those who wrong us! Our desire should not be to keep
score but to love and forgive. This is not natural—it is supernatural. Only God can
give us the strength to love as he does. Instead of planning vengeance, pray for
those who hurt you.

*God's purpose behind this law was to limit vengeance and help
the court administer punishment that was neither too strict nor
too lenient.*

Jesus teaches about loving enemies

*"But to you who are willing to listen, I say, love your enemies! Do good to
those who hate you. Bless those who curse you. Pray for those who hurt you. If
someone slaps you on one cheek, offer the other cheek also. If someone demands
your coat, offer your shirt also. Give to anyone who asks; and when things are
taken away from you, don't try to get them back. Do to others as you would like
them to do to you.*

*"If you love only those who love you, why should you get credit for that? Even
sinners love those who love them! And if you do good only to those who do good
to you, why should you get credit? Even sinners do that much! And if you lend
money only to those who can repay you, why should you get credit? Even sinners
will lend to other sinners for a full return.*

*"Love your enemies! Do good to them. Lend to them without expecting to be
repaid. Then your reward from heaven will be very great, and you will truly be
acting as children of the Most High, for he is kind to those who are unthankful
and wicked. You must be compassionate, just as your Father is compassionate."*

LUKE 6:27-36 *(see also Matthew 5:43-48)*

LOVING YOUR ENEMIES

By telling us not to retaliate, Jesus keeps us from taking the law into our own
hands. By loving and praying for our enemies, we can overcome evil with good. If
you love your enemies and treat them well, you will truly show that Jesus is Lord of
your life. This is possible only for those who give themselves fully to God because
only he can deliver people from natural selfishness. Loving our enemies means
acting in their best interests. We can pray for them and think of ways to help them.
Jesus loved the whole world, even though the world was in rebellion against God.
Jesus asks us to follow his example by loving our enemies. Grant your enemies the
same respect and rights as you desire for yourself.

*Jesus wasn't talking about having affection for enemies; he was
talking about an act of will. You can't "fall into" this kind of love—
it takes conscious effort. We must trust the Holy Spirit to help us
show love to those for whom we may not feel love.*

Jesus teaches about giving to the needy

"Watch out! Don't do your good deeds publicly, to be admired by others, for you will lose the reward from your Father in heaven. When you give to someone in need, don't do as the hypocrites do—blowing trumpets in the synagogues and streets to call attention to their acts of charity! I tell you the truth, they have received all the reward they will ever get. But when you give to someone in need, don't let your left hand know what your right hand is doing. Give your gifts in private, and your Father, who sees everything, will reward you."

MATTHEW 6:1-4

GOOD SECRETS

When Jesus says not to let the left hand know what the right hand is doing, he is teaching that our motives for giving to God and to others must be pure. It's easier to do what is right when we gain recognition and praise. To be sure that our motives are not selfish, we should do our good works quietly or in secret, with no thought of reward. Our actions should not be self-centered but God-centered, done not to make us look good but to make God look good. The reward God promises is not material, and it is never given to those who seek it. Doing something only for ourselves is not a loving sacrifice. With your next good deed, ask yourself, *Would I still do this if no one would ever know I did it?*

The term hypocrites, as used here, describes people who do good acts for appearances only—not out of compassion or other good motives. Their actions may be good, but their motives are hollow.

Jesus teaches about prayer

"When you pray, don't be like the hypocrites who love to pray publicly on street corners and in the synagogues where everyone can see them. I tell you the truth, that is all the reward they will ever get. But when you pray, go away by yourself, shut the door behind you, and pray to your Father in private. Then your Father, who sees everything, will reward you.

"When you pray, don't babble on and on as people of other religions do. They think their prayers are answered merely by repeating their words again and again. Don't be like them, for your Father knows exactly what you need even before you ask him!" MATTHEW 6:5-8

OVER AND OVER

Repeating the same words over and over like an incantation is no way to ensure that God will hear your prayer. It's not wrong to come to God many times with the same requests—Jesus encourages *persistent* prayer. But he condemns the mindless repetition of words that are not offered with a sincere heart. We can never pray too much if our prayers are honest and sincere. Before you start to pray, make sure you mean what you say.

Some people, especially the religious leaders, wanted to be seen as "holy," and public prayer was one way to get attention. Jesus saw through their self-righteous acts, however, and taught that the essence of prayer is not public style but private communication with God.

Jesus teaches about prayer

"Pray like this: 'Our Father in heaven, may your name be kept holy. May your Kingdom come soon. May your will be done on earth, as it is in heaven. Give us today the food we need, and forgive us our sins, as we have forgiven those who sin against us. And don't let us yield to temptation, but rescue us from the evil one.'

"If you forgive those who sin against you, your heavenly Father will forgive you. But if you refuse to forgive others, your Father will not forgive your sins."

MATTHEW 6:9-15

FORGIVENESS

Jesus gives a startling warning about forgiveness: If we refuse to forgive others, God will also refuse to forgive us. Why? Because when we don't forgive others, we are denying our common ground as sinners in need of God's forgiveness. God's forgiveness of sin is not the direct result of our forgiving others, but it is based on our realizing what forgiveness means (Ephesians 4:32). It is easy to ask God for forgiveness but difficult to grant it to others. Whenever we ask God to forgive us for sin, we should ask ourselves, *Have I forgiven the people who have wronged me?*

This is often called the Lord's Prayer because Jesus gave it to the disciples. It can be a pattern for our prayers.

Jesus teaches about fasting

"And when you fast, don't make it obvious, as the hypocrites do, for they try to look miserable and disheveled so people will admire them for their fasting. I tell you the truth, that is the only reward they will ever get. But when you fast, comb your hair and wash your face. Then no one will notice that you are fasting, except your Father, who knows what you do in private. And your Father, who sees everything, will reward you."   MATTHEW 6:16-18

SPIRITUAL DISCIPLINE

Fasting—going without food in order to spend time in prayer—is noble *and* difficult. It gives us time to pray, teaches self-discipline, reminds us that we can live with a lot less, and helps us appreciate God's gifts. Jesus was not condemning fasting, but hypocrisy—fasting in order to gain public approval. Fasting was mandatory for the Jewish people once a year, on the Day of Atonement (Leviticus 23:32). The Pharisees voluntarily fasted twice a week to impress the people with their "holiness." Jesus commended acts of self-sacrifice done quietly and sincerely. He wanted people to adopt spiritual disciplines for the right reasons, not from a selfish desire for praise.

By separating yourself from the daily routine of food preparation and eating, you can devote extra time to prayer. Hunger pangs remind you of your weakness and your dependence upon God. Fasting can still be helpful today as you seek God's will in special situations.

Jesus teaches about money

"Don't store up treasures here on earth, where moths eat them and rust destroys them, and where thieves break in and steal. Store your treasures in heaven, where moths and rust cannot destroy, and thieves do not break in and steal. Wherever your treasure is, there the desires of your heart will also be.

"Your eye is a lamp that provides light for your body. When your eye is good, your whole body is filled with light. But when your eye is bad, your whole body is filled with darkness. And if the light you think you have is actually darkness, how deep that darkness is!

"No one can serve two masters. For you will hate one and love the other; you will be devoted to one and despise the other. You cannot serve both God and money."   MATTHEW 6:19-24

ONE MASTER

Jesus says we can have only one master. We live in a materialistic society where many people serve money. They spend all their lives collecting and storing it, only to die and leave it behind. Their desire for money and what it can buy far outweighs their commitment to God and spiritual matters. You will spend much of your time and energy thinking about whatever you have stored up. Don't fall into the materialism trap, because "the love of money is the root of all kinds of evil" (1 Timothy 6:10). Can you honestly say that God, and not money, is your master? One test is to ask which one occupies more of your thoughts, time, and efforts.

Spiritual vision is the capacity to see clearly what God wants us to do and to see the world from his point of view. But this spiritual insight can be easily clouded. Self-serving desires, interests, and goals block that vision. Serving God is the best way to restore it. A "pure" eye is one that is fixed on God.

Jesus teaches about worry

"That is why I tell you not to worry about everyday life—whether you have enough food and drink, or enough clothes to wear. Isn't life more than food, and your body more than clothing? Look at the birds. They don't plant or harvest or store food in barns, for your heavenly Father feeds them. And aren't you far more valuable to him than they are? Can all your worries add a single moment to your life?

"And why worry about your clothing? Look at the lilies of the field and how they grow. They don't work or make their clothing, yet Solomon in all his glory was not dressed as beautifully as they are. And if God cares so wonderfully for wildflowers that are here today and thrown into the fire tomorrow, he will certainly care for you. Why do you have so little faith?"   MATTHEW 6:25-30

WHY WORRY?

Because of the ill effects of worry, Jesus tells us not to worry about those needs that God promises to supply. Worry may (1) damage your health, (2) cause the object of your worry to consume your thoughts, (3) disrupt your productivity, (4) negatively affect the way you treat others, and (5) reduce your ability to trust in God. How many ill effects of worry are you experiencing? Here is the difference between worry and genuine concern—worry immobilizes, but concern moves you to action. Take your worry and turn it into prayer. Do you want to worry less? Then pray more! Whenever you start to worry, stop and pray.

Jesus referred to King Solomon "in all his glory." When Solomon asked for wisdom, God promised him riches and honor as well (1 Kings 3:13). Solomon's riches became legendary. Yet the great glory of his expensive robes and jewels cannot compare with the beauty of God's creation in the form of the tiniest flowers.

Jesus teaches about worry

"So don't worry about these things, saying, 'What will we eat? What will we drink? What will we wear?' These things dominate the thoughts of unbelievers, but your heavenly Father already knows all your needs. Seek the Kingdom of God above all else, and live righteously, and he will give you everything you need.

"So don't worry about tomorrow, for tomorrow will bring its own worries. Today's trouble is enough for today."   MATTHEW 6:31-34

WHO'S ON FIRST?

To make the Kingdom of God your primary concern means that your thoughts are so centered on God and his will for your life that you desire to serve and obey him in everything. What is really important to you? People, objects, goals, and other desires all compete for priority. *Any* of these can quickly bump God out of first place if you don't actively choose to give him first place in *every* area of your life.

Planning for tomorrow is time well spent; worrying about tomorrow is time wasted. Sometimes it's difficult to tell the difference. Careful planning is thinking ahead about goals, steps, and schedules and trusting in God's guidance.

April 16 READ LUKE 6:37-42

Jesus teaches about criticizing others

"Do not judge others, and you will not be judged. Do not condemn others, or it will all come back against you. Forgive others, and you will be forgiven. Give, and you will receive. Your gift will return to you in full—pressed down, shaken together to make room for more, running over, and poured into your lap. The amount you give will determine the amount you get back."

Then Jesus gave the following illustration: "Can one blind person lead another? Won't they both fall into a ditch? Students are not greater than their teacher. But the student who is fully trained will become like the teacher.

"And why worry about a speck in your friend's eye when you have a log in your own? How can you think of saying, 'Friend, let me help you get rid of that speck in your eye,' when you can't see past the log in your own eye? Hypocrite! First get rid of the log in your own eye; then you will see well enough to deal with the speck in your friend's eye." LUKE 6:37-42 *(see also Matthew 7:1-6)*

VISION TEST

Jesus doesn't mean we should ignore wrongdoing, but that we should not be so worried about others' sins that we overlook our own. Jesus tells us to examine our own motives and conduct instead of judging others. The traits that bother us in others are often the habits we dislike in ourselves. Our untamed bad habits and behavior patterns are the very ones that we most want to change in others. Do you find it easy to magnify others' faults while excusing your own? If you are ready to criticize someone, check to see if you deserve the same criticism. Judge yourself first, and then lovingly forgive and help your neighbor. Remember your own "logs" when you feel like criticizing, and you may find that you have less to say.

An object in the eye quickly blurs a person's vision, causing him or her to see things imagined, blurred, or double. When one's vision is clear, that person will be better able to help someone else remove a speck in his or her eye (if one actually exists).

Jesus teaches about asking, seeking, knocking

"Keep on asking, and you will receive what you ask for. Keep on seeking, and you will find. Keep on knocking, and the door will be opened to you. For everyone who asks, receives. Everyone who seeks, finds. And to everyone who knocks, the door will be opened.

"You parents—if your children ask for a loaf of bread, do you give them a stone instead? Or if they ask for a fish, do you give them a snake? Of course not! So if you sinful people know how to give good gifts to your children, how much more will your heavenly Father give good gifts to those who ask him."

MATTHEW 7:7-11

ASKING FOR SNAKES

When children ask their parents for food, their request is usually granted. Parents most certainly would not give their children a stone or a poisonous snake instead! As we learn to know God better as a loving Father, we will come to realize that he desires to grant us only good gifts.

Jesus told us to persist in pursuing God. People often give up after a few halfhearted efforts and conclude that God cannot be found. But knowing God takes faith, focus, and follow-through. Jesus assures us that we will be rewarded.

Jesus teaches how to relate to others

"Do to others whatever you would like them to do to you. This is the essence of all that is taught in the law and the prophets."   MATTHEW 7:12

GOLDEN ACTIONS

This is commonly known as the Golden Rule. In many religions it is stated negatively: "Don't do to others what you don't want done to you." By stating the principle positively, Jesus made it more significant. Refraining from harming others is not very difficult; it is much more difficult to take the initiative in doing something good for them. The Golden Rule as Jesus formulated it is the foundation of active goodness and mercy—the kind of love God shows to us every day. Think of a good and merciful action you can do today.

Jesus called this the "essence of all that is taught in the law and the prophets." If we do to others what we want done to us, we will naturally keep all the laws. This looks at God's law positively. Rather than worrying about all we should not do, we should concentrate on all we can do to show our love for God and others.

Jesus teaches about the way to heaven

"You can enter God's Kingdom only through the narrow gate. The highway to hell is broad, and its gate is wide for the many who choose that way. But the gateway to life is very narrow and the road is difficult, and only a few ever find it." MATTHEW 7:13-14

ONE WAY

The gate that leads to eternal life is called "narrow." This does not mean that it is difficult to become a Christian but that there is only *one* door to eternal life with God, and only a few decide to enter that door. Believing in Jesus is the only way to heaven because he alone died for our sins and opened the door. Going Jesus' way may not be popular, but it is true and right. Thank God there *is* one way!

In John 10:7, Jesus called himself "the gate for the sheep." Jesus is the only way into God's Kingdom. Only by accepting his sacrifice on your behalf can you find eternal life.

Jesus teaches about fruit in people's lives

"Beware of false prophets who come disguised as harmless sheep but are really vicious wolves. You can identify them by their fruit, that is, by the way they act. Can you pick grapes from thornbushes, or figs from thistles? A good tree produces good fruit, and a bad tree produces bad fruit. A good tree can't produce bad fruit, and a bad tree can't produce good fruit. So every tree that does not produce good fruit is chopped down and thrown into the fire. Yes, just as you can identify a tree by its fruit, so you can identify people by their actions."

MATTHEW 7:15-20 *(see also Luke 6:43-45)*

FRUIT CHECK

We should evaluate Bible teachers' words by examining their lives. Just as trees are consistent in the kind of fruit they produce, good teachers consistently exhibit good behavior and high moral character as they attempt to live out the truths of Scripture. This does not mean we should throw out church teachers, pastors, and others who are less than perfect. Every one of us is subject to sin, and we must show the same mercy to others that we need for ourselves. When Jesus talks about bad trees, he means teachers who deliberately teach false doctrine. We must examine teachers' motives, the directions they are taking, and the results they are seeking.

False prophets were common in Old Testament times. They prophesied only what the king and the people wanted to hear, claiming it was God's message. False teachers are just as common today. Jesus said to beware of those whose words sound religious but who are motivated by money, fame, or power.

Jesus teaches about those who build houses on rock and sand

"Not everyone who calls out to me, 'Lord! Lord!' will enter the Kingdom of Heaven. Only those who actually do the will of my Father in heaven will enter. On judgment day many will say to me, 'Lord! Lord! We prophesied in your name and cast out demons in your name and performed many miracles in your name.' But I will reply, 'I never knew you. Get away from me, you who break God's laws.'

"Anyone who listens to my teaching and follows it is wise, like a person who builds a house on solid rock. Though the rain comes in torrents and the floodwaters rise and the winds beat against that house, it won't collapse because it is built on bedrock. But anyone who hears my teaching and doesn't obey it is foolish, like a person who builds a house on sand. When the rains and floods come and the winds beat against that house, it will collapse with a mighty crash."

When Jesus had finished saying these things, the crowds were amazed at his teaching, for he taught with real authority—quite unlike their teachers of religious law.   MATTHEW 7:21-29 *(see also Luke 6:46-49)*

A SOLID FOUNDATION

Like a house of cards, the fool's life crumbles under pressure. Most people do not deliberately seek to build on a false or inferior foundation; instead, they just don't think about the purpose for their lives. Many people are headed for destruction, not out of stubbornness but out of thoughtlessness. Part of our responsibility as believers is to help others stop and think about where their lives are headed and to point out the consequences of ignoring Christ's message. Obeying God is like building a house on a strong, solid foundation that stands firm when storms come. When life is calm, our foundations don't seem to matter. But when crises come, our foundations are tested. Be sure your life is built on the solid foundation of knowing and trusting Jesus Christ.

Living on the edge of a desert, Jesus' listeners were well aware of sand—its shifts and sudden movements in the wind. Tents, not houses, were used on sand. The people were also very aware of the deceptive nature of water, having experienced violent storms on the Sea of Galilee.

April 22 READ LUKE 7:1-10

A Roman soldier demonstrates faith

When Jesus had finished saying all this to the people, he returned to Capernaum. At that time the highly valued slave of a Roman officer was sick and near death. When the officer heard about Jesus, he sent some respected Jewish elders to ask him to come and heal his slave. So they earnestly begged Jesus to help the man. "If anyone deserves your help, he does," they said, "for he loves the Jewish people and even built a synagogue for us."

So Jesus went with them. But just before they arrived at the house, the officer sent some friends to say, "Lord, don't trouble yourself by coming to my home, for I am not worthy of such an honor. I am not even worthy to come and meet you. Just say the word from where you are, and my servant will be healed. I know this because I am under the authority of my superior officers, and I have authority over my soldiers. I only need to say, 'Go,' and they go, or 'Come,' and they come. And if I say to my slaves, 'Do this,' they do it."

When Jesus heard this, he was amazed. Turning to the crowd that was following him, he said, "I tell you, I haven't seen faith like this in all Israel!" And when the officer's friends returned to his house, they found the slave completely healed.   LUKE 7:1-10 *(see also Matthew 8:5-13)*

BETWEEN YOU AND JESUS

This officer was a centurion, which meant he was in charge of one hundred men in the Roman army. This man turned to Jesus, not as a last resort or a magic charm but because he believed Jesus was sent from God. Yet he didn't come himself to Jesus, and he didn't expect Jesus to come to him. Just as this officer did not need to be present to have his orders carried out, so Jesus did not need to be present to heal. The captain's faith was especially amazing because he was a Gentile who had not been brought up to know a loving God. The Roman officer could have let many obstacles stand between him and Jesus—pride, doubt, money, language, distance, time, self-sufficiency, power, race. But he didn't. Neither should we.

Since he was well aware of the Jewish hatred for Roman soldiers, the Roman army officer may not have wanted to interrupt a Jewish gathering. As a centurion, he daily delegated work and sent groups on missions, so this was how he chose to get his message to Jesus.

Jesus raises a widow's son from the dead

Soon afterward Jesus went with his disciples to the village of Nain, and a large crowd followed him. A funeral procession was coming out as he approached the village gate. The young man who had died was a widow's only son, and a large crowd from the village was with her. When the Lord saw her, his heart overflowed with compassion. "Don't cry!" he said. Then he walked over to the coffin and touched it, and the bearers stopped. "Young man," he said, "I tell you, get up." Then the dead boy sat up and began to talk! And Jesus gave him back to his mother.

Great fear swept the crowd, and they praised God, saying, "A mighty prophet has risen among us," and "God has visited his people today." And the news about Jesus spread throughout Judea and the surrounding countryside.

LUKE 7:11-17

ACCEPT THE GIFT

This story illustrates salvation. The whole world was dead in sin (Ephesians 2:1), just as the widow's son was dead. Being dead, we could do nothing to help ourselves—we couldn't even ask for help. But God had compassion on us, and he sent Jesus to raise us to life with him (Ephesians 2:4-7). The dead boy did not earn his second chance at life, and we cannot earn our new life in Christ. But we can accept God's gift of life, praise God for it, and use our lives to do his will.

Honoring the dead was important in Jewish tradition. A funeral procession—the relatives of the dead person following the body, which was wrapped and carried on a kind of stretcher—would make its way through town, and bystanders would be expected to join the procession. In addition, hired mourners would cry aloud and draw attention to the procession.

Jesus eases John's doubt

The disciples of John the Baptist told John about everything Jesus was doing. So John called for two of his disciples, and he sent them to the Lord to ask him, "Are you the Messiah we've been expecting, or should we keep looking for someone else?"

John's two disciples found Jesus and said to him, "John the Baptist sent us to ask, 'Are you the Messiah we've been expecting, or should we keep looking for someone else?'"

At that very time, Jesus cured many people of their diseases, illnesses, and evil spirits, and he restored sight to many who were blind. Then he told John's disciples, "Go back to John and tell him what you have seen and heard—the blind see, the lame walk, the lepers are cured, the deaf hear, the dead are raised to life, and the Good News is being preached to the poor. And tell him, 'God blesses those who do not turn away because of me.'"

After John's disciples left, Jesus began talking about him to the crowds. "What kind of man did you go into the wilderness to see? Was he a weak reed, swayed by every breath of wind? Or were you expecting to see a man dressed in expensive clothes? No, people who wear beautiful clothes and live in luxury are found in palaces. Were you looking for a prophet? Yes, and he is more than a prophet. John is the man to whom the Scriptures refer when they say, 'Look, I am sending my messenger ahead of you, and he will prepare your way before you.' I tell you, of all who have ever lived, none is greater than John. Yet even the least person in the Kingdom of God is greater than he is!" LUKE 7:18-28 *(see also Matthew 11:1-15)*

DEALING WITH DOUBTS

John was confused because the reports he received about Jesus were unexpected and incomplete. John's doubts were natural, and Jesus didn't rebuke him for them. Instead, Jesus responded in a way that John would understand: Jesus explained that he had accomplished what the Messiah was supposed to accomplish. God can handle our doubts, and he welcomes our questions. Do you have questions about Jesus—about who he is or what he expects of you? Admit them to yourself and to God, and begin looking for answers. Only as you face your doubts honestly can you begin to resolve them.

Of all people, no one fulfilled his God-given purpose better than John. Yet in God's Kingdom, all who come after John have a greater spiritual heritage because they have clearer knowledge of the purpose of Jesus' death and resurrection.

Jesus exposes hypocrisy

When they heard this, all the people—even the tax collectors—agreed that God's way was right, for they had been baptized by John. But the Pharisees and experts in religious law rejected God's plan for them, for they had refused John's baptism.

"To what can I compare the people of this generation?" Jesus asked. "How can I describe them? They are like children playing a game in the public square. They complain to their friends, 'We played wedding songs, and you didn't dance, so we played funeral songs, and you didn't weep.' For John the Baptist didn't spend his time eating bread or drinking wine, and you say, 'He's possessed by a demon.' The Son of Man, on the other hand, feasts and drinks, and you say, 'He's a glutton and a drunkard, and a friend of tax collectors and other sinners!' But wisdom is shown to be right by the lives of those who follow it."

LUKE 7:29-35 *(see also Matthew 11:16-19)*

HYPOCRISY

The religious leaders hated anyone who exposed their hypocrisy and spoke the truth, and they did not bother to be consistent in their faultfinding. They criticized John the Baptist because he fasted and drank no wine; they criticized Jesus because he ate heartily and drank wine with tax collectors and "lowlifes." Their real objection to both men, of course, had nothing to do with dietary habits. What the Pharisees and experts in the law couldn't stand was being exposed for their hypocrisy. Most of us can find compelling reasons to do or believe whatever suits our purposes. If we do not examine our ideas in the light of God's truth, however, we may be just as obviously self-serving as the Pharisees.

The tax collectors (who embodied evil in most people's minds) and common people heard John's message and repented. In contrast, the Pharisees and experts in religious law rejected his words. Wanting to live their own way, they justified their own point of view and refused to listen to other ideas.

Jesus denounces unbelief

Then Jesus began to denounce the towns where he had done so many of his miracles, because they hadn't repented of their sins and turned to God. "What sorrow awaits you, Korazin and Bethsaida! For if the miracles I did in you had been done in wicked Tyre and Sidon, their people would have repented of their sins long ago, clothing themselves in burlap and throwing ashes on their heads to show their remorse. I tell you, Tyre and Sidon will be better off on judgment day than you.

"And you people of Capernaum, will you be honored in heaven? No, you will go down to the place of the dead. For if the miracles I did for you had been done in wicked Sodom, it would still be here today. I tell you, even Sodom will be better off on judgment day than you."   MATTHEW 11:20-24

NO EXCUSES

Tyre, Sidon, and Sodom were ancient cities with a long-standing reputation for wickedness (Genesis 18–19; Ezekiel 27–28). Each was destroyed by God for its evil. The people of Bethsaida, Korazin, and Capernaum saw Jesus firsthand, and yet they stubbornly refused to repent of their sins and believe in him. Jesus said that if some of the wickedest cities in the world had seen him, they would have repented. Because Bethsaida, Korazin, and Capernaum saw Jesus and didn't believe, they would suffer even greater punishment than the wicked cities that hadn't seen Jesus. Similarly, nations and cities with churches on every corner and Bibles in every home will have no excuse on Judgment Day if they do not repent and believe. What evidence do you have for the truth of the gospel? How have you responded to the truth?

God had promised to spare Sodom if only ten godly people could be found in the city (Genesis 18:32), but not even ten could be found. The cities of Tyre and Sidon on the sea were beautiful, but the beauty was a source of pride, guaranteeing their judgment.

Jesus promises rest for the soul

At that time Jesus prayed this prayer: "O Father, Lord of heaven and earth, thank you for hiding these things from those who think themselves wise and clever, and for revealing them to the childlike. Yes, Father, it pleased you to do it this way!

"My Father has entrusted everything to me. No one truly knows the Son except the Father, and no one truly knows the Father except the Son and those to whom the Son chooses to reveal him."

Then Jesus said, "Come to me, all of you who are weary and carry heavy burdens, and I will give you rest. Take my yoke upon you. Let me teach you, because I am humble and gentle at heart, and you will find rest for your souls. For my yoke is easy to bear, and the burden I give you is light."

MATTHEW 11:25-30

THE YOKE

A yoke is a heavy wooden harness that fits over the shoulders of oxen and other animals. It is attached to a piece of equipment the animals are to pull. A person, also, may be carrying heavy burdens of (1) sin; (2) excessive demands of religious leaders (Matthew 23:4; Acts 15:10); (3) oppression and persecution; or (4) weariness in searching for God. Jesus frees people from all these burdens. He promises us his love, healing, and rest for our souls. A relationship with God changes meaningless, wearisome toil into spiritual productivity and purpose. Come to Jesus with your burdens. Turn them over to him—he will give you rest.

Jesus mentions two kinds of people in his prayer: The "wise"— arrogant in their own knowledge—and the "childlike"—humbly open to receive the truth of God's Word. Are you wise in your own eyes, or do you seek the truth in childlike faith, realizing that only God holds all the answers?

A sinful woman anoints Jesus' feet

One of the Pharisees asked Jesus to have dinner with him, so Jesus went to his home and sat down to eat. When a certain immoral woman from that city heard he was eating there, she brought a beautiful alabaster jar filled with expensive perfume. Then she knelt behind him at his feet, weeping. Her tears fell on his feet, and she wiped them off with her hair. Then she kept kissing his feet and putting perfume on them.

When the Pharisee who had invited him saw this, he said to himself, "If this man were a prophet, he would know what kind of woman is touching him. She's a sinner!"

Then Jesus answered his thoughts. "Simon," he said to the Pharisee, "I have something to say to you."

"Go ahead, Teacher," Simon replied.

Then Jesus told him this story: "A man loaned money to two people—500 pieces of silver to one and 50 pieces to the other. But neither of them could repay him, so he kindly forgave them both, canceling their debts. Who do you suppose loved him more after that?"

Simon answered, "I suppose the one for whom he canceled the larger debt."

"That's right," Jesus said. Then he turned to the woman and said to Simon, "Look at this woman kneeling here. When I entered your home, you didn't offer me water to wash the dust from my feet, but she has washed them with her tears and wiped them with her hair. You didn't greet me with a kiss, but from the time I first came in, she has not stopped kissing my feet. You neglected the courtesy of olive oil to anoint my head, but she has anointed my feet with rare perfume.

"I tell you, her sins—and they are many—have been forgiven, so she has shown me much love. But a person who is forgiven little shows only little love." Then Jesus said to the woman, "Your sins are forgiven."

The men at the table said among themselves, "Who is this man, that he goes around forgiving sins?"

And Jesus said to the woman, "Your faith has saved you; go in peace."

LUKE 7:36-50

COMPLETE FORGIVENESS

Simon had committed several social errors in neglecting to wash Jesus' feet (a courtesy extended to guests because sandaled feet got very dirty), to anoint his head with oil, or to offer him the kiss of greeting. Did Simon perhaps feel that he was too good to treat Jesus as an equal? The immoral woman, by contrast, lavished tears, expensive perfume, and kisses on her Savior. In this story it is this grateful woman, not the stingy religious leader, whose sins were forgiven. Although it is God's grace through faith that saves us and not acts of love or generosity, this woman demonstrated true faith, and Jesus honored her faith. Overflowing love is the natural response to forgiveness and the appropriate consequence of faith. But only those who realize the depth of their sin can appreciate the complete forgiveness God offers them. Do you appreciate the wideness of God's mercy? Are you grateful for his forgiveness?

In Jesus' day, it was customary to recline while eating. Dinner guests would lie on couches with their heads near the table, propping themselves up on one elbow and stretching their feet out behind them. The woman could easily anoint Jesus' feet without approaching the table.

Women accompany Jesus and his disciples

Soon afterward Jesus began a tour of the nearby towns and villages, preaching and announcing the Good News about the Kingdom of God. He took his twelve disciples with him, along with some women who had been cured of evil spirits and diseases. Among them were Mary Magdalene, from whom he had cast out seven demons; Joanna, the wife of Chuza, Herod's business manager; Susanna; and many others who were contributing their own resources to support Jesus and his disciples.　LUKE 8:1-3

EQUAL IN VALUE

Jesus lifted up women from the agony of degradation and servitude to the joy of fellowship and service. In Jewish culture, women were not supposed to learn from rabbis. By allowing these women to travel with him, Jesus was showing that all people are valuable under God. These women supported Jesus' ministry with their own money. They owed a great debt to him because he had driven demons out of some of them and had healed others. Here we catch a glimpse of a few of the people behind the scenes in Jesus' ministry. The ministry of those in the foreground is often supported by those whose work is less visible but just as essential. Offer your resources to God, whether or not you will be on center stage.

God equips men and women for various tasks, but all lead to the same goal—honoring God. Each has a role that carries exclusive privileges, which should eliminate any attitudes about an inferior or superior sex.

Religious leaders accuse Jesus of being Satan

A demon-possessed man, who was blind and couldn't speak, was brought to Jesus. He healed the man so that he could both speak and see. The crowd was amazed and asked, "Could it be that Jesus is the Son of David, the Messiah?"

But when the Pharisees heard about the miracle, they said, "No wonder he can cast out demons. He gets his power from Satan, the prince of demons."

Jesus knew their thoughts and replied, "Any kingdom divided by civil war is doomed. A town or family splintered by feuding will fall apart. And if Satan is casting out Satan, he is divided and fighting against himself. His own kingdom will not survive. And if I am empowered by Satan, what about your own exorcists? They cast out demons, too, so they will condemn you for what you have said. But if I am casting out demons by the Spirit of God, then the Kingdom of God has arrived among you. For who is powerful enough to enter the house of a strong man like Satan and plunder his goods? Only someone even stronger—someone who could tie him up and then plunder his house.

"Anyone who isn't with me opposes me, and anyone who isn't working with me is actually working against me.

"So I tell you, every sin and blasphemy can be forgiven—except blasphemy against the Holy Spirit, which will never be forgiven. Anyone who speaks against the Son of Man can be forgiven, but anyone who speaks against the Holy Spirit will never be forgiven, either in this world or in the world to come."

MATTHEW 12:22-32 *(see also Mark 3:20-30)*

THE UNFORGIVABLE SIN

The Pharisees blasphemed against the Holy Spirit when they attributed the power by which Christ did miracles to Satan (Matthew 12:24) instead of to the Spirit. The unforgivable sin is the deliberate refusal to acknowledge God's power in Christ. It indicates an irreversible hardness of heart. Sometimes believers worry that they have accidentally committed this unforgivable sin. But only those who have turned their backs on God and rejected faith in Christ have any need to worry. Jesus said they can't be forgiven—not because their sin is worse than any other, but because they will never ask for forgiveness. Those who reject the prompting of the Holy Spirit remove themselves from the only force that can lead them to repentance and restoration to God.

Religious leaders accuse Jesus of being Satan

"A tree is identified by its fruit. If a tree is good, its fruit will be good. If a tree is bad, its fruit will be bad. You brood of snakes! How could evil men like you speak what is good and right? For whatever is in your heart determines what you say. A good person produces good things from the treasury of a good heart, and an evil person produces evil things from the treasury of an evil heart. And I tell you this, you must give an account on judgment day for every idle word you speak. The words you say will either acquit you or condemn you."

MATTHEW 12:33-37

MOUTHWASH

Jesus reminds us that what we say reveals what is in our hearts. What kinds of words come from your mouth? They are an indication of what your heart is really like. You can't solve your heart problem, however, just by cleaning up your speech. You must allow the Holy Spirit to fill you with new attitudes and motives; then your speech will be cleansed at its source.

Jesus Christ has been given the authority to judge all the earth (Romans 14:9-11; Philippians 2:9-11). Although his judgment is already at work in our lives, there will be a future, final judgment when Christ returns (Matthew 25:31-46) and everyone's life is reviewed and evaluated.

Religious leaders ask Jesus for a miracle

One day some teachers of religious law and Pharisees came to Jesus and said, "Teacher, we want you to show us a miraculous sign to prove your authority."

But Jesus replied, "Only an evil, adulterous generation would demand a miraculous sign; but the only sign I will give them is the sign of the prophet Jonah. For as Jonah was in the belly of the great fish for three days and three nights, so will the Son of Man be in the heart of the earth for three days and three nights.

"The people of Nineveh will stand up against this generation on judgment day and condemn it, for they repented of their sins at the preaching of Jonah. Now someone greater than Jonah is here—but you refuse to repent. The queen of Sheba will also stand up against this generation on judgment day and condemn it, for she came from a distant land to hear the wisdom of Solomon. Now someone greater than Solomon is here—but you refuse to listen."

MATTHEW 12:38-42

MORE EVIDENCE?

The Pharisees were asking for another miraculous sign, but they were not sincerely seeking to know Jesus. Jesus knew they had already seen enough miraculous proof to convince them that he was the Messiah if they would just open their hearts. But they had already decided not to believe in him, and more miracles would not change that.

Many people have said, "If I could just see a real miracle, then I could believe in God." But Jesus' response to the Pharisees applies to us. We have plenty of evidence—Jesus' birth, death, resurrection, and ascension, as well as centuries of his work in believers around the world. Instead of looking for additional evidence or miracles, accept what God has already given and move forward. He may use your life as evidence to reach another person.

Jonah was a prophet sent to the Assyrian city of Nineveh (see the book of Jonah). Because Assyria was such a cruel and warlike nation, Jonah tried to run from his assignment and ended up spending three days in the stomach of a huge fish. When Jonah got out, he grudgingly went to Nineveh, preached God's message, and saw the city repent. By contrast, when Jesus came to his people, they refused to repent.

Religious leaders ask Jesus for a miracle

"When an evil spirit leaves a person, it goes into the desert, seeking rest but finding none. Then it says, 'I will return to the person I came from.' So it returns and finds its former home empty, swept, and in order. Then the spirit finds seven other spirits more evil than itself, and they all enter the person and live there. And so that person is worse off than before. That will be the experience of this evil generation."   MATTHEW 12:43-45

EMPTY IT OUT, FILL IT UP

Jesus was describing the attitude of the nation of Israel, and the religious leaders in particular. Just cleaning up one's life without filling it with God leaves plenty of room for Satan to enter. The book of Ezra records how the people rid themselves of idolatry but failed to replace it with love for God and obedience to him. Ridding our lives of sin is only the first step. We must also take the second step: filling our lives with God's Word and the Holy Spirit. Unfilled and complacent people are easy targets for Satan.

Jesus told this parable to warn the Jewish religious leaders, who were opposing him. The nation had benefited from the exorcisms and miracles of Jesus. But because they rejected the Savior, the nation would now be defenseless against evil and be worse off than before—just like the person in the parable.

Jesus describes his true family

Jesus' mother and brothers came to see him. They stood outside and sent word for him to come out and talk with them. There was a crowd sitting around Jesus, and someone said, "Your mother and your brothers are outside asking for you."

Jesus replied, "Who is my mother? Who are my brothers?" Then he looked at those around him and said, "Look, these are my mother and brothers. Anyone who does God's will is my brother and sister and mother."

MARK 3:31-35 *(see also Matthew 12:46-50; Luke 8:19-21)*

GOD'S FAMILY

God's family is to be accepting and not exclude anyone. Although Jesus cared for his mother and brothers, he also cared for all those who loved him. Jesus did not show partiality; he allowed everyone the privilege of obeying God and becoming part of his family. In our increasingly computerized, impersonal world, warm relationships among members of God's family take on major importance. The church can give the loving, personalized care found nowhere else.

———————————●●———————————

Jesus' family did not yet fully understand his ministry. Jesus explained that in our spiritual family, the relationships are ultimately more important and longer lasting than those formed in our physical families.

———————————●●———————————

May 5 READ MARK 4:1-9

Jesus tells the parable of the four soils

Once again Jesus began teaching by the lakeshore. A very large crowd soon gathered around him, so he got into a boat. Then he sat in the boat while all the people remained on the shore. He taught them by telling many stories in the form of parables, such as this one:

"Listen! A farmer went out to plant some seed. As he scattered it across his field, some of the seed fell on a footpath, and the birds came and ate it. Other seed fell on shallow soil with underlying rock. The seed sprouted quickly because the soil was shallow. But the plant soon wilted under the hot sun, and since it didn't have deep roots, it died. Other seed fell among thorns that grew up and choked out the tender plants so they produced no grain. Still other seeds fell on fertile soil, and they sprouted, grew, and produced a crop that was thirty, sixty, and even a hundred times as much as had been planted!" Then he said, "Anyone with ears to hear should listen and understand."

MARK 4:1-9 *(see also Matthew 13:1-9; Luke 8:4-8)*

KEEP ON SOWING

This parable should encourage spiritual "sowers"—those who teach, preach, and lead others. The farmer sowed good seed, but not all the seed sprouted, and even the plants that grew had varying yields. Don't be discouraged if you do not always see results as you faithfully teach the Word. Belief does not follow a formula (for example, a 4:1 ratio of seeds planted to seeds sprouted). Rather, it is a miracle of God's Holy Spirit as he uses your words to lead others to him.

Jesus taught the people by telling parables, short stories using familiar scenes to explain spiritual truth. This method of teaching compels the listener to think. It conceals the truth from those who are too stubborn or prejudiced to hear what is being taught. Most parables have one main point, so we must be careful not to go beyond what Jesus intended to teach.

Jesus explains the parable of the four soils

Later, when Jesus was alone with the twelve disciples and with the others who were gathered around, they asked him what the parables meant.

He replied, "You are permitted to understand the secret of the Kingdom of God. But I use parables for everything I say to outsiders, so that the Scriptures might be fulfilled: 'When they see what I do, they will learn nothing. When they hear what I say, they will not understand. Otherwise, they will turn to me and be forgiven.'"

Then Jesus said to them, "If you can't understand the meaning of this parable, how will you understand all the other parables? The farmer plants seed by taking God's word to others. The seed that fell on the footpath represents those who hear the message, only to have Satan come at once and take it away. The seed on the rocky soil represents those who hear the message and immediately receive it with joy. But since they don't have deep roots, they don't last long. They fall away as soon as they have problems or are persecuted for believing God's word. The seed that fell among the thorns represents others who hear God's word, but all too quickly the message is crowded out by the worries of this life, the lure of wealth, and the desire for other things, so no fruit is produced. And the seed that fell on good soil represents those who hear and accept God's word and produce a harvest of thirty, sixty, or even a hundred times as much as had been planted!"

Then Jesus asked them, "Would anyone light a lamp and then put it under a basket or under a bed? Of course not! A lamp is placed on a stand, where its light will shine. For everything that is hidden will eventually be brought into the open, and every secret will be brought to light. Anyone with ears to hear should listen and understand."

Then he added, "Pay close attention to what you hear. The closer you listen, the more understanding you will be given—and you will receive even more. To those who listen to my teaching, more understanding will be given. But for those who are not listening, even what little understanding they have will be taken away from them."

MARK 4:10-25 *(see also Matthew 13:10-23; Luke 8:9-18)*

SOIL AGAIN

The four soils represent four different ways people respond to God's message. Usually we think that Jesus was talking about four different kinds of people. But he may also have been talking about (1) different times or phases in a person's life or (2) how we willingly receive God's message in some areas of our lives and resist it in others. For example, you may be open to God about your future but closed concerning how you spend your money. You may respond like good soil to God's demand for worship but like rocky soil to his demand to give to people in need. We must strive to be like good soil in every area of our lives at all times.

We hear with our ears, but there is a deeper kind of listening with the mind and heart that is necessary in order to gain spiritual understanding from Jesus' words. Some people in the crowd were looking for evidence to use against Jesus; others truly wanted to learn and grow. Jesus' words were for the honest seekers.

Jesus tells the parable of the growing seed

Jesus also said, "The Kingdom of God is like a farmer who scatters seed on the ground. Night and day, while he's asleep or awake, the seed sprouts and grows, but he does not understand how it happens. The earth produces the crops on its own. First a leaf blade pushes through, then the heads of wheat are formed, and finally the grain ripens. And as soon as the grain is ready, the farmer comes and harvests it with a sickle, for the harvest time has come." MARK 4:26-29

KINGDOM GROWTH

This parable about the Kingdom of God, recorded only by Mark, reveals that spiritual growth is a continual, gradual process that is finally consummated in a harvest of spiritual maturity. We can understand the process of spiritual growth by comparing it to the slow but certain growth of a plant. God's Kingdom grows. We don't know how. We do our part and God does his, so that in due time a harvest is ready. Are you doing your part in helping the Kingdom of God grow to maturity?

Seed was sown by hand. As the farmer walked across a field, he threw handfuls of seed onto the ground from a large bag slung across his shoulders.

Jesus tells the parable of the weeds

Here is another story Jesus told: "The Kingdom of Heaven is like a farmer who planted good seed in his field. But that night as the workers slept, his enemy came and planted weeds among the wheat, then slipped away. When the crop began to grow and produce grain, the weeds also grew.

"The farmer's workers went to him and said, 'Sir, the field where you planted that good seed is full of weeds! Where did they come from?'

"'An enemy has done this!' the farmer exclaimed.

"'Should we pull out the weeds?' they asked.

"'No,' he replied, 'you'll uproot the wheat if you do. Let both grow together until the harvest. Then I will tell the harvesters to sort out the weeds, tie them into bundles, and burn them, and to put the wheat in the barn.'"

MATTHEW 13:24-30

THE COMING HARVEST

The young weeds and the young blades of wheat look the same and can't be distinguished until they are grown and ready for harvest. Weeds (unbelievers) and wheat (believers) must live side by side in this world. God allows unbelievers to remain for a while, just as a farmer allows weeds to remain in his field so the surrounding wheat isn't uprooted with them. At the harvest, however, the weeds will be uprooted and thrown away. God's harvest (judgment) of all people is coming. We are to make ourselves ready by making sure that our faith is sincere.

The Kingdom of Heaven is not a geographic location but a spiritual realm where God rules and where we share in his eternal life. We join that Kingdom when we trust in Christ as Savior.

Jesus tells the parable of the mustard seed

Jesus said, "How can I describe the Kingdom of God? What story should I use to illustrate it? It is like a mustard seed planted in the ground. It is the smallest of all seeds, but it becomes the largest of all garden plants; it grows long branches, and birds can make nests in its shade."

Jesus used many similar stories and illustrations to teach the people as much as they could understand. In fact, in his public ministry he never taught without using parables; but afterward, when he was alone with his disciples, he explained everything to them. MARK 4:30-34 *(see also Matthew 13:31-32)*

WORLDWIDE FELLOWSHIP

Jesus adapted his methods to his audience's ability and desire to understand. He didn't speak in parables to confuse people but to challenge sincere seekers to discover the meaning of his words. Jesus used this parable to explain that although Christianity had very small beginnings, it would grow into a worldwide community of believers. When you feel alone in your stand for Christ, realize that God is building a worldwide Kingdom. He has faithful followers in every part of the world, and your faith, no matter how small, can join with that of others to accomplish great things.

The mustard seed was the smallest seed a farmer used. Jesus used this parable to show that the Kingdom has small beginnings but will grow and produce great results.

Jesus tells the parable of the yeast

Jesus also used this illustration: "The Kingdom of Heaven is like the yeast a woman used in making bread. Even though she put only a little yeast in three measures of flour, it permeated every part of the dough."

Jesus always used stories and illustrations like these when speaking to the crowds. In fact, he never spoke to them without using such parables. This fulfilled what God had spoken through the prophet: "I will speak to you in parables. I will explain things hidden since the creation of the world."

MATTHEW 13:33-35

JUST ONE SEED

In other Bible passages, yeast is used as a symbol of evil or uncleanness. Here it is a positive symbol of growth. Although yeast looks like a minor ingredient, it permeates the whole loaf. Although the Kingdom of God began small and was nearly invisible, it would soon grow and have a great impact on the world. You may wonder what kind of impact you as just one person can make on your world. But as the Kingdom grows from one small seed, so it grows from individual believers who serve God. Ask God what you can do to help his Kingdom grow.

All the parables in Matthew 13 teach us about God and his Kingdom. They explain what the Kingdom is really like as opposed to our expectations of it.

Jesus explains the parable of the weeds

Then, leaving the crowds outside, Jesus went into the house. His disciples said, "Please explain to us the story of the weeds in the field."

Jesus replied, "The Son of Man is the farmer who plants the good seed. The field is the world, and the good seed represents the people of the Kingdom. The weeds are the people who belong to the evil one. The enemy who planted the weeds among the wheat is the devil. The harvest is the end of the world, and the harvesters are the angels.

"Just as the weeds are sorted out and burned in the fire, so it will be at the end of the world. The Son of Man will send his angels, and they will remove from his Kingdom everything that causes sin and all who do evil. And the angels will throw them into the fiery furnace, where there will be weeping and gnashing of teeth. Then the righteous will shine like the sun in their Father's Kingdom. Anyone with ears to hear should listen and understand!"

MATTHEW 13:36-43

FINAL JUDGMENT

At the end of the world, angels will separate the evil from the good. There are true and false believers in churches today, but we should be cautious in our judgments because only Christ is qualified to make the final separation. If you start judging, you may damage some of the good "plants." It's more important to judge our own response to God than to analyze others' responses.

Those who receive God's favor stand in bright contrast to those who receive his judgment. The weeping indicates sorrow or remorse, and gnashing of teeth shows extreme anxiety or pain.

Jesus tells the parable of hidden treasure

"The Kingdom of Heaven is like a treasure that a man discovered hidden in a field. In his excitement, he hid it again and sold everything he owned to get enough money to buy the field."   MATTHEW 13:44

TOTAL RULE

The Kingdom of Heaven is more valuable than anything else we can have, and a person must be willing to give up everything to obtain it. The man who discovered the treasure in the field stumbled upon it by accident but knew its value when he found it. When we decide to become part of God's Kingdom, we are accepted by God. Yet to truly experience citizenship in that Kingdom, we may need to give up some actions or attitudes. Have you set aside "the world" in order to have God's Kingdom? Do you live in such a way that people know your true citizenship?

Believers live in this world, but they're not "of" it; their home is really in heaven. We often feel like strangers in a world that would prefer to ignore God. But we have citizenship in the Kingdom of Heaven.

Jesus tells the parable of the pearl merchant

"Again, the Kingdom of Heaven is like a merchant on the lookout for choice pearls. When he discovered a pearl of great value, he sold everything he owned and bought it!" MATTHEW 13:45-46

THE KINGDOM'S VALUE

The merchant was earnestly searching for the pearl of great value, and when he found it he sold everything he had to purchase it. Why is the Kingdom so valuable? Because someday, after God judges and destroys all sin, the Kingdom of Heaven will rule every corner of this earth. We will be with Christ in a way not possible in this life. John saw this day in a vision, and he cried out, "Look, God's home is now among his people! He will live with them, and they will be his people. God himself will be with them" (Revelation 21:3). Our true loyalty is not to the things of this earth, which will be destroyed. It is to God's truth, his way of life, his perfect creation. Are you willing to put aside everything else in order to have God and his Kingdom?

Heaven is where God dwells, and it operates according to God's principles and values. It is eternal and unshakable. Our hope is in the certainty of heaven.

Jesus tells the parable of the fishing net

"Again, the Kingdom of Heaven is like a fishing net that was thrown into the water and caught fish of every kind. When the net was full, they dragged it up onto the shore, sat down, and sorted the good fish into crates, but threw the bad ones away. That is the way it will be at the end of the world. The angels will come and separate the wicked people from the righteous, throwing the wicked into the fiery furnace, where there will be weeping and gnashing of teeth. Do you understand all these things?"

"Yes," they said, "we do."

Then he added, *"Every teacher of religious law who becomes a disciple in the Kingdom of Heaven is like a homeowner who brings from his storeroom new gems of truth as well as old."*   MATTHEW 13:47-52

FINAL SORTING

The parable of the fishing net has the same meaning as the parable of the wheat and weeds. We are to obey God and tell others about his grace and goodness, but we cannot determine who is part of the Kingdom of Heaven and who is not. This sorting will be done at the Last Judgment by those infinitely more qualified than we are. On the Day of Judgment we will appear before Christ and be held account-able for our lives. With God living in us through Christ, we have no reason to fear this day because we have been saved from punishment. Instead, we can look for-ward to the judgment because it will mean the end of sin and the beginning of a face-to-face relationship with Jesus Christ. Be careful of judging another person's relationship with God. Only God is the true and reliable Judge.

Revelation 14:14-17 describes Christ's separating the faithful from the unfaithful like a farmer harvesting his crops. This will be a time of joy for Christians.

Jesus calms the storm

As evening came, Jesus said to his disciples, "Let's cross to the other side of the lake." So they took Jesus in the boat and started out, leaving the crowds behind (although other boats followed). But soon a fierce storm came up. High waves were breaking into the boat, and it began to fill with water.

Jesus was sleeping at the back of the boat with his head on a cushion. The disciples woke him up, shouting, "Teacher, don't you care that we're going to drown?"

When Jesus woke up, he rebuked the wind and said to the waves, "Silence! Be still!" Suddenly the wind stopped, and there was a great calm. Then he asked them, "Why are you afraid? Do you still have no faith?"

The disciples were absolutely terrified. "Who is this man?" they asked each other. "Even the wind and waves obey him!"

MARK 4:35-41 *(see also Matthew 8:23-27; Luke 8:22-25)*

CALMING THE STORMS

Although the disciples had witnessed many miracles, they panicked in this storm. As experienced sailors, they knew its danger; what they did not know was that Christ could control the forces of nature. There is often a stormy area of our human nature where we feel God can't or won't work. When we truly understand who God is, however, we will realize that he controls both the storms of nature and the storms of the troubled heart. Jesus' power that calmed this storm can also help us deal with the problems we face. Jesus is willing to help if only we ask him. We should never discount his power, even in terrible trials.

The Sea of Galilee is an unusual body of water. It is relatively small (thirteen miles long, seven miles wide), but it is 150 feet deep, and the shoreline is 680 feet below sea level. Sudden storms can appear over the surrounding mountains with little warning, stirring the water into violent, twenty-foot waves.

Jesus sends the demons into a herd of pigs

So they arrived at the other side of the lake, in the region of the Gerasenes. When Jesus climbed out of the boat, a man possessed by an evil spirit came out from a cemetery to meet him. This man lived among the burial caves and could no longer be restrained, even with a chain. Whenever he was put into chains and shackles—as he often was—he snapped the chains from his wrists and smashed the shackles. No one was strong enough to subdue him. Day and night he wandered among the burial caves and in the hills, howling and cutting himself with sharp stones.

When Jesus was still some distance away, the man saw him, ran to meet him, and bowed low before him. With a shriek, he screamed, "Why are you interfering with me, Jesus, Son of the Most High God? In the name of God, I beg you, don't torture me!" For Jesus had already said to the spirit, "Come out of the man, you evil spirit."

Then Jesus demanded, "What is your name?"

And he replied, "My name is Legion, because there are many of us inside this man." Then the evil spirits begged him again and again not to send them to some distant place.   MARK 5:1-10 *(see also Matthew 8:28-29; Luke 8:26-31)*

CHRIST'S AUTHORITY

These demons recognized Jesus and his authority immediately. They knew who Jesus was and what his great power could do to them. Demons, Satan's messengers, are powerful and destructive. Still active today, they attempt to distort and destroy people's relationship with God. Demons and demon possession are real. It is vital that believers recognize the power of Satan and his demons, but we shouldn't let curiosity lead us to get involved with demonic forces (Deuteronomy 18:10-12). Demons have no authority over those who trust in Jesus. If we resist the devil, he will leave us alone (James 4:7).

The demons begged Jesus not to send them to "some distant place" (to spare them from the abyss, which is also mentioned in Revelation 9:1 and 20:1-3 as the place of confinement for Satan and his messengers). The demons, of course, knew all about this place of confinement, and they didn't want to go there.

Jesus sends the demons into a herd of pigs

There happened to be a large herd of pigs feeding on the hillside nearby. "Send us into those pigs," the spirits begged. "Let us enter them."

So Jesus gave them permission. The evil spirits came out of the man and entered the pigs, and the entire herd of 2,000 pigs plunged down the steep hillside into the lake and drowned in the water.

The herdsmen fled to the nearby town and the surrounding countryside, spreading the news as they ran. People rushed out to see what had happened. A crowd soon gathered around Jesus, and they saw the man who had been possessed by the legion of demons. He was sitting there fully clothed and perfectly sane, and they were all afraid. Then those who had seen what happened told the others about the demon-possessed man and the pigs. And the crowd began pleading with Jesus to go away and leave them alone.

As Jesus was getting into the boat, the man who had been demon possessed begged to go with him. But Jesus said, "No, go home to your family, and tell them everything the Lord has done for you and how merciful he has been." So the man started off to visit the Ten Towns of that region and began to proclaim the great things Jesus had done for him; and everyone was amazed at what he told them. MARK 5:11-20 *(see also Matthew 8:30-34; Luke 8:32-39)*

WHAT'S MORE IMPORTANT?

The demons destroyed the pigs, which hurt the finances of those tending the pigs, but can animals and money compare with a human life? Even though a man had been freed from the devil's power, the people thought only about their livestock. People have always tended to value financial gain above needy people. Throughout history, most wars have been fought to protect economic interests. Much injustice and oppression, both at home and abroad, are the direct result of some individual's or company's urge to get rich. People are continually being sacrificed to the god of money. Don't think more highly of "swine" than of people. Think carefully about how your decisions will affect other human beings, and be willing to choose a simpler lifestyle if it will keep other people from being harmed.

Why didn't Jesus send these demons to the abyss? Because his time for that had not yet come. But it will come. The book of Revelation portrays the future victory of Jesus over Satan, his demons, and all evil.

Jesus heals a bleeding woman

Jesus got into the boat again and went back to the other side of the lake, where a large crowd gathered around him on the shore. Then a leader of the local synagogue, whose name was Jairus, arrived. When he saw Jesus, he fell at his feet, pleading fervently with him. "My little daughter is dying," he said. "Please come and lay your hands on her; heal her so she can live."

Jesus went with him, and all the people followed, crowding around him. A woman in the crowd had suffered for twelve years with constant bleeding. She had suffered a great deal from many doctors, and over the years she had spent everything she had to pay them, but she had gotten no better. In fact, she had gotten worse. She had heard about Jesus, so she came up behind him through the crowd and touched his robe. For she thought to herself, "If I can just touch his robe, I will be healed." Immediately the bleeding stopped, and she could feel in her body that she had been healed of her terrible condition.

Jesus realized at once that healing power had gone out from him, so he turned around in the crowd and asked, "Who touched my robe?"

His disciples said to him, "Look at this crowd pressing around you. How can you ask, 'Who touched me?'"

But he kept on looking around to see who had done it. Then the frightened woman, trembling at the realization of what had happened to her, came and fell to her knees in front of him and told him what she had done. And he said to her, "Daughter, your faith has made you well. Go in peace. Your suffering is over."   MARK 5:21-34 *(see also Matthew 9:18-22; Luke 8:40-48)*

AVAILABLE POWER

Many people surrounded Jesus as he made his way toward Jairus's house. It was virtually impossible to get through the multitude, but one woman desperately fought her way through the crowd in order to touch Jesus. As soon as she did so, she was healed. What a difference there is between the crowds that are curious about Jesus and the few who reach out and touch him! Today, many people are vaguely familiar with Jesus, but nothing in their lives is changed or improved by this passing acquaintance. It is only faith that releases God's healing power. Are you just curious about God, or do you reach out to him in faith, knowing that his mercy will bring healing to your body, soul, and spirit?

Jesus restores a girl to life

While he was still speaking to her, messengers arrived from the home of Jairus, the leader of the synagogue. They told him, "Your daughter is dead. There's no use troubling the Teacher now."

But Jesus overheard them and said to Jairus, "Don't be afraid. Just have faith."

Then Jesus stopped the crowd and wouldn't let anyone go with him except Peter, James, and John (the brother of James). When they came to the home of the synagogue leader, Jesus saw much commotion and weeping and wailing. He went inside and asked, "Why all this commotion and weeping? The child isn't dead; she's only asleep."

The crowd laughed at him. But he made them all leave, and he took the girl's father and mother and his three disciples into the room where the girl was lying. Holding her hand, he said to her, "Talitha koum," which means "Little girl, get up!" And the girl, who was twelve years old, immediately stood up and walked around! They were overwhelmed and totally amazed. Jesus gave them strict orders not to tell anyone what had happened, and then he told them to give her something to eat.   MARK 5:35-43 *(see also Matthew 9:23-26; Luke 8:49-56)*

POWER OVER DEATH

The leader of the synagogue didn't come to Jesus until his daughter was near death—it was too late for anyone else to help. But Jesus simply went to the girl and raised her! In our lives Christ can make a difference when it is too late for anyone else to help. He can bring restoration to broken relationships, release from bad habits, and forgiveness and healing to emotional scars. If your situation looks hopeless, remember that Christ can do the impossible.

Jesus told the girl's parents not to spread the news of the miracle. He wanted the facts to speak for themselves, and the time was not yet right for a major confrontation with the religious leaders. Jesus still had much to accomplish, and he didn't want people following him just to see his miracles.

Jesus heals the blind and mute

After Jesus left the girl's home, two blind men followed along behind him, shouting, "Son of David, have mercy on us!"

They went right into the house where he was staying, and Jesus asked them, "Do you believe I can make you see?"

"Yes, Lord," they told him, "we do."

Then he touched their eyes and said, "Because of your faith, it will happen." Then their eyes were opened, and they could see! Jesus sternly warned them, "Don't tell anyone about this." But instead, they went out and spread his fame all over the region.

When they left, a demon-possessed man who couldn't speak was brought to Jesus. So Jesus cast out the demon, and then the man began to speak. The crowds were amazed. "Nothing like this has ever happened in Israel!" they exclaimed.

But the Pharisees said, "He can cast out demons because he is empowered by the prince of demons." MATTHEW 9:27-34

HEALING POWER

These blind men were persistent. They went right into the house where Jesus was staying. They knew Jesus could heal them. "Son of David" was a popular way of addressing Jesus as the Messiah because it was known that the Messiah would be a descendant of David (Isaiah 9:7). This is the first time the title is used in Matthew. Jesus' ability to give sight to the blind was prophesied in Isaiah 29:18; 35:5; 42:7. These men let nothing stop them from finding the Messiah. That's real faith in action. If you believe Jesus is the answer to your every need, don't let anything or anyone stop you from reaching him.

While the Pharisees questioned, debated, and dissected Jesus, people were being healed and lives were changed right in front of them. Their skepticism was based not on insufficient evidence but on jealousy of Jesus' popularity.

The people of Nazareth refuse to believe

Jesus left that part of the country and returned with his disciples to Nazareth, his hometown. The next Sabbath he began teaching in the synagogue, and many who heard him were amazed. They asked, "Where did he get all this wisdom and the power to perform such miracles?" Then they scoffed, "He's just a carpenter, the son of Mary and the brother of James, Joseph, Judas, and Simon. And his sisters live right here among us." They were deeply offended and refused to believe in him.

Then Jesus told them, "A prophet is honored everywhere except in his own hometown and among his relatives and his own family." And because of their unbelief, he couldn't do any miracles among them except to place his hands on a few sick people and heal them. And he was amazed at their unbelief.

Then Jesus went from village to village, teaching the people.

MARK 6:1-6 *(see also Matthew 13:53-58)*

SEEING THE REAL JESUS

Jesus was teaching effectively and wisely, but the people of his hometown saw him as just a carpenter. They were offended that others could be impressed by Jesus and follow him. They rejected his authority because he was one of their peers. They thought they knew him, but their preconceived notions about who he is made it impossible for them to accept his message. Don't let prejudice blind you to truth. As you learn more about Jesus, try to see him for who he really is.

Jesus could have done greater miracles in Nazareth, but he chose not to because of the people's pride and unbelief. The miracles he did had little effect on the people because they did not accept his message or believe that he was from God.

Jesus urges the disciples to pray for workers

Jesus traveled through all the towns and villages of that area, teaching in the synagogues and announcing the Good News about the Kingdom. And he healed every kind of disease and illness. When he saw the crowds, he had compassion on them because they were confused and helpless, like sheep without a shepherd. He said to his disciples, "The harvest is great, but the workers are few. So pray to the Lord who is in charge of the harvest; ask him to send more workers into his fields." MATTHEW 9:35-38

HELP WANTED

Jesus looked at the crowds following him and referred to them as fields ripe for harvest. Many people are ready to give their lives to Christ if someone will show them how. Jesus commands us to pray that people will respond to this need for workers. Often when we pray for something, God answers our prayers by using *us*. Be prepared for God to use you to show another person the way to him. Jesus needs workers who know how to deal with people's problems. We can comfort others and show them the way to live because we have been helped with our problems by God and his laborers.

The gospel of the Kingdom was that the promised and long-awaited Messiah had finally come. His healing miracles were a sign that his teaching was true.

Jesus sends out the twelve disciples

Jesus called his twelve disciples together and gave them authority to cast out evil spirits and to heal every kind of disease and illness. Here are the names of the twelve apostles: first, Simon (also called Peter), then Andrew (Peter's brother), James (son of Zebedee), John (James's brother), Philip, Bartholomew, Thomas, Matthew (the tax collector), James (son of Alphaeus), Thaddaeus, Simon (the zealot), Judas Iscariot (who later betrayed him).

Jesus sent out the twelve apostles with these instructions: "Don't go to the Gentiles or the Samaritans, but only to the people of Israel—God's lost sheep. Go and announce to them that the Kingdom of Heaven is near. Heal the sick, raise the dead, cure those with leprosy, and cast out demons. Give as freely as you have received!

"Don't take any money in your money belts—no gold, silver, or even copper coins. Don't carry a traveler's bag with a change of clothes and sandals or even a walking stick. Don't hesitate to accept hospitality, because those who work deserve to be fed.

"Whenever you enter a city or village, search for a worthy person and stay in his home until you leave town. When you enter the home, give it your blessing. If it turns out to be a worthy home, let your blessing stand; if it is not, take back the blessing. If any household or town refuses to welcome you or listen to your message, shake its dust from your feet as you leave. I tell you the truth, the wicked cities of Sodom and Gomorrah will be better off than such a town on the judgment day." MATTHEW 10:1-15 *(see also Mark 6:7-13; Luke 9:1-6)*

USED BY GOD

The list of Jesus' twelve disciples doesn't give us many details—probably because there weren't many impressive details to tell. Jesus called people from all walks of life—fishermen, political activists, tax collectors. He called common people and uncommon leaders, rich and poor, educated and uneducated. Today many people think only certain people are fit to follow Christ, but this was not the attitude of the Master himself. Jesus *called* his twelve disciples. He didn't draft them, force them, or ask them to volunteer; he chose them to serve him in a special way. Christ calls us today. He doesn't twist our arms and make us do something we don't want to do. We can choose to join him or go our own way. God can use anyone, no matter how insignificant he or she appears. God uses ordinary people to do his extraordinary work. Be one who is used by God.

May 24

Jesus prepares the disciples for persecution

"Look, I am sending you out as sheep among wolves. So be as shrewd as snakes and harmless as doves. But beware! For you will be handed over to the courts and will be flogged with whips in the synagogues. You will stand trial before governors and kings because you are my followers. But this will be your opportunity to tell the rulers and other unbelievers about me. When you are arrested, don't worry about how to respond or what to say. God will give you the right words at the right time. For it is not you who will be speaking—it will be the Spirit of your Father speaking through you.

"A brother will betray his brother to death, a father will betray his own child, and children will rebel against their parents and cause them to be killed. And all nations will hate you because you are my followers. But everyone who endures to the end will be saved. When you are persecuted in one town, flee to the next. I tell you the truth, the Son of Man will return before you have reached all the towns of Israel." MATTHEW 10:16-23

BE PREPARED

Jesus told the disciples that when they were arrested for preaching the gospel, they should not worry about what to say in their defense—God's Spirit would speak through them. This promise was fulfilled in Acts 4:8-14 and elsewhere. Some mistakenly think this means that we don't have to prepare to present the gospel because God will take care of everything. Scripture makes it clear, however, that we *are* to be prepared to tell others about Jesus (2 Timothy 4:2; 1 Peter 3:15). Jesus' teaching is not that we would be unprepared but that we would be unworried about what to say.

Enduring to the end is not a way to be saved but rather the evidence that a person is really committed to Jesus. Persistence is not a means to earn salvation; it is the by-product of a truly devoted life.

Jesus prepares the disciples for persecution

"Students are not greater than their teacher, and slaves are not greater than their master. Students are to be like their teacher, and slaves are to be like their master. And since I, the master of the household, have been called the prince of demons, the members of my household will be called by even worse names!

"But don't be afraid of those who threaten you. For the time is coming when everything that is covered will be revealed, and all that is secret will be made known to all. What I tell you now in the darkness, shout abroad when daybreak comes. What I whisper in your ear, shout from the housetops for all to hear!

"Don't be afraid of those who want to kill your body; they cannot touch your soul. Fear only God, who can destroy both soul and body in hell. What is the price of two sparrows—one copper coin? But not a single sparrow can fall to the ground without your Father knowing it. And the very hairs on your head are all numbered. So don't be afraid; you are more valuable to God than a whole flock of sparrows.

"Everyone who acknowledges me publicly here on earth, I will also acknowledge before my Father in heaven. But everyone who denies me here on earth, I will also deny before my Father in heaven."   MATTHEW 10:24-33

COVERED BY GOD

Jesus said that God is aware of everything that happens, even to sparrows, and you are far more valuable to him than they are. You are so valuable that God sent his only Son to die for you (John 3:16). Because God places such value on you, you need never fear personal threats or difficult trials. These can't shake God's love or dislodge his Spirit from within you.

But this doesn't mean that God will take away all your troubles (Matthew 10:16). The real test of value is how well something holds up under the wear, tear, and abuse of everyday life. Those who stand up for Christ in spite of their troubles truly have lasting value and will receive great rewards (Matthew 5:11-12). Despite your struggles and trials, remember that you are valuable to God and that he is making you more like Christ (Romans 8:29).

The Pharisees did, in fact, say that Jesus was "empowered by the prince of demons" (Matthew 9:34). Good is sometimes labeled evil. If Jesus, who is perfect, was called evil, his followers should expect that similar accusations will be directed at them. But those who endure will be saved (Matthew 10:22).

Jesus prepares the disciples for persecution

"Don't imagine that I came to bring peace to the earth! I came not to bring peace, but a sword. 'I have come to set a man against his father, a daughter against her mother, and a daughter-in-law against her mother-in-law. Your enemies will be right in your own household!'

"If you love your father or mother more than you love me, you are not worthy of being mine; or if you love your son or daughter more than me, you are not worthy of being mine. If you refuse to take up your cross and follow me, you are not worthy of being mine. If you cling to your life, you will lose it; but if you give up your life for me, you will find it."   MATTHEW 10:34-39

FREE TO FOLLOW

Matthew 10:39 is a positive and a negative statement of the same truth: Clinging to this life may cause us to forfeit the best from Christ in this world *and* in the next. The more we love this life's rewards (leisure, power, popularity, financial security), the more we will discover how empty they really are. The best way to enjoy life, therefore, is to loosen our greedy grasp on earthly rewards so that we can be free to follow Christ. In doing so, we will inherit eternal life and begin at once to experience the benefits of following Christ. To what are you holding tightly for security and meaning in life? Let go!

To take our cross and follow Jesus means to be willing to publicly identify with him, to experience almost certain opposition, and to be committed to face even suffering and death for his sake.

Jesus prepares the disciples for persecution

"Anyone who receives you receives me, and anyone who receives me receives the Father who sent me. If you receive a prophet as one who speaks for God, you will be given the same reward as a prophet. And if you receive righteous people because of their righteousness, you will be given a reward like theirs. And if you give even a cup of cold water to one of the least of my followers, you will surely be rewarded." MATTHEW 10:40-42

LOVE'S MEASUREMENT

How much we love God can be measured by how well we treat others. Jesus' example of giving a cup of cold water to one of his servants is a good model of unselfish service. People in full-time ministry often can't return the favor. God notices every good deed we do or don't do as if he were the one receiving it. Is there something unselfish you can do for someone else today? Although no one else may see you, God will notice.

Jesus gave the disciples a principle to guide their actions as they ministered to others: "Give as freely as you have received!" (Matthew 10:8). Because God has showered us with his blessings, we should give generously to others of our time, love, and possessions.

Herod kills John the Baptist

Herod Antipas, the king, soon heard about Jesus, because everyone was talking about him. Some were saying, "This must be John the Baptist raised from the dead. That is why he can do such miracles." Others said, "He's the prophet Elijah." Still others said, "He's a prophet like the other great prophets of the past."

When Herod heard about Jesus, he said, "John, the man I beheaded, has come back from the dead." MARK 6:14-16 *(see also Matthew 14:1-2; Luke 9:7-9)*

CHRIST'S TRUE IDENTITY

It was so difficult for the people to accept Jesus as the Son of God that they tried to come up with other solutions—most of which sound quite unbelievable to us. Many thought that he must be someone who had come back to life, perhaps John the Baptist or another prophet. Some suggested that he was Elijah, the great prophet who did not die but was taken to heaven in a chariot of fire (2 Kings 2:1-11). Very few found the correct answer, as Peter did (Luke 9:20).

Many people still find it difficult to accept Jesus as the fully human yet fully divine Son of God. People are still trying to find alternate explanations—so they call Jesus a great prophet, a radical political leader, a self-deceived rabble-rouser. None of these explanations can account for Jesus' miracles or, especially, his glorious resurrection—so these realities, too, have to be explained away. In the end, the attempts to explain away Jesus are far more difficult to believe than the truth. But people still have to make up their minds about Jesus. Some think that if they can name what he is—prophet, teacher, good man—they can weaken the power of his claim on their lives. But what they *think* does not change who Jesus *is*. Jesus is the God-man; he is God. Does he rule in your life?

Herod was a tetrarch—one of four rulers over the four districts of Palestine. His territory included the regions of Galilee and Perea. He was the son of Herod the Great, who had ordered the killing of the babies in Bethlehem (Matthew 2:16). Also known as Herod Antipas, he heard Jesus' case before Jesus' crucifixion (Luke 23:6-12).

Herod kills John the Baptist

For Herod had sent soldiers to arrest and imprison John as a favor to Herodias. She had been his brother Philip's wife, but Herod had married her. John had been telling Herod, "It is against God's law for you to marry your brother's wife." So Herodias bore a grudge against John and wanted to kill him. But without Herod's approval she was powerless, for Herod respected John; and knowing that he was a good and holy man, he protected him. Herod was greatly disturbed whenever he talked with John, but even so, he liked to listen to him.

Herodias's chance finally came on Herod's birthday. He gave a party for his high government officials, army officers, and the leading citizens of Galilee. Then his daughter, also named Herodias, came in and performed a dance that greatly pleased Herod and his guests. "Ask me for anything you like," the king said to the girl, "and I will give it to you." He even vowed, "I will give you whatever you ask, up to half my kingdom!"

She went out and asked her mother, "What should I ask for?"

Her mother told her, "Ask for the head of John the Baptist!"

So the girl hurried back to the king and told him, "I want the head of John the Baptist, right now, on a tray!"

Then the king deeply regretted what he had said; but because of the vows he had made in front of his guests, he couldn't refuse her. So he immediately sent an executioner to the prison to cut off John's head and bring it to him. The soldier beheaded John in the prison, brought his head on a tray, and gave it to the girl, who took it to her mother. When John's disciples heard what had happened, they came to get his body and buried it in a tomb.

MARK 6:17-29 *(see also Matthew 14:3-12)*

DETERMINE TO DO RIGHT

As a ruler under Roman authority, Herod had no kingdom to give. The offer of half his kingdom was Herod's way of saying that he would give Herodias's daughter almost anything she wanted. When Herodias asked for John's head, Herod would have been greatly embarrassed in front of his guests if he had denied her request. Words are powerful. Because they can lead to great sin, we should use them with great care. How easy it is to give in to the crowd and to let ourselves be pressured into doing wrong. Don't get in a situation where it might be embarrassing to do what is right. But determine to do what is right, no matter how embarrassing or painful it may be.

May 30 READ MARK 6:30-34

Jesus feeds five thousand

The apostles returned to Jesus from their ministry tour and told him all they had done and taught. Then Jesus said, "Let's go off by ourselves to a quiet place and rest awhile." He said this because there were so many people coming and going that Jesus and his apostles didn't even have time to eat.

So they left by boat for a quiet place, where they could be alone. But many people recognized them and saw them leaving, and people from many towns ran ahead along the shore and got there ahead of them. Jesus saw the huge crowd as he stepped from the boat, and he had compassion on them because they were like sheep without a shepherd. So he began teaching them many things. MARK 6:30-34 *(see also Matthew 14:13-14; Luke 9:10-11; John 6:1-4)*

JESUS LOVED PEOPLE

Jesus had tried to slip quietly away from the crowds, but they found out where he was going and followed him. Instead of showing impatience at this interruption, Jesus welcomed the people and ministered to their needs. This crowd was as pitiful as a flock of sheep without a shepherd. Sheep are easily scattered; without a shepherd they are in grave danger. Jesus was the shepherd who could teach them what they needed to know and keep them from straying from God. How do you view people who interrupt your schedule—as nuisances, or as the reason for your life and ministry?

When the disciples returned from their mission, Jesus took them away to rest. Doing God's work is very important, but Jesus recognized that to do it effectively we need periodic rest and renewal.

Jesus feeds five thousand

Late in the afternoon his disciples came to him and said, "This is a remote place, and it's already getting late. Send the crowds away so they can go to the nearby farms and villages and buy something to eat."

But Jesus said, "You feed them."

"With what?" they asked. "We'd have to work for months to earn enough money to buy food for all these people!"

"How much bread do you have?" he asked. "Go and find out."

They came back and reported, "We have five loaves of bread and two fish."

Then Jesus told the disciples to have the people sit down in groups on the green grass. So they sat down in groups of fifty or a hundred.

Jesus took the five loaves and two fish, looked up toward heaven, and blessed them. Then, breaking the loaves into pieces, he kept giving the bread to the disciples so they could distribute it to the people. He also divided the fish for everyone to share. They all ate as much as they wanted, and afterward, the disciples picked up twelve baskets of leftover bread and fish. A total of 5,000 men and their families were fed from those loaves!

MARK 6:35-44 *(see also Matthew 14:15-21; Luke 9:12-17; John 6:5-13)*

GIVE WHAT YOU HAVE

Jesus multiplied five loaves and two fish to feed more than five thousand people. What he was originally given seemed insufficient, but in his hands it became more than enough. We often feel that our contribution to Jesus is meager, but he can use and multiply whatever we give him, whether it is talent, time, or treasure. It is when we give them to Jesus that our resources are multiplied. God gives in abundance. He takes whatever we can offer him in time, ability, or resources and multiplies its effectiveness beyond our wildest expectations. If you take the first step in making yourself available to God, he will show you how greatly you can be used to advance the work of his Kingdom.

The text states that there were five thousand men present, besides women and children. Therefore the total number of people Jesus fed could have been ten to fifteen thousand. The number of men is listed separately because in the Jewish culture of the day, men and women usually ate separately when in public. The children ate with the women.

June 1

Jesus walks on water

Immediately after this, Jesus insisted that his disciples get back into the boat and cross to the other side of the lake, while he sent the people home. After sending them home, he went up into the hills by himself to pray. Night fell while he was there alone.

Meanwhile, the disciples were in trouble far away from land, for a strong wind had risen, and they were fighting heavy waves.

MATTHEW 14:22-24 *(see also Mark 6:45-46; John 6:16-18)*

TIME ALONE

Seeking solitude was an important priority for Jesus (see also Matthew 14:13). He made room in his busy schedule to be alone with the Father. Spending time with God in prayer nurtures a vital relationship and equips us to meet life's challenges and struggles. Finding time to pray is not easy, but prayer is the vital link between us and God. Like Jesus, we must break away from others to talk with God, even if we have to get up very early in the morning to do it! Develop the discipline of spending time alone with God—it will help you grow spiritually and become more and more like Christ.

The miraculous feeding of the five thousand occurred on the shores of the Sea of Galilee. Jesus sent his disciples across the lake while he went up into the rolling hills to spend time in prayer.

Jesus walks on water

About three o'clock in the morning Jesus came toward them, walking on the water. When the disciples saw him walking on the water, they were terrified. In their fear, they cried out, "It's a ghost!"

But Jesus spoke to them at once. "Don't be afraid," he said. "Take courage. I am here!"

Then Peter called to him, "Lord, if it's really you, tell me to come to you, walking on the water."

"Yes, come," Jesus said.

So Peter went over the side of the boat and walked on the water toward Jesus. But when he saw the strong wind and the waves, he was terrified and began to sink. "Save me, Lord!" he shouted.

Jesus immediately reached out and grabbed him. "You have so little faith," Jesus said. "Why did you doubt me?"

When they climbed back into the boat, the wind stopped. Then the disciples worshiped him. "You really are the Son of God!" they exclaimed.

MATTHEW 14:25-33 *(see also Mark 6:47-52; John 6:19-21)*

TRANSFER THE TRUTH

The disciples didn't want to believe, perhaps because (1) they couldn't accept the fact that this human named Jesus was really the Son of God; (2) they dared not believe that the Messiah would choose them as his followers—it was too good to be true; or (3) they still did not understand the real purpose for Jesus' coming to earth. Their disbelief took the form of misunderstanding.

Even after watching Jesus miraculously feed five thousand people, they still could not take the final step of faith and believe that he was God's Son. If they had, they would not have been amazed that Jesus could walk on water. The disciples did not transfer the truth they already knew about Jesus to their own lives. We read that Jesus walked on the water, and yet we often marvel that he is able to work in our lives. We must not only believe that these miracles really occurred, we must also transfer the truth to our own life situations.

The disciples were afraid, but Jesus' presence calmed their fears. We all experience fear. Do we try to deal with it ourselves, or do we let Jesus deal with it? In times of fear and uncertainty, it is calming to know that Christ is always with us.

Jesus heals all who touch him

After they had crossed the lake, they landed at Gennesaret. They brought the boat to shore and climbed out. The people recognized Jesus at once, and they ran throughout the whole area, carrying sick people on mats to wherever they heard he was. Wherever he went—in villages, cities, or the countryside—they brought the sick out to the marketplaces. They begged him to let the sick touch at least the fringe of his robe, and all who touched him were healed.

MARK 6:53-56 *(see also Matthew 14:34-36)*

THE GREAT HEALER

The people recognized Jesus as a great healer, but how many understood who he truly was? They came to Jesus for physical healing, but did they come for spiritual healing? They came to prolong their lives on earth, but did they come to secure eternal life for themselves? People may seek Jesus to learn valuable lessons from his life or in hopes of finding relief from pain. But we miss Jesus' whole message if we seek him to heal our bodies but not our souls—if we look to him for help only in this life and do not consider his eternal plan for us. Only when we understand the real Jesus Christ can we appreciate how he can truly change our lives.

Gennesaret was a small fertile plain located on the west side of the Sea of Galilee. Capernaum, Jesus' home, sat at the northern edge of this plain.

Jesus is the true Bread from heaven

The next day the crowd that had stayed on the far shore saw that the disciples had taken the only boat, and they realized Jesus had not gone with them. Several boats from Tiberias landed near the place where the Lord had blessed the bread and the people had eaten. So when the crowd saw that neither Jesus nor his disciples were there, they got into the boats and went across to Capernaum to look for him. They found him on the other side of the lake and asked, "Rabbi, when did you get here?"

Jesus replied, "I tell you the truth, you want to be with me because I fed you, not because you understood the miraculous signs. But don't be so concerned about perishable things like food. Spend your energy seeking the eternal life that the Son of Man can give you. For God the Father has given me the seal of his approval."

They replied, "We want to perform God's works, too. What should we do?"

Jesus told them, "This is the only work God wants from you: Believe in the one he has sent." JOHN 6:22-29

WE MUST BELIEVE

Many sincere seekers after God are puzzled about what he wants them to do. The world's religions are humankind's attempts to answer this question. But Jesus' reply is brief and simple: We must believe on him whom God has sent. Satisfying God does not come from the work we *do* but from whom we *believe*. The first step is accepting that Jesus is who he claims to be. All spiritual development is built on this affirmation. Declare to Jesus that he is "the Messiah, the Son of the living God" (Matthew 16:16), and embark on a life of belief that is satisfying to your Creator.

Jesus criticized the people who followed him only for the physical and temporal benefits and not for the satisfying of their spiritual hunger. Many people use religion to gain prestige, comfort, or even political votes. But those are self-centered motives.

June 5 READ JOHN 6:30-40

Jesus is the true Bread from heaven

They answered, "Show us a miraculous sign if you want us to believe in you. What can you do? After all, our ancestors ate manna while they journeyed through the wilderness! The Scriptures say, 'Moses gave them bread from heaven to eat.'"

Jesus said, "I tell you the truth, Moses didn't give you bread from heaven. My Father did. And now he offers you the true bread from heaven. The true bread of God is the one who comes down from heaven and gives life to the world."

"Sir," they said, "give us that bread every day."

Jesus replied, "I am the bread of life. Whoever comes to me will never be hungry again. Whoever believes in me will never be thirsty. But you haven't believed in me even though you have seen me. However, those the Father has given me will come to me, and I will never reject them. For I have come down from heaven to do the will of God who sent me, not to do my own will. And this is the will of God, that I should not lose even one of all those he has given me, but that I should raise them up at the last day. For it is my Father's will that all who see his Son and believe in him should have eternal life. I will raise them up at the last day." JOHN 6:30-40

SPIRITUAL HUNGER

People eat bread to satisfy physical hunger and to sustain physical life. We can satisfy spiritual hunger and sustain spiritual life only by having a right relationship with Jesus Christ. No wonder he called himself the Bread of Life. But bread must be eaten to sustain life, and Christ must be invited into our daily walk to sustain spiritual life.

Jesus did not work independently of God the Father but in union with him. Jesus' purpose was to do the will of God, not to satisfy human desires.

The Jews disagree that Jesus is from heaven

Then the people began to murmur in disagreement because he had said, "I am the bread that came down from heaven." They said, "Isn't this Jesus, the son of Joseph? We know his father and mother. How can he say, 'I came down from heaven'?"

But Jesus replied, "Stop complaining about what I said. For no one can come to me unless the Father who sent me draws them to me, and at the last day I will raise them up. As it is written in the Scriptures, 'They will all be taught by God.' Everyone who listens to the Father and learns from him comes to me. (Not that anyone has ever seen the Father; only I, who was sent from God, have seen him.)

"I tell you the truth, anyone who believes has eternal life. Yes, I am the bread of life! Your ancestors ate manna in the wilderness, but they all died. Anyone who eats the bread from heaven, however, will never die. I am the living bread that came down from heaven. Anyone who eats this bread will live forever; and this bread, which I will offer so the world may live, is my flesh." JOHN 6:41-51

SATISFACTION

The religious leaders frequently asked Jesus to prove to them why he was better than the prophets they already had. Jesus was referring to the manna that Moses had given their ancestors in the wilderness (Exodus 16). That bread was physical and temporal. The people had eaten it, and it had sustained them for a day. But they had to get more bread every day, and this bread could not keep them from dying. Jesus, who is much greater than Moses, offers himself as the spiritual bread from heaven that satisfies completely and leads to eternal life. God, not man, plays the most active role in salvation. When someone chooses to believe in Jesus Christ as Savior, he or she does so only in response to the urging of God's Holy Spirit. God does the urging and gives the faith; the person then decides whether or not to believe. Thus, no one can believe in Jesus without God's help. If you know Christ as Savior, thank him for his powerful work in your life.

The religious leaders grumbled because they could not accept Jesus' claim of divinity. They saw him only as a carpenter from Nazareth. They refused to believe that Jesus was God's divine Son, and they could not tolerate his message.

The Jews disagree that Jesus is from heaven

Then the people began arguing with each other about what he meant. "How can this man give us his flesh to eat?" they asked.

So Jesus said again, "I tell you the truth, unless you eat the flesh of the Son of Man and drink his blood, you cannot have eternal life within you. But anyone who eats my flesh and drinks my blood has eternal life, and I will raise that person at the last day. For my flesh is true food, and my blood is true drink. Anyone who eats my flesh and drinks my blood remains in me, and I in him. I live because of the living Father who sent me; in the same way, anyone who feeds on me will live because of me. I am the true bread that came down from heaven. Anyone who eats this bread will not die as your ancestors did (even though they ate the manna) but will live forever."

He said these things while he was teaching in the synagogue in Capernaum.

JOHN 6:52-59

THE LIVING BREAD

How can Jesus give us his flesh as bread to eat? This was a shocking message—to eat flesh and drink blood sounded cannibalistic. The idea of drinking any blood, let alone human blood, was repugnant to the religious leaders because the law forbade it (Leviticus 17:10-11). Jesus was not talking about literal blood, of course; he was saying that his life had to become their own. But they could not accept this concept. The apostle Paul later used the body and blood imagery in talking about Communion (1 Corinthians 11:23-26). To eat the living bread means to accept Christ into our lives and become united with him. We are united with Christ in two ways: (1) by believing in his death (the sacrifice of his flesh) and resurrection and (2) by devoting ourselves to living as he requires, depending on his teaching for guidance and trusting in the Holy Spirit for power. If you are united with Christ, he is living through you by his Holy Spirit. In what ways do you reflect Christ to your family and friends?

Those who put their faith in Christ will be resurrected from physical death to everlasting life with God when Christ comes again (1 Corinthians 15:52; 1 Thessalonians 4:16).

Many disciples desert Jesus

Many of his disciples said, "This is very hard to understand. How can anyone accept it?"

Jesus was aware that his disciples were complaining, so he said to them, "Does this offend you? Then what will you think if you see the Son of Man ascend to heaven again? The Spirit alone gives eternal life. Human effort accomplishes nothing. And the very words I have spoken to you are spirit and life. But some of you do not believe me." (For Jesus knew from the beginning which ones didn't believe, and he knew who would betray him.) Then he said, "That is why I said that people can't come to me unless the Father gives them to me." JOHN 6:60-65

WHY TURN AWAY?

Why were Jesus' words so difficult for many of his followers to understand? (1) They may have realized that he wasn't going to be the conquering Messiah-King they expected. (2) He refused to give in to their self-centered requests. (3) He emphasized faith, not works. (4) His teachings were difficult to understand, and some of his words were offensive. As we grow in our faith, we may be tempted to turn away because Jesus' lessons are difficult. Will your response be to give up, ignore certain teachings, or reject Christ? Instead, ask God to show you what the teachings mean and how they apply to your life. Then have the courage to act on God's truth.

The Holy Spirit gives spiritual life; without the work of the Holy Spirit, we cannot even see our need for new life (John 14:17). All spiritual renewal begins and ends with God. He reveals truth to us, lives within us, and then enables us to respond to that truth.

Many disciples desert Jesus

At this point many of his disciples turned away and deserted him. Then Jesus turned to the Twelve and asked, "Are you also going to leave?"

Simon Peter replied, "Lord, to whom would we go? You have the words that give eternal life. We believe, and we know you are the Holy One of God."

Then Jesus said, "I chose the twelve of you, but one is a devil." He was speaking of Judas, son of Simon Iscariot, one of the Twelve, who would later betray him.   JOHN 6:66-71

NO OTHER WAY

After many of his followers had deserted him, Jesus asked the twelve disciples if they were also going to leave. Peter replied, "To whom would we go?" In his straightforward way, Peter answered for all of us—there is no other way to God. Though there are many philosophies and self-styled authorities, Jesus alone has the words of eternal life. People look everywhere for eternal life and miss Christ, the only source. Many people today turn away; others pretend to follow, going to church for status, approval of family and friends, or business contacts. But there are only two real responses to Jesus—you either accept him or reject him. How have you responded to Christ?

The more the people heard Jesus' real message, the more they divided into two camps—the honest seekers who wanted to understand more, and those who rejected Jesus because they didn't like what they had heard.

Jesus teaches about inner purity

One day some Pharisees and teachers of religious law arrived from Jerusalem to see Jesus. They noticed that some of his disciples failed to follow the Jewish ritual of hand washing before eating. (The Jews, especially the Pharisees, do not eat until they have poured water over their cupped hands, as required by their ancient traditions. Similarly, they don't eat anything from the market until they immerse their hands in water. This is but one of many traditions they have clung to—such as their ceremonial washing of cups, pitchers, and kettles.)

So the Pharisees and teachers of religious law asked him, "Why don't your disciples follow our age-old tradition? They eat without first performing the hand-washing ceremony."

Jesus replied, "You hypocrites! Isaiah was right when he prophesied about you, for he wrote, 'These people honor me with their lips, but their hearts are far from me. Their worship is a farce, for they teach man-made ideas as commands from God.' For you ignore God's law and substitute your own tradition."

Then he said, "You skillfully sidestep God's law in order to hold on to your own tradition. For instance, Moses gave you this law from God: 'Honor your father and mother,' and 'Anyone who speaks disrespectfully of father or mother must be put to death.' But you say it is all right for people to say to their parents, 'Sorry, I can't help you. For I have vowed to give to God what I would have given to you.' In this way, you let them disregard their needy parents. And so you cancel the word of God in order to hand down your own tradition. And this is only one example among many others." MARK 7:1-13 *(see also Matthew 15:1-9)*

HYPOCRISY

Hypocrisy is pretending to be something you are not and have no intention of being. Jesus called the Pharisees hypocrites because they worshiped God for the wrong reasons. Their worship was not motivated by love but by a desire to attain profit, to appear holy, and to increase their status. We become hypocrites when we (1) pay more attention to reputation than to character, (2) carefully follow certain religious practices while allowing our hearts to remain distant from God, and (3) emphasize our virtues but others' sins. Why do you go to church?

———————————◆◆———————————

The Pharisees added hundreds of their own petty rules and regulations to God's holy laws, and then they tried to force people to follow these rules. These men claimed to know God's will in every detail of life.

———————————◆◆———————————

Jesus teaches about inner purity

Then Jesus called to the crowd to come and hear. "All of you listen," he said, "and try to understand. It's not what goes into your body that defiles you; you are defiled by what comes from your heart."

Then Jesus went into a house to get away from the crowd, and his disciples asked him what he meant by the parable he had just used. "Don't you understand either?" he asked. "Can't you see that the food you put into your body cannot defile you? Food doesn't go into your heart, but only passes through the stomach and then goes into the sewer." (By saying this, he declared that every kind of food is acceptable in God's eyes.)

MARK 7:14-19 *(see also Matthew 15:10-17)*

INSIDE OUT

Do we worry more about what is in our diets than what is in our hearts and minds? As they interpreted the dietary laws (Leviticus 11), the Jews believed they could be clean before God because of what they refused to eat. But Jesus pointed out that sin actually begins in the attitudes and intentions of the inner person. Jesus did not degrade the law, but he paved the way for the change made clear in Acts 10:9-29, when God removed the cultural restrictions regarding food. We are not pure because of outward acts—we become pure on the inside as Christ renews our minds and transforms us into his image.

It is idolatry to claim that your interpretation of God's Word is as important as God's Word itself. It is especially dangerous to set up unbiblical standards for others to follow. Instead, look to Christ for guidance about your own behavior, and let him lead others in the details of their lives.

Jesus teaches about inner purity

And then he added, "It is what comes from inside that defiles you. For from within, out of a person's heart, come evil thoughts, sexual immorality, theft, murder, adultery, greed, wickedness, deceit, lustful desires, envy, slander, pride, and foolishness. All these vile things come from within; they are what defile you."

MARK 7:20-23 *(see also Matthew 15:18-20)*

A SINGLE THOUGHT

An evil action begins with a single thought. Allowing our minds to dwell on lust, envy, hatred, or revenge will lead to sin. Don't defile yourself by focusing on evil. What we put into our minds determines what comes out in our words and actions. The apostle Paul tells us to fix our thoughts on what is true, honorable, right, pure, lovely, admirable, excellent, and praiseworthy (Philippians 4:8). Do you have problems with impure thoughts and daydreams? Examine what you are putting into your mind through television, books, conversations, movies, and magazines. Replace harmful input with wholesome material. Above all, read God's Word and pray. Ask God to help you focus your mind on what is good and pure. It takes practice, but it can be done.

There is a downward spiral. First, people reject a command of God; next, they make up their own ideas about God. Then, they allow evil thoughts to lead them into evil actions. Finally, they grow to hate God. Only Christ can break this progression and help people escape the downward spiral.

Jesus sends a demon out of a girl

Then Jesus left Galilee and went north to the region of Tyre. He didn't want anyone to know which house he was staying in, but he couldn't keep it a secret. Right away a woman who had heard about him came and fell at his feet. Her little girl was possessed by an evil spirit, and she begged him to cast out the demon from her daughter.

Since she was a Gentile, born in Syrian Phoenicia, Jesus told her, "First I should feed the children—my own family, the Jews. It isn't right to take food from the children and throw it to the dogs."

She replied, "That's true, Lord, but even the dogs under the table are allowed to eat the scraps from the children's plates."

"Good answer!" he said. "Now go home, for the demon has left your daughter." And when she arrived home, she found her little girl lying quietly in bed, and the demon was gone. MARK 7:24-30 *(see also Matthew 15:21-28)*

AVAILABLE TO ALL

Jesus' words do not contradict the truth that God's message is for all people (Psalm 22:27; Isaiah 56:7; Matthew 28:19; Romans 15:9-12). Remember, when Jesus said these words, he was in Gentile territory on a mission to Gentile people. He ministered to Gentiles on many other occasions also. Jesus was simply telling the woman that Jews were to have the first opportunity to accept him as the Messiah because God wanted them to present the message of salvation to the rest of the world (Genesis 12:3). Jesus was not rejecting the Syrophoenician woman. He may have wanted to test her faith, or he may have wanted to use the situation as another opportunity to teach that faith is available to all kinds of people. Ironically, many Jews would lose God's spiritual healing because of their rejection of Jesus, while many Gentiles, whom the Jews rejected, would find salvation because of their recognition of Jesus. Whom do you know who seems to be beyond the gospel? Don't count them out. Continue to pray that God will bring them to faith, and look for ways to tell them about God's love.

Dog *was a term the Jews commonly applied to Gentiles because the Jews considered these heathen people no more likely than dogs to receive God's blessing. Jesus was not degrading the woman by using this term; he was reflecting the Jews' attitude so as to contrast it with his own.*

The crowd marvels at Jesus' healings

esus left Tyre and went up to Sidon before going back to the Sea of Galilee and the region of the Ten Towns. A deaf man with a speech impediment was brought to him, and the people begged Jesus to lay his hands on the man to heal him.

Jesus led him away from the crowd so they could be alone. He put his fingers into the man's ears. Then, spitting on his own fingers, he touched the man's tongue. Looking up to heaven, he sighed and said, "Ephphatha," which means, "Be opened!" Instantly the man could hear perfectly, and his tongue was freed so he could speak plainly!

Jesus told the crowd not to tell anyone, but the more he told them not to, the more they spread the news. They were completely amazed and said again and again, "Everything he does is wonderful. He even makes the deaf to hear and gives speech to those who cannot speak."

MARK 7:31-37 *(see also Matthew 15:29-31)*

HEALING POWER

Many people were brought to Jesus to be healed, and he healed them all. Jesus is still able to heal broken lives, and we can be the ones who bring suffering people to him. Do you know people who need Christ's healing touch? You can bring them to Jesus by prayer or through explaining to them the reason for the hope that you have (1 Peter 3:15). Then let Christ do the healing.

Jesus asked the people not to talk about this healing because he didn't want to be seen simply as a miracle worker. He didn't want the people to miss his real message. We must not be so concerned about what Jesus can do for us that we forget to listen to his message.

Jesus feeds four thousand

About this time another large crowd had gathered, and the people ran out of food again. Jesus called his disciples and told them, "I feel sorry for these people. They have been here with me for three days, and they have nothing left to eat. If I send them home hungry, they will faint along the way. For some of them have come a long distance."

His disciples replied, "How are we supposed to find enough food to feed them out here in the wilderness?"

Jesus asked, "How much bread do you have?"

"Seven loaves," they replied.

So Jesus told all the people to sit down on the ground. Then he took the seven loaves, thanked God for them, and broke them into pieces. He gave them to his disciples, who distributed the bread to the crowd. A few small fish were found, too, so Jesus also blessed these and told the disciples to distribute them.

They ate as much as they wanted. Afterward, the disciples picked up seven large baskets of leftover food. There were about 4,000 people in the crowd that day, and Jesus sent them home after they had eaten.

MARK 8:1-9 *(see also Matthew 15:32-39)*

FOOD FOR THOUGHT

This is a different miracle from the feeding of the five thousand described earlier. At that time, those fed were mostly Jews. This time Jesus was ministering to a non-Jewish crowd in the Gentile region of the Decapolis. Jesus had already fed more than five thousand people with five loaves and two fish. Here, in a similar situation, the disciples were again perplexed. How easily we despair when faced with difficult situations. Like the disciples, we often forget that if God has cared for us in the past, he will do the same now. When facing a perplexing problem or a tough task, remember how God has cared for you and trust him to work faithfully again.

Magadan (Matthew 15:39) was located on the west shore of the Sea of Galilee. Also known as Magdala or Dalmanutha (Mark 8:10), this was Mary Magdalene's hometown.

Religious leaders ask for a sign in the sky

One day the Pharisees and Sadducees came to test Jesus, demanding that he show them a miraculous sign from heaven to prove his authority.

He replied, "You know the saying, 'Red sky at night means fair weather tomorrow; red sky in the morning means foul weather all day.' You know how to interpret the weather signs in the sky, but you don't know how to interpret the signs of the times! Only an evil, adulterous generation would demand a miraculous sign, but the only sign I will give them is the sign of the prophet Jonah." MATTHEW 16:1-4 *(see also Mark 8:10-12)*

MIRACLES

These Jewish leaders said they wanted to see a miracle so that they could believe. But Jesus knew that miracles never convince the skeptical. Jesus had been healing, raising people from the dead, and feeding thousands, and still people wanted him to prove himself. Do you doubt Christ because you haven't *seen* a miracle? Do you expect God to prove himself to you personally before you choose to believe? Jesus says, "Blessed are those who believe without seeing me" (John 20:29). We have all the miracles recorded in the Old and New Testaments, two thousand years of church history, and the witness of thousands of believers. With all this evidence, those who won't believe are either too proud or too stubborn. If you simply step forward in faith and believe, then you will begin to see the miracles that God can do with your life!

———————————◆●◆———————————

The Pharisees had tried to explain away Jesus' previous miracles by claiming they happened by luck, coincidence, or evil power. Here they demanded a sign from heaven—something only God could do. Jesus refused their demand because he knew that even this kind of miracle would not convince them. They had already decided not to believe.

———————————◆●◆———————————

Jesus warns against wrong teaching

So he got back into the boat and left them, and he crossed to the other side of the lake.

But the disciples had forgotten to bring any food. They had only one loaf of bread with them in the boat. As they were crossing the lake, Jesus warned them, "Watch out! Beware of the yeast of the Pharisees and of Herod."

At this they began to argue with each other because they hadn't brought any bread. Jesus knew what they were saying, so he said, "Why are you arguing about having no bread? Don't you know or understand even yet? Are your hearts too hard to take it in? 'You have eyes—can't you see? You have ears—can't you hear?' Don't you remember anything at all? When I fed the 5,000 with five loaves of bread, how many baskets of leftovers did you pick up afterward?"

"Twelve," they said.

"And when I fed the 4,000 with seven loaves, how many large baskets of leftovers did you pick up?"

"Seven," they said.

"Don't you understand yet?" he asked them.

MARK 8:13-21 *(see also Matthew 16:5-12)*

OPEN HEARTS AND MINDS

How could the disciples experience so many of Jesus' miracles and yet be so slow to comprehend who he was? They had already seen Jesus feed more than five thousand men and their families with five loaves and two fish (Mark 6:35-44), yet here they doubted whether he could feed them.

Sometimes we are also slow to catch on. Although Christ has brought us through trials and temptations in the past, we don't believe that he will do it in the future. Is your heart too closed to take in all that God can do for you? Don't be like the disciples. Remember what Christ has done, and have faith that he will do it again.

———————————●———————————

Yeast in this passage symbolizes evil. Just as only a small amount of yeast is needed to make a batch of bread rise, so the hard-heartedness of the religious and political leaders could permeate and contaminate the entire society and make it rise up against Jesus.

———————————●———————————

Jesus restores sight to a blind man

When they arrived at Bethsaida, some people brought a blind man to Jesus, and they begged him to touch the man and heal him. Jesus took the blind man by the hand and led him out of the village. Then, spitting on the man's eyes, he laid his hands on him and asked, "Can you see anything now?"

The man looked around. "Yes," he said, "I see people, but I can't see them very clearly. They look like trees walking around."

Then Jesus placed his hands on the man's eyes again, and his eyes were opened. His sight was completely restored, and he could see everything clearly. Jesus sent him away, saying, "Don't go back into the village on your way home."

MARK 8:22-26

OPEN EYES

Why did Jesus touch the man a second time before he could see? This miracle was not too difficult for Jesus, but he chose to do it in stages, possibly to show the disciples that some healing would be gradual rather than instantaneous or to demonstrate that spiritual truth is not always perceived clearly at first. Before Jesus left, however, the man was healed completely. Sometimes it takes time for us to understand. Christ stays with us, helping us to finally "see" clearly. Trust him to help you when you don't understand.

Jesus took the man out of the village to heal him and then told him not to go back into the village. Jesus had compassion to heal, but he did not want to be seen as merely a miracle worker.

June 19 READ MATTHEW 16:13-20

Peter says Jesus is the Messiah

When Jesus came to the region of Caesarea Philippi, he asked his disciples, "Who do people say that the Son of Man is?"

"Well," they replied, "some say John the Baptist, some say Elijah, and others say Jeremiah or one of the other prophets."

Then he asked them, "But who do you say I am?"

Simon Peter answered, "You are the Messiah, the Son of the living God."

Jesus replied, "You are blessed, Simon son of John, because my Father in heaven has revealed this to you. You did not learn this from any human being. Now I say to you that you are Peter (which means 'rock'), and upon this rock I will build my church, and all the powers of hell will not conquer it. And I will give you the keys of the Kingdom of Heaven. Whatever you forbid on earth will be forbidden in heaven, and whatever you permit on earth will be permitted in heaven."

Then he sternly warned the disciples not to tell anyone that he was the Messiah.   MATTHEW 16:13-20 *(see also Mark 8:27-30; Luke 9:18-21)*

WHO DO YOU SAY HE IS?

The disciples answered Jesus' question with the common view—that Jesus was one of the great prophets come back to life. This belief may have stemmed from Deuteronomy 18:18, where God said he would raise up a prophet from among the people. Peter, however, confessed Jesus as divine and as the promised and long-awaited Messiah. It is not enough to know what others say about Jesus: You must know, understand, and accept for yourself that he is the Messiah. You must move from curiosity to commitment, from admiration to adoration. If Jesus were to ask you this question, how would you answer? Is he your Lord and Messiah?

The rock on which Jesus would build his church has been identified as (1) Jesus himself (his work of salvation by dying for us on the cross); (2) Peter (the first great leader of the church at Jerusalem); or (3) the confession of faith that Peter gave and that all subsequent true believers would give.

Jesus predicts his death the first time

Then Jesus began to tell them that the Son of Man must suffer many terrible things and be rejected by the elders, the leading priests, and the teachers of religious law. He would be killed, but three days later he would rise from the dead. As he talked about this openly with his disciples, Peter took him aside and began to reprimand him for saying such things.

Jesus turned around and looked at his disciples, then reprimanded Peter. "Get away from me, Satan!" he said. "You are seeing things merely from a human point of view, not from God's."

Then, calling the crowd to join his disciples, he said, "If any of you wants to be my follower, you must turn from your selfish ways, take up your cross, and follow me. If you try to hang on to your life, you will lose it. But if you give up your life for my sake and for the sake of the Good News, you will save it. And what do you benefit if you gain the whole world but lose your own soul? Is anything worth more than your soul? If anyone is ashamed of me and my message in these adulterous and sinful days, the Son of Man will be ashamed of that person when he returns in the glory of his Father with the holy angels."

Jesus went on to say, "I tell you the truth, some standing here right now will not die before they see the Kingdom of God arrive in great power!"

MARK 8:31–9:1 *(see also Matthew 16:21-28; Luke 9:21-27)*

LOST AND FOUND

Many people spend all their energy seeking pleasure. Jesus said, however, that a world of pleasure centered on possessions, position, or power is ultimately worthless. Whatever you have on earth is only temporary; it cannot be exchanged for your soul. If you work hard at getting what you want, you might eventually have a pleasurable life, but in the end you will find it hollow and empty. We should be willing to lose our lives for the sake of the gospel, not because our lives are useless, but because nothing—not even life itself—can compare to what we gain with Christ. Jesus wants us to *choose* to follow him rather than to lead a life of sin and self-satisfaction. He wants us to stop trying to control our own destiny and to let him direct us. This makes good sense because, as the Creator, Christ knows better than we do what real life is about. He asks for submission, not self-hatred; he asks us to lose our self-centered determination to be in charge.

June 21

Jesus is transfigured on the mountain

About eight days later Jesus took Peter, John, and James up on a mountain to pray. And as he was praying, the appearance of his face was transformed, and his clothes became dazzling white. Suddenly, two men, Moses and Elijah, appeared and began talking with Jesus. They were glorious to see. And they were speaking about his exodus from this world, which was about to be fulfilled in Jerusalem. LUKE 9:28-31 *(see also Matthew 17:1-3; Mark 9:2-4)*

THE INNER CIRCLE

When Jesus said that some of his disciples would see the Kingdom of God arrive (Luke 9:27), he may have been referring to the three disciples who would see the Transfiguration. We don't know why Jesus singled out Peter, James, and John for this special revelation of his glory and purity. Perhaps they were the ones most ready to understand and accept this great truth. These three disciples were the inner circle of the group of twelve. They were among the first to hear Jesus' call (Mark 1:16-20). They headed the lists of disciples (Mark 3:16-17) in the Gospels. And they were present at certain healings where others were excluded (Luke 8:51). God calls different people to certain areas of service for him. Some are more visible than others, but all are needed to accomplish his work in the world. Are you doing what God called you to do?

Moses and Elijah were the two greatest prophets in the Old Testament. Moses represents the law, or the old covenant. He wrote the Pentateuch and predicted the coming of a great prophet (Deuteronomy 18:15-19). Elijah represents the prophets who foretold the coming of the Messiah (Malachi 4:5-6). Moses' and Elijah's presence with Jesus confirmed Jesus' messianic mission—to fulfill God's law and the words of God's prophets.

Jesus is transfigured on the mountain

Peter and the others had fallen asleep. When they woke up, they saw Jesus' glory and the two men standing with him. As Moses and Elijah were starting to leave, Peter, not even knowing what he was saying, blurted out, "Master, it's wonderful for us to be here! Let's make three shelters as memorials—one for you, one for Moses, and one for Elijah." But even as he was saying this, a cloud overshadowed them, and terror gripped them as the cloud covered them.

Then a voice from the cloud said, "This is my Son, my Chosen One. Listen to him." When the voice finished, Jesus was there alone. They didn't tell anyone at that time what they had seen.

LUKE 9:32-36 *(see also Matthew 17:4-13; Mark 9:5-13)*

GOD'S SON

The Transfiguration revealed Christ's divine nature. God's voice exalted Jesus above Moses and Elijah as the long-awaited Messiah with full divine authority. Moses represented the law, and Elijah, the prophets. Their appearance showed Jesus as the fulfillment of both the Old Testament law and the prophetic promises.

Jesus was not a reincarnation of Elijah or Moses. He was not merely one of the prophets. As God's only Son, he far surpasses them in authority and power. Many voices try to tell us how to live and how to know God personally. Some of these are helpful; many are not. We must first listen to the Bible and then evaluate all other authorities in light of God's revelation.

Jesus told Peter, James, and John not to speak about what they had seen because they would not fully understand it until Jesus had risen from the dead. Then they would realize that only through dying could Jesus show his power over death and his authority to be King of all. The disciples could not be powerful witnesses for God until they had grasped this truth.

June 23 READ MARK 9:14-29

Jesus heals a demon-possessed boy

When they returned to the other disciples, they saw a large crowd surrounding them, and some teachers of religious law were arguing with them. When the crowd saw Jesus, they were overwhelmed with awe, and they ran to greet him.

"What is all this arguing about?" Jesus asked.

One of the men in the crowd spoke up and said, "Teacher, I brought my son so you could heal him. He is possessed by an evil spirit that won't let him talk. And whenever this spirit seizes him, it throws him violently to the ground. Then he foams at the mouth and grinds his teeth and becomes rigid. So I asked your disciples to cast out the evil spirit, but they couldn't do it."

Jesus said to them, "You faithless people! How long must I be with you? How long must I put up with you? Bring the boy to me."

So they brought the boy. But when the evil spirit saw Jesus, it threw the child into a violent convulsion, and he fell to the ground, writhing and foaming at the mouth.

"How long has this been happening?" Jesus asked the boy's father.

He replied, "Since he was a little boy. The spirit often throws him into the fire or into water, trying to kill him. Have mercy on us and help us, if you can."

"What do you mean, 'If I can'?" Jesus asked. "Anything is possible if a person believes."

The father instantly cried out, "I do believe, but help me overcome my unbelief!"

When Jesus saw that the crowd of onlookers was growing, he rebuked the evil spirit. "Listen, you spirit that makes this boy unable to hear and speak," he said. "I command you to come out of this child and never enter him again!"

Then the spirit screamed and threw the boy into another violent convulsion and left him. The boy appeared to be dead. A murmur ran through the crowd as people said, "He's dead." But Jesus took him by the hand and helped him to his feet, and he stood up.

Afterward, when Jesus was alone in the house with his disciples, they asked him, "Why couldn't we cast out that evil spirit?"

Jesus replied, "This kind can be cast out only by prayer."

MARK 9:14-29 *(see also Matthew 17:14-21; Luke 9:37-43)*

ANYTHING WITH FAITH

Jesus did not mean that we can automatically obtain anything we want if we just think positively. Jesus meant that anything is *possible* if we believe, because nothing is too difficult for God. We cannot have everything we pray for as if by magic; but with faith, we can have everything we need to serve him. The attitude of trust and confidence that the Bible calls *belief* or *faith* (Hebrews 11:1, 6) is not something we can obtain without help. Faith is a gift from God (Ephesians 2:8-9). No matter how much faith we have, we never reach the point of being self-sufficient. Faith is not stored away like money in the bank. Growing in faith is a constant process of daily renewing our trust in Jesus.

Why couldn't the disciples drive out the evil spirit that had caused the boy to be mute? They had special authority to do so, but perhaps their faith was faltering. Mark tells this story to show that the battle with Satan is a difficult, ongoing struggle.

Jesus predicts his death the second time

Leaving that region, they traveled through Galilee. Jesus didn't want anyone to know he was there, for he wanted to spend more time with his disciples and teach them. He said to them, "The Son of Man is going to be betrayed into the hands of his enemies. He will be killed, but three days later he will rise from the dead." They didn't understand what he was saying, however, and they were afraid to ask him what he meant.

MARK 9:30-32 *(see also Matthew 17:22-23; Luke 9:44-45)*

CALLED TO BELIEVE

Once again Jesus predicted his death (see also Matthew 16:21); but more important, he told of his resurrection. Unfortunately, the disciples heard only the first part of Jesus' words and became discouraged. They couldn't understand why Jesus wanted to go back to Jerusalem, where he would walk right into trouble.

The disciples didn't fully comprehend the purpose of Jesus' death and resurrection until Pentecost (Acts 2). They didn't understand why Jesus kept talking about his death, because they expected him to set up a political kingdom. His death, they thought, would dash their hopes. They didn't know that Jesus' death and resurrection would make his Kingdom possible. We shouldn't get upset at ourselves for being slow to understand everything about Jesus. After all, the disciples were with him, saw his miracles, heard his words, and still had difficulty understanding. Despite their questions and doubts, however, they believed. We should do no less.

At times, Jesus limited his public ministry in order to train his disciples in depth. He knew the importance of equipping them to carry on when he returned to heaven. Leaving Caesarea Philippi, Jesus began his last tour through the region of Galilee.

READ MATTHEW 17:24-27 **June 25**

Peter finds the coin in the fish's mouth

On their arrival in Capernaum, the collectors of the Temple tax came to Peter and asked him, "Doesn't your teacher pay the Temple tax?"

"Yes, he does," Peter replied. Then he went into the house.

But before he had a chance to speak, Jesus asked him, "What do you think, Peter? Do kings tax their own people or the people they have conquered?"

"They tax the people they have conquered," Peter replied.

"Well, then," Jesus said, "the citizens are free! However, we don't want to offend them, so go down to the lake and throw in a line. Open the mouth of the first fish you catch, and you will find a large silver coin. Take it and pay the tax for both of us." MATTHEW 17:24-27

GOOD AMBASSADORS

As usual, Peter answered a question without really knowing the answer, putting Jesus and the disciples in an awkward position. Jesus used this situation, however, to emphasize his kingly role. Just as kings pay no taxes and collect none from their family, Jesus, the King, owed no taxes. But he supplied the tax payment for both himself and Peter rather than offend those who didn't understand his kingship. As God's people, we are foreigners on earth because our loyalty is always to our real King—Jesus. Still, we have to cooperate with the authorities and be responsible citizens. An ambassador to another country keeps the local laws in order to represent well the country he came from. We are Christ's ambassadors (2 Corinthians 5:20). Are you being a good foreign ambassador for him to this world?

All Jewish males had to pay a Temple tax to support Temple upkeep (Exodus 30:11-16). Tax collectors set up booths to collect these taxes. Only Matthew records this incident, perhaps because he had been a tax collector himself.

The disciples argue about who would be the greatest

After they arrived at Capernaum and settled in a house, Jesus asked his disciples, "What were you discussing out on the road?" But they didn't answer, because they had been arguing about which of them was the greatest. He sat down, called the twelve disciples over to him, and said, "Whoever wants to be first must take last place and be the servant of everyone else."

Then he put a little child among them. Taking the child in his arms, he said to them, "Anyone who welcomes a little child like this on my behalf welcomes me, and anyone who welcomes me welcomes not only me but also my Father who sent me." MARK 9:33-37 *(see also Matthew 18:1-6; Luke 9:46-48)*

THE GREATEST

The disciples, caught up in their constant struggle for personal success, were embarrassed to answer Jesus' question. It is always painful to compare our motives with Christ's. It is not wrong for believers to be industrious or ambitious. But when ambition pushes obedience and service to one side, it becomes sin. Pride or insecurity can cause us to overvalue position and prestige. In God's Kingdom, such motives are destructive. The only safe ambition is directed toward Christ's Kingdom, not our own advancement. It is possible for thoughtless, selfish people to gain a measure of greatness in the world's eyes, but enduring greatness is measured only by God's standards. What do you use as your measure of greatness—personal achievement or unselfish service?

Children are trusting by nature. They trust adults, and through that trust their capacity to trust God grows. God holds parents and other adults who influence young children accountable for how they affect these little ones' ability to trust.

The disciples forbid another to use Jesus' name

John said to Jesus, "Teacher, we saw someone using your name to cast out demons, but we told him to stop because he wasn't in our group."

"Don't stop him!" Jesus said. "No one who performs a miracle in my name will soon be able to speak evil of me. Anyone who is not against us is for us. If anyone gives you even a cup of water because you belong to the Messiah, I tell you the truth, that person will surely be rewarded.

"But if you cause one of these little ones who trusts in me to fall into sin, it would be better for you to be thrown into the sea with a large millstone hung around your neck." MARK 9:38-42 *(see also Luke 9:49-50)*

COMMON FAITH, COMMON GOAL

The disciples were jealous of a man who healed in Jesus' name because they were more concerned about their own group's position than about helping to free those troubled by demons. We do the same when we refuse to participate in worthy causes because (1) other people or groups are not affiliated with our denomination, (2) the projects do not involve the kind of people with whom we feel most comfortable, (3) others don't do things the way we are used to doing them, or (4) our efforts won't receive enough recognition. Correct theology is important but should never be an excuse to avoid helping people in need. People who are on Jesus' side have the same goal of building up the Kingdom of God, and they should not let their differences hinder them from attaining it. Those who share a common faith in Christ should cooperate. People don't have to be just like us to be following Jesus with us.

In Mark 9:40, Jesus was not saying that being indifferent or neutral toward him is as good as being committed. The statement is spoken in a different way in Matthew 12:30: "Anyone who isn't working with me is actually working against me." In both cases Jesus was pointing out that neutrality toward him is not possible.

Jesus warns against temptation

"If your hand causes you to sin, cut it off. It's better to enter eternal life with only one hand than to go into the unquenchable fires of hell with two hands. If your foot causes you to sin, cut it off. It's better to enter eternal life with only one foot than to be thrown into hell with two feet. And if your eye causes you to sin, gouge it out. It's better to enter the Kingdom of God with only one eye than to have two eyes and be thrown into hell, 'where the maggots never die and the fire never goes out.'

"For everyone will be tested with fire. Salt is good for seasoning. But if it loses its flavor, how do you make it salty again? You must have the qualities of salt among yourselves and live in peace with each other."

MARK 9:43-50 *(see also Matthew 18:7-9)*

SALTY ENOUGH?

Jesus used salt to illustrate three qualities that should be found in his people: (1) *We should remember God's faithfulness,* just as salt when used with a sacrifice recalled God's covenant with his people (Leviticus 2:13). (2) *We should make a difference in the "flavor" of the world we live in,* just as salt changes meat's flavor (Matthew 5:13). (3) *We should counteract the moral decay in society,* just as salt preserves food from decay. When we lose this desire to "salt" the earth with the love and message of God, we become useless to him. Think of how you can be salty this week.

Jesus used startling language to stress the importance of cutting sin out of our lives. Painful discipline is required of his true followers. Giving up a relationship, job, or habit that is against God's will may seem just as painful as cutting off a hand. Nothing should stand in the way of faith.

Jesus warns against looking down on others

"Beware that you don't look down on any of these little ones. For I tell you that in heaven their angels are always in the presence of my heavenly Father.

"If a man has a hundred sheep and one of them wanders away, what will he do? Won't he leave the ninety-nine others on the hills and go out to search for the one that is lost? And if he finds it, I tell you the truth, he will rejoice over it more than over the ninety-nine that didn't wander away! In the same way, it is not my heavenly Father's will that even one of these little ones should perish."

MATTHEW 18:10-14

GUIDANCE

Just as a shepherd is concerned enough about one lost sheep to search the hills for it, so God is concerned about every human being he has created ("he does not want anyone to be destroyed" [2 Peter 3:9]). At home, at school, in church, and in the neighborhood you come in contact with children who need Christ. Steer them toward Christ by your example, your words, and your acts of kindness.

Certain angels are assigned to watch over children, and they have direct access to God. If their angels have constant access to God, the least we can do is to allow children to approach us easily in spite of our far-too-busy schedules.

Jesus teaches how to treat a believer who sins

"If another believer sins against you, go privately and point out the offense. If the other person listens and confesses it, you have won that person back. But if you are unsuccessful, take one or two others with you and go back again, so that everything you say may be confirmed by two or three witnesses. If the person still refuses to listen, take your case to the church. Then if he or she won't accept the church's decision, treat that person as a pagan or a corrupt tax collector.

"I tell you the truth, whatever you forbid on earth will be forbidden in heaven, and whatever you permit on earth will be permitted in heaven."

MATTHEW 18:15-18

SINNED AGAINST

These are Jesus' guidelines for dealing with those who sin against us. They were meant for (1) Christians, not unbelievers; (2) sins committed against *you* and not others; and (3) conflict resolution in the context of the church, not the community at large. Jesus' words are not a license for a frontal attack on every person who hurts or slights us. They are not a license to start a destructive gossip campaign or to call for a church trial. These guidelines are designed to reconcile those who disagree so that all Christians can live in harmony.

When someone wrongs us, we often do the opposite of what Jesus recommends. We turn away in hatred or resentment, seek revenge, or engage in gossip. By contrast, we should go to that person *first*, as difficult as that may be. Then we should forgive that person as often as he or she needs it (Matthew 18:21-22). This will create a much better chance of restoring the relationship.

This prohibiting and allowing refers to the decisions of churches with conflicts. Among believers, there is no court higher than the church. Ideally, a church's decisions should be God guided and based on discernment of his Word. Believers have the responsibility to bring their problems to the church, and the church has the responsibility to use God's guidance in seeking to resolve them.

Jesus promises to be with us in prayer

"I also tell you this: If two of you agree here on earth concerning anything you ask, my Father in heaven will do it for you. For where two or three gather together as my followers, I am there among them." MATTHEW 18:19-20

PRAYER POWER

Jesus looked ahead to a new day when he would be present with his followers, not physically, but through his Holy Spirit. When two or three of Jesus' followers agree in prayer, Jesus is with them, and the Father listens. Two or more believers, filled with the Holy Spirit, will pray according to God's will, not their own; thus their requests will be granted. Although God is all-powerful and all-knowing, he has chosen to let us help him change the world through our prayers. How this works is a mystery to us because of our limited understanding, but it is a reality. Our earnest prayers will have powerful results (James 5:16). Make prayer a regular part of your life, alone and with other believers.

God is three persons in one—Father, Son, and Holy Spirit. God became a man in Jesus so that Jesus could die for our sins. When Jesus ascended into heaven, his physical presence left the earth, but he promised to send the Holy Spirit so that his spiritual presence would still be among us.

Jesus tells the parable of the unforgiving debtor

Then Peter came to him and asked, "Lord, how often should I forgive someone who sins against me? Seven times?"

"No, not seven times," Jesus replied, "but seventy times seven!"

MATTHEW 18:21-22

FORGIVEN

When Jesus explained that we should forgive others "seventy times seven," he meant that we shouldn't even keep track of how many times we forgive someone. We should always forgive those who are truly repentant, no matter how many times they ask. As Christians, we should forgive as we have been forgiven. True forgiveness means we treat the one we've forgiven as we would want to be treated. As we understand God's mercy, we will want to be like him. Having received forgiveness, we will pass it on to others. Is there someone you say you have forgiven, but who still needs your kindness?

The rabbis taught that people should forgive those who offended them—but only three times. Peter, trying to be especially generous, asked Jesus if seven (the "perfect" number) was enough times to forgive someone.

Jesus tells the parable of the unforgiving debtor

"Therefore, the Kingdom of Heaven can be compared to a king who decided to bring his accounts up to date with servants who had borrowed money from him. In the process, one of his debtors was brought in who owed him millions of dollars. He couldn't pay, so his master ordered that he be sold—along with his wife, his children, and everything he owned—to pay the debt.

"But the man fell down before his master and begged him, 'Please, be patient with me, and I will pay it all.' Then his master was filled with pity for him, and he released him and forgave his debt.

"But when the man left the king, he went to a fellow servant who owed him a few thousand dollars. He grabbed him by the throat and demanded instant payment.

"His fellow servant fell down before him and begged for a little more time. 'Be patient with me, and I will pay it,' he pleaded. But his creditor wouldn't wait. He had the man arrested and put in prison until the debt could be paid in full.

"When some of the other servants saw this, they were very upset. They went to the king and told him everything that had happened. Then the king called in the man he had forgiven and said, 'You evil servant! I forgave you that tremendous debt because you pleaded with me. Shouldn't you have mercy on your fellow servant, just as I had mercy on you?' Then the angry king sent the man to prison to be tortured until he had paid his entire debt.

"That's what my heavenly Father will do to you if you refuse to forgive your brothers and sisters from your heart."   MATTHEW 18:23-35

HARD TO FORGIVE

If we love others the way Christ loves us, we will be willing to forgive. If we have experienced God's grace, we will want to pass it on. Forgiveness involves both attitudes and actions. If you find it difficult to *feel* forgiving of someone who has hurt you, try *acting* forgiving. Many times right actions can lead to right feelings. Because God has forgiven all our sins, we should not withhold forgiveness from others. Realizing how completely Christ has forgiven us should produce a free and generous attitude of forgiveness on our part. When we don't forgive others, we are setting ourselves outside and above Christ's law of love. Those who are unwilling to forgive have not become one with Christ.

Jesus' brothers ridicule him

After this, Jesus traveled around Galilee. He wanted to stay out of Judea, where the Jewish leaders were plotting his death. But soon it was time for the Jewish Festival of Shelters, and Jesus' brothers said to him, "Leave here and go to Judea, where your followers can see your miracles! You can't become famous if you hide like this! If you can do such wonderful things, show yourself to the world!" For even his brothers didn't believe in him.

Jesus replied, "Now is not the right time for me to go, but you can go anytime. The world can't hate you, but it does hate me because I accuse it of doing evil. You go on. I'm not going to this festival, because my time has not yet come." After saying these things, Jesus remained in Galilee. JOHN 7:1-9

THE EVIDENCE

Jesus' brothers had a difficult time believing in him. Some of these brothers would eventually become leaders in the church (James, for example), but for several years they were embarrassed by Jesus. After Jesus died and rose again, they finally believed. Today we have every reason to believe because we have the full record of Jesus' miracles, death, and resurrection. We also have the evidence of what the gospel has done in people's lives through the centuries. We have no excuses.

———————————◆◆◆———————————

The Festival of Shelters, also called the Feast of Tabernacles, is described in Leviticus 23:33-43. This event occurred in October, about six months after the Passover celebration. The feast commemorated the days when the Israelites wandered in the wilderness and lived in tents (Leviticus 23:43).

———————————◆◆◆———————————

Jesus teaches about the cost of following him

As the time drew near for him to ascend to heaven, Jesus resolutely set out for Jerusalem. He sent messengers ahead to a Samaritan village to prepare for his arrival. But the people of the village did not welcome Jesus because he was on his way to Jerusalem. When James and John saw this, they said to Jesus, "Lord, should we call down fire from heaven to burn them up?" But Jesus turned and rebuked them. So they went on to another village. LUKE 9:51-56

REVENGE

When James and John were rejected by the Samaritan village, they didn't want to stop at shaking the dust from their feet (Luke 9:5). They wanted to retaliate by calling down fire from heaven on the people as Elijah had done on the servants of a wicked king of Israel (2 Kings 1). When others reject or scorn us, we, too, may feel like retaliating. We must remember that judgment belongs to God, and we must not expect him to use his power to carry out our personal vendettas.

After Assyria invaded Israel, the northern kingdom, and resettled it with its own people (2 Kings 17:24-41), the mixed race that developed became known as the Samaritans. "Purebred" Jews hated these "half-breeds"; the Samaritans, in turn, hated the Jews.

Jesus teaches about the cost of following him

As they were walking along, someone said to Jesus, "I will follow you wherever you go."

But Jesus replied, "Foxes have dens to live in, and birds have nests, but the Son of Man has no place even to lay his head."

He said to another person, "Come, follow me."

The man agreed, but he said, "Lord, first let me return home and bury my father."

But Jesus told him, "Let the spiritually dead bury their own dead! Your duty is to go and preach about the Kingdom of God."

Another said, "Yes, Lord, I will follow you, but first let me say good-bye to my family."

But Jesus told him, "Anyone who puts a hand to the plow and then looks back is not fit for the Kingdom of God."   LUKE 9:57-62 *(see also Matthew 8:18-22)*

CROSS AND CROWN

What does Jesus want from us? Total dedication, not halfhearted commitment. Following Jesus is not always easy or comfortable. Often it means great cost and sacrifice, with no earthly rewards or security. Jesus didn't have a place to call home. You may find that following Christ costs you popularity, friendships, leisure time, or treasured habits. But while the cost of following Christ is high, the value of being Christ's disciple is even higher. Discipleship is an investment that lasts for eternity and yields incredible rewards. We can't pick and choose among Jesus' ideas and follow him selectively; we have to accept the cross along with the crown, judgment as well as mercy. We must count the cost and be willing to abandon everything else that has given us security. Focusing on Jesus, we should allow nothing to distract us from the manner of living that he calls good and true.

Jesus was always direct with those who wanted to follow him. He made sure they counted the cost and set aside any conditions they might have for following him. As God's Son, Jesus did not hesitate to demand complete loyalty. Even family loyalty was not to take priority over the demands of obedience.

Jesus teaches openly at the Temple

But after his brothers left for the festival, Jesus also went, though secretly, staying out of public view. The Jewish leaders tried to find him at the festival and kept asking if anyone had seen him. There was a lot of grumbling about him among the crowds. Some argued, "He's a good man," but others said, "He's nothing but a fraud who deceives the people." But no one had the courage to speak favorably about him in public, for they were afraid of getting in trouble with the Jewish leaders. JOHN 7:10-13

SPEAK UP

Jesus offered the greatest gift ever, so why did he often act secretly? The religious leaders hated him, and many would refuse his gift of salvation, no matter what he said or did. The more Jesus taught and worked in public, the more these leaders would cause trouble for him and his followers. So it was necessary for Jesus to teach and work as quietly as possible. Many people today have the privilege of teaching, preaching, and worshiping publicly with little persecution. These believers should be grateful and make the most of their opportunities to proclaim the gospel. Although many people talk about Christ in church, when it comes to making a public statement about their faith, they are often embarrassed. Jesus says that he will acknowledge us before God if we acknowledge him before others (Matthew 10:32). Be courageous! Speak up for Christ!

─────────●●─────────

The religious leaders had a great deal of power over the common people. Apparently these leaders couldn't do much to Jesus at this time, but they threatened anyone who might publicly support him. Excommunication from the synagogue was one of the reprisals for believing in Jesus (John 9:22). To a Jew, this was a severe punishment.

─────────●●─────────

Jesus teaches openly at the Temple

Then, midway through the festival, Jesus went up to the Temple and began to teach. The people were surprised when they heard him. "How does he know so much when he hasn't been trained?" they asked.

So Jesus told them, "My message is not my own; it comes from God who sent me. Anyone who wants to do the will of God will know whether my teaching is from God or is merely my own. Those who speak for themselves want glory only for themselves, but a person who seeks to honor the one who sent him speaks truth, not lies. Moses gave you the law, but none of you obeys it! In fact, you are trying to kill me."

The crowd replied, "You're demon possessed! Who's trying to kill you?"

Jesus replied, "I did one miracle on the Sabbath, and you were amazed. But you work on the Sabbath, too, when you obey Moses' law of circumcision. (Actually, this tradition of circumcision began with the patriarchs, long before the law of Moses.) For if the correct time for circumcising your son falls on the Sabbath, you go ahead and do it so as not to break the law of Moses. So why should you be angry with me for healing a man on the Sabbath? Look beneath the surface so you can judge correctly." JOHN 7:14-24

MORE THAN REQUIRED

The Pharisees spent their days trying to achieve holiness by keeping the meticulous rules that they had added to God's laws. Jesus' accusation that they didn't keep Moses' laws stung them deeply. In spite of their pompous pride in themselves and their rules, they did not even fulfill a legalistic religion, for they were living far below what the law of Moses required. Their plot to commit murder was certainly against the law. Jesus' followers should do *more* than the moral law requires, not by adding to its requirements, but by going beyond and beneath the mere dos and don'ts of the law to the spirit of the law. This means being kind and forgiving, serving others, and showing love.

Have you ever listened to religious speakers and wondered if they were telling the truth? Test them: (1) Their words should agree with, not contradict, the Bible; and (2) their words should point to God and his will, not to themselves.

READ JOHN 7:25-31 **July 9**

Jesus teaches openly at the Temple

Some of the people who lived in Jerusalem started to ask each other, "Isn't this the man they are trying to kill? But here he is, speaking in public, and they say nothing to him. Could our leaders possibly believe that he is the Messiah? But how could he be? For we know where this man comes from. When the Messiah comes, he will simply appear; no one will know where he comes from."

While Jesus was teaching in the Temple, he called out, "Yes, you know me, and you know where I come from. But I'm not here on my own. The one who sent me is true, and you don't know him. But I know him because I come from him, and he sent me to you." Then the leaders tried to arrest him; but no one laid a hand on him, because his time had not yet come.

Many among the crowds at the Temple believed in him. "After all," they said, "would you expect the Messiah to do more miraculous signs than this man has done?" JOHN 7:25-31

NO NEUTRAL GROUND

Many consider neutrality to be a sign of maturity and objectivity. Maintaining a neutral position toward Christ may be popular, but it is dangerous. People stay undecided about Jesus under the pretense of not wanting to make a hasty or wrong judgment. But Jesus never allowed indecision. He confronted men and women with the unavoidable choice of belief or unbelief. Today those who remain undecided must understand that they remain, by that choice, in opposition to Christ. You can't sit on the fence; whose side are you on?

There was a popular tradition that the Messiah would simply appear. But those who believed this tradition were ignoring the Scriptures that clearly predicted the Messiah's birthplace (Micah 5:2).

Religious leaders attempt to arrest Jesus

When the Pharisees heard that the crowds were whispering such things, they and the leading priests sent Temple guards to arrest Jesus. But Jesus told them, "I will be with you only a little longer. Then I will return to the one who sent me. You will search for me but not find me. And you cannot go where I am going."

The Jewish leaders were puzzled by this statement. "Where is he planning to go?" they asked. "Is he thinking of leaving the country and going to the Jews in other lands? Maybe he will even teach the Greeks! What does he mean when he says, 'You will search for me but not find me,' and 'You cannot go where I am going'?"

On the last day, the climax of the festival, Jesus stood and shouted to the crowds, "Anyone who is thirsty may come to me! Anyone who believes in me may come and drink! For the Scriptures declare, 'Rivers of living water will flow from his heart.'" (When he said "living water," he was speaking of the Spirit, who would be given to everyone believing in him. But the Spirit had not yet been given, because Jesus had not yet entered into his glory.)

When the crowds heard him say this, some of them declared, "Surely this man is the Prophet we've been expecting." Others said, "He is the Messiah." Still others said, "But he can't be! Will the Messiah come from Galilee? For the Scriptures clearly state that the Messiah will be born of the royal line of David, in Bethlehem, the village where King David was born." So the crowd was divided about him. Some even wanted him arrested, but no one laid a hand on him. JOHN 7:32-44

COME AND DRINK

Jesus used the term *living water* in John 4:10 to indicate eternal life. Here he used the term to refer to the Holy Spirit. The two go together: When a person trusts Jesus as Savior, the Holy Spirit is given as a guarantee of eternal life. Jesus' words "come and drink" alluded to the theme of many Bible passages that talk about the Messiah's life-giving blessings (Isaiah 12:2-3; 44:3-4; 58:11). In promising to give the Holy Spirit to all who believed, Jesus was claiming to be the Messiah, for that was something only the Messiah could do. The Holy Spirit was first given to Jesus' followers at Pentecost (Acts 2) and is still given today to all who believe in Jesus as Savior. If you know Christ, you have the Holy Spirit living in you and can depend on him for power for living the Christian life.

Religious leaders attempt to arrest Jesus

When the Temple guards returned without having arrested Jesus, the leading priests and Pharisees demanded, "Why didn't you bring him in?"

"We have never heard anyone speak like this!" the guards responded.

"Have you been led astray, too?" the Pharisees mocked. "Is there a single one of us rulers or Pharisees who believes in him? This foolish crowd follows him, but they are ignorant of the law. God's curse is on them!"

Then Nicodemus, the leader who had met with Jesus earlier, spoke up. "Is it legal to convict a man before he is given a hearing?" he asked.

They replied, "Are you from Galilee, too? Search the Scriptures and see for yourself—no prophet ever comes from Galilee!"   JOHN 7:45-52

KEEPERS OF THE TRUTH

Nicodemus confronted the Pharisees with their failure to keep their own laws. The Pharisees were losing ground—the Temple guards came back impressed by Jesus (John 7:46), and one of the Pharisees' own, Nicodemus, was defending him. With their hypocritical motives being exposed and their prestige slowly eroding, they began to move to protect themselves. Pride would interfere with their ability to reason, and soon they would become obsessed with getting rid of Jesus just to save face. What was good and right no longer mattered. It is easy for us, too, to think that we have the truth and that those who disagree with us do not have any truth at all. But God's truth is available to everyone. Don't copy the Pharisees' self-centered and narrow attitude.

Nicodemus was the Pharisee who visited Jesus at night (John 3). Apparently Nicodemus had become a secret believer. Most of the Pharisees hated Jesus and wanted to kill him, so Nicodemus risked his reputation and high position when he spoke up for Jesus.

July 12

Jesus forgives an adulterous woman

Jesus returned to the Mount of Olives, but early the next morning he was back again at the Temple. A crowd soon gathered, and he sat down and taught them. As he was speaking, the teachers of religious law and the Pharisees brought a woman who had been caught in the act of adultery. They put her in front of the crowd.

"Teacher," they said to Jesus, "this woman was caught in the act of adultery. The law of Moses says to stone her. What do you say?"

They were trying to trap him into saying something they could use against him, but Jesus stooped down and wrote in the dust with his finger. They kept demanding an answer, so he stood up again and said, "All right, but let the one who has never sinned throw the first stone!" Then he stooped down again and wrote in the dust.

When the accusers heard this, they slipped away one by one, beginning with the oldest, until only Jesus was left in the middle of the crowd with the woman. Then Jesus stood up again and said to the woman, "Where are your accusers? Didn't even one of them condemn you?"

"No, Lord," she said.

And Jesus said, "Neither do I. Go and sin no more." JOHN 8:1-11

THE FIRST STONE

This is a significant statement about judging others. Because Jesus upheld the legal penalty for adultery, stoning, he could not be accused of being against the law. But by saying that only a sinless person could throw the first stone, he highlighted the importance of compassion and forgiveness. When others are caught in sin, are you quick to pass judgment? To do so is to act as though you have never sinned. It is God's role to judge, not ours. Our role is to show forgiveness and compassion. Jesus didn't condemn the woman accused of adultery, but neither did he ignore or condone her sin. He told the woman to leave her life of sin. Jesus stands ready to forgive any sin in your life, but confession and repentance mean a change of heart. With God's help we can accept Christ's forgiveness and stop our wrongdoing.

The Jewish leaders had already disregarded the law by arresting only the woman. The law required that both parties to adultery be stoned (Leviticus 20:10; Deuteronomy 22:22). The leaders were using the woman as a trap so they could trick Jesus.

Jesus is the Light of the world

Jesus spoke to the people once more and said, "I am the light of the world. If you follow me, you won't have to walk in darkness, because you will have the light that leads to life." JOHN 8:12

THE LIGHT OF THE WORLD

What does following Christ mean? As a soldier follows his captain, so we should follow Christ, our Commander. As a slave follows his master, so we should follow Christ, our Lord. As we follow the advice of a trusted counselor, so we should follow Jesus' commands to us in Scripture. As we follow the laws of our nation, so we should follow the laws of the Kingdom of Heaven. When we follow Jesus, the true light, we can avoid walking blindly and falling into sin. He lights the path ahead of us so we can see how to live. He removes the darkness of sin from our lives. Have you allowed the light of Christ to shine into your life? Let Christ guide your life, and you'll never need to stumble in darkness. Is he the light of *your* world?

Jesus was speaking in the part of the Temple where the offerings were put, where candles burned to symbolize the pillar of fire that led the people of Israel through the wilderness (Exodus 13:21-22). In this context, Jesus called himself the Light of the world. The pillar of fire represented God's presence, protection, and guidance. Jesus brings God's presence, protection, and guidance.

Jesus is the Light of the world

The Pharisees replied, "You are making those claims about yourself! Such testimony is not valid."

Jesus told them, "These claims are valid even though I make them about myself. For I know where I came from and where I am going, but you don't know this about me. You judge me by human standards, but I do not judge anyone. And if I did, my judgment would be correct in every respect because I am not alone. The Father who sent me is with me. Your own law says that if two people agree about something, their witness is accepted as fact. I am one witness, and my Father who sent me is the other."

"Where is your father?" they asked.

Jesus answered, "Since you don't know who I am, you don't know who my Father is. If you knew me, you would also know my Father." Jesus made these statements while he was teaching in the section of the Temple known as the Treasury. But he was not arrested, because his time had not yet come.

JOHN 8:13-20

THE TRUTH

The Pharisees thought that Jesus was either a lunatic or a liar. Jesus provided them with a third alternative—that he was the Son of God. Because most of the Pharisees refused to consider the third alternative, they never recognized him as Messiah and Lord. If you are seeking to know who Jesus is, do not close any door before looking through it honestly. Only with an open mind will you know the truth, that he is Messiah and Lord.

The Pharisees argued that Jesus' claim was legally invalid because he had no other witnesses. Jesus responded that his confirming witness was God himself. Jesus and the Father made two witnesses, the number required by the law (Deuteronomy 19:15).

Jesus warns of coming judgment

Later Jesus said to them again, "I am going away. You will search for me but will die in your sin. You cannot come where I am going."

The people asked, "Is he planning to commit suicide? What does he mean, 'You cannot come where I am going'?"

Jesus continued, "You are from below; I am from above. You belong to this world; I do not. That is why I said that you will die in your sins; for unless you believe that I AM who I claim to be, you will die in your sins."

"Who are you?" they demanded.

Jesus replied, "The one I have always claimed to be. I have much to say about you and much to condemn, but I won't. For I say only what I have heard from the one who sent me, and he is completely truthful." But they still didn't understand that he was talking about his Father.

So Jesus said, "When you have lifted up the Son of Man on the cross, then you will understand that I AM he. I do nothing on my own but say only what the Father taught me. And the one who sent me is with me—he has not deserted me. For I always do what pleases him." JOHN 8:21-29

WHAT DO YOU WANT?

Those questioning Jesus were convinced they understood God's plan. They thought they had a clear idea of exactly what kind of savior they needed, and Jesus did not fit that pattern. Are you trusting Jesus to be your Savior because he knows best, or are you reserving final judgment just in case a "better" option comes along? Are you trusting God to graciously meet your needs even when you do not fully understand them, or are you clinging to the belief that you know best what God can do for you? Are you still shopping for a better offer? Only Jesus can give forgiveness and eternal life.

If the Jewish religious leaders would not believe in Jesus while he was with them, they would run the risk of not having any further opportunity. They would die in their sin because they had rejected the only one who could save them.

July 16 READ JOHN 8:30-33

Jesus speaks about God's true children

Then many who heard him say these things believed in him.

Jesus said to the people who believed in him, "You are truly my disciples if you remain faithful to my teachings. And you will know the truth, and the truth will set you free."

"But we are descendants of Abraham," they said. "We have never been slaves to anyone. What do you mean, 'You will be set free'?"   JOHN 8:30-33

SET FREE

Sin has a way of enslaving us, controlling us, dominating us, and dictating our actions. Jesus can free us from this slavery, which keeps us from becoming what God created us to be. If sin is restraining, mastering, or enslaving us, Jesus can break its power over our lives. He frees us from the consequences of sin, from self-deception, and from deception by Satan. He shows us clearly the way to everlasting life with God. Thus, Jesus does not give us freedom to do what we want but freedom to follow God. As we seek to serve God, Jesus' perfect truth frees us to be all that God meant us to be.

To know the truth is to know God's revelation to people. That revelation is Jesus himself. Therefore, Jesus is the truth that makes us free (John 8:36). He is the source of truth, the perfect standard of what is right.

Jesus speaks about God's true children

Jesus replied, "I tell you the truth, everyone who sins is a slave of sin. A slave is not a permanent member of the family, but a son is part of the family forever. So if the Son sets you free, you are truly free. Yes, I realize that you are descendants of Abraham. And yet some of you are trying to kill me because there's no room in your hearts for my message. I am telling you what I saw when I was with my Father. But you are following the advice of your father."

"Our father is Abraham!" they declared.

"No," Jesus replied, "for if you were really the children of Abraham, you would follow his example. Instead, you are trying to kill me because I told you the truth, which I heard from God. Abraham never did such a thing. No, you are imitating your real father."

They replied, "We aren't illegitimate children! God himself is our true Father."

Jesus told them, "If God were your Father, you would love me, because I have come to you from God. I am not here on my own, but he sent me. Why can't you understand what I am saying? It's because you can't even hear me! For you are the children of your father the devil, and you love to do the evil things he does. He was a murderer from the beginning. He has always hated the truth, because there is no truth in him. When he lies, it is consistent with his character; for he is a liar and the father of lies. So when I tell the truth, you just naturally don't believe me! Which of you can truthfully accuse me of sin? And since I am telling you the truth, why don't you believe me? Anyone who belongs to God listens gladly to the words of God. But you don't listen because you don't belong to God." JOHN 8:34-47

WHOSE CHILD?

Jesus made a distinction between hereditary children and *true* children. The religious leaders were hereditary children of Abraham (founder of the Jewish nation) and therefore claimed to be children of God. But their actions showed them to be true children of Satan, for they followed the advice of Satan. True children of Abraham (faithful followers of God) would not act as they did. Your church membership and family connections will not make you a true child of God. Your true father is the one you imitate and obey.

The attitudes and actions of these leaders clearly identified them as followers of Satan. They may not have been conscious of this, but their hatred of truth, their lies, and their murderous intentions indicated how much control the devil had over them.

Jesus states he is eternal

The people retorted, "You Samaritan devil! Didn't we say all along that you were possessed by a demon?"

"No," Jesus said, "I have no demon in me. For I honor my Father—and you dishonor me. And though I have no wish to glorify myself, God is going to glorify me. He is the true judge. I tell you the truth, anyone who obeys my teaching will never die!"

The people said, "Now we know you are possessed by a demon. Even Abraham and the prophets died, but you say, 'Anyone who obeys my teaching will never die!' Are you greater than our father Abraham? He died, and so did the prophets. Who do you think you are?"

Jesus answered, "If I want glory for myself, it doesn't count. But it is my Father who will glorify me. You say, 'He is our God,' but you don't even know him. I know him. If I said otherwise, I would be as great a liar as you! But I do know him and obey him. Your father Abraham rejoiced as he looked forward to my coming. He saw it and was glad."

The people said, "You aren't even fifty years old. How can you say you have seen Abraham?"

Jesus answered, "I tell you the truth, before Abraham was even born, I AM!" At that point they picked up stones to throw at him. But Jesus was hidden from them and left the Temple. JOHN 8:48-59

THE TRUE SON OF GOD

This is one of the most powerful statements uttered by Jesus. When he said that he existed before Abraham was born, he undeniably proclaimed his divinity. This claim demands a response. It cannot be ignored. The Jewish leaders tried to stone Jesus for blasphemy because he claimed equality with God. But Jesus *is* God. How have you responded to Jesus, the Son of God?

In accordance with the law in Leviticus 24:16, the religious leaders were ready to stone Jesus for claiming to be God. They well understood what Jesus was claiming, and because they didn't believe him, they charged him with blasphemy.

Jesus sends out seventy-two messengers

The Lord now chose seventy-two other disciples and sent them ahead in pairs to all the towns and places he planned to visit. These were his instructions to them: "The harvest is great, but the workers are few. So pray to the Lord who is in charge of the harvest; ask him to send more workers into his fields. Now go, and remember that I am sending you out as lambs among wolves. Don't take any money with you, nor a traveler's bag, nor an extra pair of sandals. And don't stop to greet anyone on the road.

"Whenever you enter someone's home, first say, 'May God's peace be on this house.' If those who live there are peaceful, the blessing will stand; if they are not, the blessing will return to you. Don't move around from home to home. Stay in one place, eating and drinking what they provide. Don't hesitate to accept hospitality, because those who work deserve their pay.

"If you enter a town and it welcomes you, eat whatever is set before you. Heal the sick, and tell them, 'The Kingdom of God is near you now.' But if a town refuses to welcome you, go out into its streets and say, 'We wipe even the dust of your town from our feet to show that we have abandoned you to your fate. And know this—the Kingdom of God is near!' I assure you, even wicked Sodom will be better off than such a town on judgment day.

"What sorrow awaits you, Korazin and Bethsaida! For if the miracles I did in you had been done in wicked Tyre and Sidon, their people would have repented of their sins long ago, clothing themselves in burlap and throwing ashes on their heads to show their remorse. Yes, Tyre and Sidon will be better off on judgment day than you. And you people of Capernaum, will you be honored in heaven? No, you will go down to the place of the dead."

Then he said to the disciples, "Anyone who accepts your message is also accepting me. And anyone who rejects you is rejecting me. And anyone who rejects me is rejecting God, who sent me." LUKE 10:1-16

NO UNEMPLOYMENT

Far more than twelve people had been following Jesus. Here Jesus designated a group of seventy-two to prepare a number of towns for Jesus' later visit. Jesus was sending thirty-six teams of two to reach the multitudes. These teams were not to try to do the job without help; rather, they were to ask God for more workers. Some people, as soon as they understand the gospel, want to go to work immediately contacting unsaved people. This story suggests a different approach: Begin by mobilizing people to pray. And before praying for unsaved people, pray that other concerned disciples will join you in reaching out to them. In Christian service there is no unemployment. God has work enough for everyone. Don't just sit back and watch others work—look for ways to help with the harvest.

Jesus gave two rules for the disciples to follow as they traveled: They were to eat what was set before them—that is, they were to accept hospitality without being picky—and they were to heal the sick. Because of the healings, people would be willing to listen to the gospel.

The seventy-two messengers return

When the seventy-two disciples returned, they joyfully reported to him, "Lord, even the demons obey us when we use your name!"

"Yes," he told them, "I saw Satan fall from heaven like lightning! Look, I have given you authority over all the power of the enemy, and you can walk among snakes and scorpions and crush them. Nothing will injure you. But don't rejoice because evil spirits obey you; rejoice because your names are registered in heaven." LUKE 10:17-20

CITIZENS

The disciples had seen tremendous results as they ministered in Jesus' name and with his authority. They were elated by the victories they had witnessed, and Jesus shared their enthusiasm. He helped them get their priorities right, however, by reminding them of their most important victory—that their names were written in heaven. This honor was more important than any of their accomplishments. As we see God's wonders at work in and through us, we should not lose sight of the greatest wonder of all—our heavenly citizenship.

Some interpreters believe Luke 10:18 refers to Satan's original fall and explain that Satan's pride led to all the evil we see on earth today. To Jesus' disciples, who were thrilled with their power over evil spirits ("snakes and scorpions"), he may have been giving this stern warning: "Yours is the kind of pride that led to Satan's downfall. Be careful!"

The seventy-two messengers return

At that same time Jesus was filled with the joy of the Holy Spirit, and he said, "O Father, Lord of heaven and earth, thank you for hiding these things from those who think themselves wise and clever, and for revealing them to the childlike. Yes, Father, it pleased you to do it this way.

"My Father has entrusted everything to me. No one truly knows the Son except the Father, and no one truly knows the Father except the Son and those to whom the Son chooses to reveal him."

Then when they were alone, he turned to the disciples and said, "Blessed are the eyes that see what you have seen. I tell you, many prophets and kings longed to see what you see, but they didn't see it. And they longed to hear what you hear, but they didn't hear it."   LUKE 10:21-24

EQUALLY AVAILABLE

Jesus thanked God that spiritual truth was for everyone and not just for the elite. Many of life's rewards seem to go to the intelligent, the rich, the good-looking, or the powerful, but the Kingdom of God is equally available to all, regardless of position or abilities. We come to Jesus, not through strength or intelligence, but through childlike trust. Jesus is not opposed to engaging in scholarly pursuits; he is opposed to spiritual pride (being wise in one's own eyes). Christ's mission was to reveal God the Father to people. His words brought difficult ideas down to earth. He explained God's love through parables; teachings; and most of all, his life. By examining Jesus' actions, principles, and attitudes, we can understand God more clearly. Join Jesus in thanking God that we all have equal access to him. Trust in God's grace, not in your personal qualifications, for your citizenship in the Kingdom.

Old Testament men of God such as David and the prophet Isaiah made many God-inspired predictions that Jesus fulfilled. As Peter later wrote, these prophets wondered what their words meant and when they would be fulfilled (1 Peter 1:10-13). In Jesus' words, "many prophets and kings longed to see what you see"—the coming of God's Kingdom.

Jesus begins the parable of the Good Samaritan

One day an expert in religious law stood up to test Jesus by asking him this question: "Teacher, what should I do to inherit eternal life?"

Jesus replied, "What does the law of Moses say? How do you read it?"

The man answered, "'You must love the LORD your God with all your heart, all your soul, all your strength, and all your mind.' And, 'Love your neighbor as yourself.'"

"Right!" Jesus told him. "Do this and you will live!" LUKE 10:25-28

NOT SO DIFFERENT

Jesus went on to answer the lawyer's question by telling the parable of the Good Samaritan. There was deep hatred between Jews and Samaritans. The Jews saw themselves as pure descendants of Abraham, while the Samaritans were a mixed race produced when Jews from the northern kingdom intermarried with other peoples after Israel's exile. To this lawyer, the person least likely to act correctly would be the Samaritan (Luke 10:36-37). In fact, he could not bear to say "Samaritan" in answer to Jesus' question. The lawyer's attitude betrayed his lack of the very thing that he had earlier said the law commanded—love. In our churches today, it's our natural inclination to feel uncomfortable around people who are different from us and to gravitate toward those who are similar to us. But when we allow our differences to separate us from our fellow believers, we are disregarding clear biblical teaching. Make a point to seek out and appreciate people who are not just like you and your friends. You may find that you have a lot in common with them.

This lawyer was quoting Leviticus 19:18 and Deuteronomy 6:5. He correctly understood that the law demanded total devotion to God and love for one's neighbor.

Jesus tells the parable of the Good Samaritan

The man wanted to justify his actions, so he asked Jesus, "And who is my neighbor?"

Jesus replied with a story: "A Jewish man was traveling from Jerusalem down to Jericho, and he was attacked by bandits. They stripped him of his clothes, beat him up, and left him half dead beside the road.

"By chance a priest came along. But when he saw the man lying there, he crossed to the other side of the road and passed him by. A Temple assistant walked over and looked at him lying there, but he also passed by on the other side.

"Then a despised Samaritan came along, and when he saw the man, he felt compassion for him. Going over to him, the Samaritan soothed his wounds with olive oil and wine and bandaged them. Then he put the man on his own donkey and took him to an inn, where he took care of him. The next day he handed the innkeeper two silver coins, telling him, 'Take care of this man. If his bill runs higher than this, I'll pay you the next time I'm here.'

"Now which of these three would you say was a neighbor to the man who was attacked by bandits?" Jesus asked.

The man replied, "The one who showed him mercy."

Then Jesus said, "Yes, now go and do the same."   LUKE 10:29-37

GOOD NEIGHBOR

The lawyer treated the wounded man as a topic for discussion; the thieves treated him as an object to exploit; the priest, as a problem to avoid; and the Temple assistant, as an object of curiosity. Only the Samaritan treated him as a person to love. From the parable we learn three principles about loving our neighbor: (1) Lack of love is often easy to justify, even though it is never right; (2) our neighbor is anyone of any race, creed, or social background who is in need; and (3) love means acting to meet the person's need. Wherever you live, there are needy people close by. There is no good reason for refusing to help.

That Jesus would use as an example the road between Jerusalem and Jericho on which the man was attacked would have rung true to his audience. This road was rocky, surrounded with crags to hide bandits, and had a reputation for being dangerous to lone travelers.

Jesus visits Mary and Martha

As Jesus and the disciples continued on their way to Jerusalem, they came to a certain village where a woman named Martha welcomed him into her home. Her sister, Mary, sat at the Lord's feet, listening to what he taught. But Martha was distracted by the big dinner she was preparing. She came to Jesus and said, "Lord, doesn't it seem unfair to you that my sister just sits here while I do all the work? Tell her to come and help me."

But the Lord said to her, "My dear Martha, you are worried and upset over all these details! There is only one thing worth being concerned about. Mary has discovered it, and it will not be taken away from her." LUKE 10:38-42

SERVING WHOM?

Mary and Martha both loved Jesus. On this occasion they were both serving him. But Martha thought Mary's style of serving was inferior to hers. She didn't realize that in her desire to serve, she was actually neglecting her guest. Jesus did not blame Martha for being concerned about preparing dinner. He was only asking her to set priorities. It is possible for service to Christ to degenerate into mere busywork that is no longer full of devotion to God. Are you so busy doing things *for* Jesus that you're not spending any time *with* him? Don't let your service become self-serving.

Jesus visited his friends Mary, Martha, and Lazarus, who lived in the tiny village of Bethany, just outside Jerusalem on the Mount of Olives.

Jesus teaches his disciples about prayer

Once Jesus was in a certain place praying. As he finished, one of his disciples came to him and said, "Lord, teach us to pray, just as John taught his disciples."

Jesus said, "This is how you should pray: Father, may your name be kept holy. May your Kingdom come soon. Give us each day the food we need, and forgive us our sins, as we forgive those who sin against us. And don't let us yield to temptation."   LUKE 11:1-4

PRAISING, FORGIVING

Notice the order in this prayer. First, Jesus praised God; then, he made his requests. Praising God first puts us in the right frame of mind to tell him about our needs. Too often our prayers are more like shopping lists than conversations. When Jesus taught his disciples to pray, he made forgiveness the cornerstone of their relationship with God. God has forgiven our sins; we must now forgive those who have wronged us. To remain unforgiving shows we have not understood that we ourselves deeply need to be forgiven. Think of some people who have wronged you. Have you forgiven them? How would God deal with you if he treated you as you treat others?

God's provision is daily, not all at once. We cannot store it up and then cut off communication with God. And we dare not be self-satisfied. If you are running low on strength, consider how long you have been away from the Source.

Jesus teaches his disciples about prayer

Then, teaching them more about prayer, he used this story: "Suppose you went to a friend's house at midnight, wanting to borrow three loaves of bread. You say to him, 'A friend of mine has just arrived for a visit, and I have nothing for him to eat.' And suppose he calls out from his bedroom, 'Don't bother me. The door is locked for the night, and my family and I are all in bed. I can't help you.' But I tell you this—though he won't do it for friendship's sake, if you keep knocking long enough, he will get up and give you whatever you need because of your shameless persistence.

"And so I tell you, keep on asking, and you will receive what you ask for. Keep on seeking, and you will find. Keep on knocking, and the door will be opened to you. For everyone who asks, receives. Everyone who seeks, finds. And to everyone who knocks, the door will be opened." LUKE 11:5-10

PERSISTENCE

Have you ever grown tired of praying for something or someone? Our vigilance is an expression of our faith that God answers our prayers. Faith shouldn't die if the answers come slowly, for the delay may be God's way of working his will in our lives. When you feel tired of praying, know that God is present, always listening, always answering—maybe not in ways you had hoped but in ways that he knows are best. Persistence, or boldness, in prayer overcomes our insensitivity, not God's. To practice persistence does more to change our hearts and minds than his, and it helps us understand and express the intensity of our need. Persistence in prayer helps us recognize God's work. Are you waiting for God's timing? Trust his judgment for your best interests.

Everyone who asks will receive, if the requests are made in faith. To ask in faith is to ask with confidence that God will align our desires with his purposes.

Jesus teaches his disciples about prayer

"You fathers—if your children ask for a fish, do you give them a snake instead? Or if they ask for an egg, do you give them a scorpion? Of course not! So if you sinful people know how to give good gifts to your children, how much more will your heavenly Father give the Holy Spirit to those who ask him."

LUKE 11:11-13

GOD'S GIFT

Even though good fathers make mistakes, they treat their children well. How much better our perfect heavenly Father treats his children! The most important gift he could ever give us is the Holy Spirit (Acts 2:1-4), whom he promised to give all believers after Jesus' death, resurrection, and return to heaven (John 15:26). At Pentecost (Acts 2:4), the Holy Spirit was made available to all who believe in Jesus. We receive the Holy Spirit when we receive Jesus Christ. Pray with an attitude of positive expectancy. Your heavenly Father wants the very best for you.

God is the perfect Father. Although some fathers may not be very good examples, God can be depended on to always do what is best for his children.

Jesus answers hostile accusations

One day Jesus cast out a demon from a man who couldn't speak, and when the demon was gone, the man began to speak. The crowds were amazed, but some of them said, "No wonder he can cast out demons. He gets his power from Satan, the prince of demons." Others, trying to test Jesus, demanded that he show them a miraculous sign from heaven to prove his authority.

He knew their thoughts, so he said, "Any kingdom divided by civil war is doomed. A family splintered by feuding will fall apart. You say I am empowered by Satan. But if Satan is divided and fighting against himself, how can his kingdom survive? And if I am empowered by Satan, what about your own exorcists? They cast out demons, too, so they will condemn you for what you have said. But if I am casting out demons by the power of God, then the Kingdom of God has arrived among you. For when a strong man like Satan is fully armed and guards his palace, his possessions are safe—until someone even stronger attacks and overpowers him, strips him of his weapons, and carries off his belongings.

"Anyone who isn't with me opposes me, and anyone who isn't working with me is actually working against me.

"When an evil spirit leaves a person, it goes into the desert, searching for rest. But when it finds none, it says, 'I will return to the person I came from.' So it returns and finds that its former home is all swept and in order. Then the spirit finds seven other spirits more evil than itself, and they all enter the person and live there. And so that person is worse off than before."   LUKE 11:14-26

EMPTIED, FILLED

Jesus was illustrating an unfortunate human tendency—our desire to reform often does not last long. In Israel's history, almost as soon as a good king would pull down idols, a bad king would set them up again. It is not enough to be emptied of evil; we must then be filled with the power of the Holy Spirit to accomplish God's new purpose in our lives. If we are controlled by the Holy Spirit, we will produce the kind of fruit that pleases God (as described in Galatians 5:22-23). We do not need to fear the Spirit's control. He does not possess us against our will or treat us as robots.

Regardless of how great Satan's power is, Jesus is stronger still. Satan, who had controlled the kingdom of this world for thousands of years, was now being controlled and overpowered by Jesus and the Kingdom of Heaven. He will bind Satan and dispose of him for eternity (Revelation 20:2, 10).

Jesus places importance on obedience

As he was speaking, a woman in the crowd called out, "God bless your mother—the womb from which you came, and the breasts that nursed you!"

Jesus replied, "But even more blessed are all who hear the word of God and put it into practice." LUKE 11:27-28

OBEY FIRST

Jesus was speaking to people who put extremely high value on family ties. Their genealogies were important guarantees that they were part of God's chosen people. A man's value came from his ancestors, and a woman's value came from the sons she bore. Jesus' response to the woman meant that a person's obedience to God is even more important than his or her place on the family tree. Consistent obedience is even more important than the honor of bearing a respected son. How do you rate your obedience? God is more than willing to give you the power to obey him with all your heart.

This woman was complimenting Jesus by complimenting his mother. Jesus, however, implied that he wanted obedience far more than compliments.

Jesus warns against unbelief

As the crowd pressed in on Jesus, he said, "This evil generation keeps asking me to show them a miraculous sign. But the only sign I will give them is the sign of Jonah. What happened to him was a sign to the people of Nineveh that God had sent him. What happens to the Son of Man will be a sign to these people that he was sent by God.

"The queen of Sheba will stand up against this generation on judgment day and condemn it, for she came from a distant land to hear the wisdom of Solomon. Now someone greater than Solomon is here—but you refuse to listen. The people of Nineveh will also stand up against this generation on judgment day and condemn it, for they repented of their sins at the preaching of Jonah. Now someone greater than Jonah is here—but you refuse to repent."

LUKE 11:29-32

LIABLE TO JUDGMENT

The people of Nineveh, the capital of Assyria, repented when Jonah preached to them—and Jonah did not even care about them. The heathen queen of Sheba praised the God of Israel when she heard Solomon's wisdom, and Solomon was full of faults. By contrast, Jesus, the perfect Son of God, had come to people that he loved dearly—but they rejected him. Thus, God's chosen people made themselves more liable to judgment than either a notoriously wicked nation or a powerful heathen queen. The Ninevites and the queen of Sheba had turned to God with far less evidence than Jesus was giving his listeners—and far less than we have today. We have eyewitness reports of the risen Jesus, the continuing power of the Holy Spirit unleashed at Pentecost, easy access to the Bible, and knowledge of two thousand years of Christ's acts through his church. With the knowledge and insight available to us, our response to Christ ought to be even more complete and wholehearted. What spiritual resources do you have? How do you use them to increase your knowledge of Christ?

God had sent Jonah to announce judgment to the Gentiles (non-Jews). Jesus was affirming that he, too, had been sent by God. Matthew 12:40 adds another piece of evidence: Jesus would die and then rise after three days, just as Jonah was in the belly of the great fish for three days and was rescued.

Jesus teaches about the light within

"No one lights a lamp and then hides it or puts it under a basket. Instead, a lamp is placed on a stand, where its light can be seen by all who enter the house.

"Your eye is a lamp that provides light for your body. When your eye is good, your whole body is filled with light. But when it is bad, your body is filled with darkness. Make sure that the light you think you have is not actually darkness. If you are filled with light, with no dark corners, then your whole life will be radiant, as though a floodlight were filling you with light."   LUKE 11:33-36

SEEING THE LIGHT

The lamp is Christ; the eye represents spiritual understanding and insight. A lustful eye is less sensitive and can blot out the light of Christ's presence. If you have a hard time seeing God at work in the world and in your life, check your vision. Are any sinful desires blinding you to Christ? If so, what can you do? Our world is filled with impurity. We can stay pure in an impure environment by reading God's Word and doing what it says (Psalm 119:9).

Lust is more than inappropriate sexual desire. It can be an unnatural or greedy desire for anything (such as winning, knowledge, possessions, or power).

Jesus criticizes the religious leaders

As Jesus was speaking, one of the Pharisees invited him home for a meal. So he went in and took his place at the table. His host was amazed to see that he sat down to eat without first performing the hand-washing ceremony required by Jewish custom. Then the Lord said to him, "You Pharisees are so careful to clean the outside of the cup and the dish, but inside you are filthy—full of greed and wickedness! Fools! Didn't God make the inside as well as the outside? So clean the inside by giving gifts to the poor, and you will be clean all over.

"What sorrow awaits you Pharisees! For you are careful to tithe even the tiniest income from your herb gardens, but you ignore justice and the love of God. You should tithe, yes, but do not neglect the more important things.

"What sorrow awaits you Pharisees! For you love to sit in the seats of honor in the synagogues and receive respectful greetings as you walk in the marketplaces. Yes, what sorrow awaits you! For you are like hidden graves in a field. People walk over them without knowing the corruption they are stepping on." LUKE 11:37-44

GENEROSITY

The Pharisees loved to think of themselves as "clean," but their stinginess toward God and the poor proved that they were not as clean as they thought. How do you use the resources God has entrusted to you? Are you generous in meeting the needs around you? Your generosity reveals much about the purity of your heart. It is easy to rationalize not helping others because we have already given to the church, but a person who follows Jesus should give to those in need. While tithing is important to the life of the church, we also need to be compassionate. Where we can help, we should help.

This washing was done not for health reasons, but as a symbol of washing away contamination from touching anything unclean. Not only did the Pharisees make a public show of their washing, but they also commanded everyone else to follow a practice originally intended only for the priests.

Jesus criticizes the religious leaders

"Teacher," said an expert in religious law, "you have insulted us, too, in what you just said."

"Yes," said Jesus, "what sorrow also awaits you experts in religious law! For you crush people with unbearable religious demands, and you never lift a finger to ease the burden. What sorrow awaits you! For you build monuments for the prophets your own ancestors killed long ago. But in fact, you stand as witnesses who agree with what your ancestors did. They killed the prophets, and you join in their crime by building the monuments! This is what God in his wisdom said about you: 'I will send prophets and apostles to them, but they will kill some and persecute the others.'

"As a result, this generation will be held responsible for the murder of all God's prophets from the creation of the world—from the murder of Abel to the murder of Zechariah, who was killed between the altar and the sanctuary. Yes, it will certainly be charged against this generation.

"What sorrow awaits you experts in religious law! For you remove the key to knowledge from the people. You don't enter the Kingdom yourselves, and you prevent others from entering."

As Jesus was leaving, the teachers of religious law and the Pharisees became hostile and tried to provoke him with many questions. They wanted to trap him into saying something they could use against him. LUKE 11:45-54

TRULY CLEAN

Jesus harshly criticized the Pharisees and the teachers of religious law because they (1) cleaned their outsides but not their insides, (2) remembered to give a tenth of even their garden herbs but neglected justice, (3) loved praise and attention, (4) loaded people down with burdensome religious demands, (5) would not accept the truth about Jesus, and (6) prevented others from believing the truth as well. They went wrong by focusing on outward appearances and ignoring the inner condition of their hearts. We do the same when our service comes from a desire to be seen rather than from a pure heart and out of a love for others. People may sometimes be fooled, but God isn't. Don't be a Christian on the outside only. Bring your inner life under God's control, and your outer life will naturally reflect him.

God's prophets have been persecuted and murdered throughout history. But this generation was rejecting more than a human prophet—they were rejecting God himself, the one to whom all their history and prophecy were pointing.

Jesus speaks against hypocrisy

Meanwhile, the crowds grew until thousands were milling about and stepping on each other. Jesus turned first to his disciples and warned them, "Beware of the yeast of the Pharisees—their hypocrisy. The time is coming when everything that is covered up will be revealed, and all that is secret will be made known to all. Whatever you have said in the dark will be heard in the light, and what you have whispered behind closed doors will be shouted from the housetops for all to hear!" LUKE 12:1-3

KEEPING UP APPEARANCES

As Jesus watched the huge crowds waiting to hear him, he warned his disciples against hypocrisy—trying to appear good when one's heart is far from God. The Pharisees could not keep their attitudes hidden forever. Their selfishness would act like yeast, and soon they would expose themselves for what they really were—power-hungry impostors, not devoted religious leaders. It is easy to be angry at the blatant hypocrisy of the Pharisees, but all of us must resist the temptation to settle for the appearance of respectability when our hearts are far from God.

The Pharisees' hypocrisy was evidenced by the burdens they added to God's law. To the commandment to remember the Sabbath (Exodus 20:8), they had added instructions regarding how far a person could walk on the Sabbath. Healing a person was considered unlawful work on the Sabbath, although rescuing a trapped animal was permitted. No wonder Jesus condemned their additions to the law.

August 4 READ LUKE 12:4-7

Jesus speaks against hypocrisy

"Dear friends, don't be afraid of those who want to kill your body; they cannot do any more to you after that. But I'll tell you whom to fear. Fear God, who has the power to kill you and then throw you into hell. Yes, he's the one to fear.

"What is the price of five sparrows—two copper coins? Yet God does not forget a single one of them. And the very hairs on your head are all numbered. So don't be afraid; you are more valuable to God than a whole flock of sparrows." LUKE 12:4-7

FEAR?

Fear of opposition or ridicule can weaken our witness for Christ. Often we cling to peace and comfort, even at the cost of our walk with God. Jesus reminds us here that we should fear God, who controls eternity, and not mere temporal consequences. Our true value is God's estimate of our worth, not that of our peers. Other people evaluate and categorize us according to how we perform, what we achieve, and how we look. But God cares for us, as he does for all his creatures, because we belong to him. So we can face life without fear.

To "fear" God means to honor and respect him as the almighty, sovereign God, the ruler of the universe. We don't have to be afraid and run from him, because he loves us. But we must submit to his authority and obey him.

Jesus speaks against hypocrisy

"I tell you the truth, everyone who acknowledges me publicly here on earth, the Son of Man will also acknowledge in the presence of God's angels. But anyone who denies me here on earth will be denied before God's angels. Anyone who speaks against the Son of Man can be forgiven, but anyone who blasphemes the Holy Spirit will not be forgiven.

"And when you are brought to trial in the synagogues and before rulers and authorities, don't worry about how to defend yourself or what to say, for the Holy Spirit will teach you at that time what needs to be said." LUKE 12:8-12

DENY OR CONFESS?

We deny Jesus when we (1) hope no one will think we are Christians, (2) decide *not* to speak up for what is right, (3) are silent about our relationship with God, (4) blend into society, or (5) accept our culture's non-Christian values. By contrast, we confess him when we (1) live moral, upright, Christ-honoring lives; (2) look for opportunities to share our faith with others; (3) help others in need; (4) take a stand for justice; (5) love others; (6) acknowledge our loyalty to Christ; and (7) use our lives and resources to carry out his desires rather than our own.

Jesus said that blasphemy against the Holy Spirit is unforgivable. It involves attributing to Satan the work that the Holy Spirit accomplishes; thus, it is deliberate and ongoing rejection of the Holy Spirit's work and even of God himself.

Jesus tells the parable of the rich fool

Then someone called from the crowd, "Teacher, please tell my brother to divide our father's estate with me."

Jesus replied, "Friend, who made me a judge over you to decide such things as that?" Then he said, "Beware! Guard against every kind of greed. Life is not measured by how much you own."

Then he told them a story: "A rich man had a fertile farm that produced fine crops. He said to himself, 'What should I do? I don't have room for all my crops.' Then he said, 'I know! I'll tear down my barns and build bigger ones. Then I'll have room enough to store all my wheat and other goods. And I'll sit back and say to myself, "My friend, you have enough stored away for years to come. Now take it easy! Eat, drink, and be merry!"'

"But God said to him, 'You fool! You will die this very night. Then who will get everything you worked for?'

"Yes, a person is a fool to store up earthly wealth but not have a rich relationship with God."   LUKE 12:13-21

THE GOOD LIFE

Jesus is pointing to a higher issue—a correct attitude toward the accumulation of wealth. Life is more than material goods; far more important is our relationship with God. Jesus says that the good life has nothing to do with being wealthy, so we should be on guard against greed (desire for what we don't have). This is the exact opposite of what society usually says. Advertisers spend millions of dollars to entice us to think that if we buy more and more of their products, we will be happier, more fulfilled, more comfortable. How do you respond to the constant pressure to buy? Learn to tune out expensive enticements and concentrate instead on the truly good life—living in a relationship with God and doing his work.

The rich man in Jesus' story died before he could begin to use what was stored in his big barns. Planning for retirement— preparing for the rest of one's life on earth—is wise, but neglecting to prepare for life after death is disastrous.

Jesus warns about worry

Then, turning to his disciples, Jesus said, "That is why I tell you not to worry about everyday life—whether you have enough food to eat or enough clothes to wear. For life is more than food, and your body more than clothing. Look at the ravens. They don't plant or harvest or store food in barns, for God feeds them. And you are far more valuable to him than any birds! Can all your worries add a single moment to your life? And if worry can't accomplish a little thing like that, what's the use of worrying over bigger things?

"Look at the lilies and how they grow. They don't work or make their clothing, yet Solomon in all his glory was not dressed as beautifully as they are. And if God cares so wonderfully for flowers that are here today and thrown into the fire tomorrow, he will certainly care for you. Why do you have so little faith?

"And don't be concerned about what to eat and what to drink. Don't worry about such things. These things dominate the thoughts of unbelievers all over the world, but your Father already knows your needs. Seek the Kingdom of God above all else, and he will give you everything you need." LUKE 12:22-31

AT THE CENTER

Seeking the Kingdom of God means making Jesus the Lord and King of your life. He must control every area—your work, play, plans, relationships. Is the Kingdom only one of your many concerns, or is it central to all you do? Are you holding back any areas of your life from God's control? As Lord and Creator, he wants to help provide what you need as well as guide how you use what he provides.

Worry is pointless because it can't meet any of our needs; worry is foolish because the Creator of the universe loves us and knows what we need. He promises to meet all our real needs, but not necessarily all our desires.

August 8 READ LUKE 12:32-34

Jesus warns about worry

"So don't be afraid, little flock. For it gives your Father great happiness to give you the Kingdom.

"Sell your possessions and give to those in need. This will store up treasure for you in heaven! And the purses of heaven never get old or develop holes. Your treasure will be safe; no thief can steal it and no moth can destroy it. Wherever your treasure is, there the desires of your heart will also be." LUKE 12:32-34

TREASURE HUNT

Money seen as an end in itself quickly traps us and cuts us off from both God and the needy. The key to using money wisely is to see how much we can use for God's purposes, not how much we can accumulate for ourselves. Does God's love touch your wallet? Does your money free you to help others? Where do you put your time, money, and energy? What do you think about most? Consider how you should change the way you use your resources in order to reflect Kingdom values more accurately.

God does not command all believers to sell everything they have. What he wants is believers who hold their possessions loosely, willing to sell or give away in order to help someone else.

Jesus warns about preparing for his coming

"Be dressed for service and keep your lamps burning, as though you were waiting for your master to return from the wedding feast. Then you will be ready to open the door and let him in the moment he arrives and knocks. The servants who are ready and waiting for his return will be rewarded. I tell you the truth, he himself will seat them, put on an apron, and serve them as they sit and eat! He may come in the middle of the night or just before dawn. But whenever he comes, he will reward the servants who are ready.

"Understand this: If a homeowner knew exactly when a burglar was coming, he would not permit his house to be broken into. You also must be ready all the time, for the Son of Man will come when least expected." LUKE 12:35-40

GETTING READY

Christ's return at an unexpected time is not a trap, a trick by which God hopes to catch us off guard. In fact, God is delaying his return so more people will have the opportunity to follow him (2 Peter 3:9). Now is the time to live out our beliefs and to reflect God's love as we relate to others.

People who are ready for their Lord's return are (1) not hypocritical but sincere (Luke 12:1); (2) not fearful but ready to witness (Luke 12:4-9); (3) not worried but trusting (Luke 12:25-26); (4) not greedy but generous (Luke 12:34); and (5) not lazy but diligent (Luke 12:37). May your life be more like Christ's so that when he comes, you will be ready to greet him joyfully.

Jesus repeatedly said that he would leave this world but would return at some future time (Matthew 24–25; John 14:1-3). He also said that the Kingdom is being prepared for his followers.

August 10 READ LUKE 12:41-48

Jesus warns about preparing for his coming

Peter asked, "Lord, is that illustration just for us or for everyone?"

And the Lord replied, "A faithful, sensible servant is one to whom the master can give the responsibility of managing his other household servants and feeding them. If the master returns and finds that the servant has done a good job, there will be a reward. I tell you the truth, the master will put that servant in charge of all he owns. But what if the servant thinks, 'My master won't be back for a while,' and he begins beating the other servants, partying, and getting drunk? The master will return unannounced and unexpected, and he will cut the servant in pieces and banish him with the unfaithful.

"And a servant who knows what the master wants, but isn't prepared and doesn't carry out those instructions, will be severely punished. But someone who does not know, and then does something wrong, will be punished only lightly. When someone has been given much, much will be required in return; and when someone has been entrusted with much, even more will be required." LUKE 12:41-48

FUTURE REWARD

Jesus promises a reward for those who have been faithful to him. While we sometimes experience immediate and material rewards for our obedience to God, this is not always the case. If it were so, we would be tempted to boast about our achievements and do good only for what we get. Jesus said that if we look for rewards now, we will lose them later (Mark 8:36). Our heavenly rewards will be the most accurate reflection of what we have done on earth, and they will be far greater than we can imagine.

Watchful and faithful leaders will be given increased opportunities and responsibilities. The more resources, understanding, and talents we have, the more we are responsible to use them effectively. God will not hold us responsible for gifts he has not given us, but all of us have been given gifts and enough duties to keep us busy until Jesus comes.

Jesus warns about coming division

"I have come to set the world on fire, and I wish it were already burning! I have a terrible baptism of suffering ahead of me, and I am under a heavy burden until it is accomplished. Do you think I have come to bring peace to the earth? No, I have come to divide people against each other! From now on families will be split apart, three in favor of me, and two against—or two in favor and three against. 'Father will be divided against son and son against father; mother against daughter and daughter against mother; and mother-in-law against daughter-in-law and daughter-in-law against mother-in-law.'" LUKE 12:49-53

TAKING A RISK

By these strange and unsettling words, Jesus revealed that his claims would result in conflict. They demand a personal response, so families may be torn apart when some choose to follow him and others refuse. There is no middle ground with Jesus. A decision must be made to trust Jesus as your Savior and commit your life to him, which may result in severed relationships. Are you willing to risk your family's disapproval in order to gain eternal life?

The "baptism" to which Jesus referred was his coming crucifixion. Jesus was dreading the physical pain, of course, but even worse would be the spiritual pain of complete separation from God that would accompany his death for the sins of the world.

Jesus warns about the future crisis

Then Jesus turned to the crowd and said, "When you see clouds beginning to form in the west, you say, 'Here comes a shower.' And you are right. When the south wind blows, you say, 'Today will be a scorcher.' And it is. You fools! You know how to interpret the weather signs of the earth and sky, but you don't know how to interpret the present times.

"Why can't you decide for yourselves what is right? When you are on the way to court with your accuser, try to settle the matter before you get there. Otherwise, your accuser may drag you before the judge, who will hand you over to an officer, who will throw you into prison. And if that happens, you won't be free again until you have paid the very last penny."   LUKE 12:54-59

KINGDOM SIGNS

Jesus was announcing the coming of God's Kingdom and warning his listeners of its importance. Like a rainstorm on a sunny day, there were signs that the Kingdom would soon arrive. But Jesus' hearers, though skilled at interpreting weather signs, were intentionally ignoring the signs of the times. Jesus' question could be asked of many today: "Why can't you decide for yourselves what is right?" Have you taken Jesus at his word? See the truth for yourself.

———————————◆◆———————————

For most of recorded history, the world's principal occupation was farming. Farmers depended directly on the weather for their livelihood. They needed just the right amounts of sun and rain— not too much, not too little—to make their living, and they grew skilled at interpreting natural signs.

———————————◆◆———————————

Jesus calls the people to repent

About this time Jesus was informed that Pilate had murdered some people from Galilee as they were offering sacrifices at the Temple. "Do you think those Galileans were worse sinners than all the other people from Galilee?" Jesus asked. "Is that why they suffered? Not at all! And you will perish, too, unless you repent of your sins and turn to God. And what about the eighteen people who died when the tower in Siloam fell on them? Were they the worst sinners in Jerusalem? No, and I tell you again that unless you repent, you will perish, too." LUKE 13:1-5

TOUGH QUESTIONS

Pilate may have killed the Galileans because he thought they were rebelling against Rome; those killed by the tower of Siloam may have been working for the Romans on an aqueduct there. The Pharisees, who were opposed to using force to deal with Rome, would have said that the Galileans deserved to die for rebelling. The Zealots, a group of anti-Roman terrorists, would have said the aqueduct workers deserved to die for cooperating. Jesus said that neither the Galileans nor the workers should be blamed for their calamity. And instead of blaming others, everyone should look to his or her own day of judgment: Death may come at any time. Being a believer doesn't shield you from death or even from tragic death. Are you ready to die? Do you know for sure that you'll be with the Savior?

———————◆●◆———————

Whether a person is killed in a tragedy or miraculously survives is not a measure of righteousness. Everyone has to die; that's part of being human. But people don't need to stay dead. Jesus promises that those who believe in him will not perish but have eternal life (John 3:16).

———————◆●◆———————

Jesus teaches about bearing fruit

Then Jesus told this story: "A man planted a fig tree in his garden and came again and again to see if there was any fruit on it, but he was always disappointed. Finally, he said to his gardener, 'I've waited three years, and there hasn't been a single fig! Cut it down. It's just taking up space in the garden.'

"The gardener answered, 'Sir, give it one more chance. Leave it another year, and I'll give it special attention and plenty of fertilizer. If we get figs next year, fine. If not, then you can cut it down.'" LUKE 13:6-9

NO FRUIT

In the Old Testament, a fruitful tree was often used as a symbol of godly living (see, for example, Psalm 1:3 and Jeremiah 17:7-8). Jesus pointed out what would happen to the other kind of tree—the kind that took valuable time and space and still produced nothing for the patient gardener. This was one way Jesus warned his listeners that God would not tolerate forever their lack of productivity. (Luke 3:9 records John the Baptist's version of the same message.) Have you been enjoying God's special treatment without giving anything in return? If so, respond to the Gardener's patient care and begin to bear the fruit God has created you to produce.

Fig trees were plentiful in Israel. In this parable, the fig tree also represents the nation of Israel. The fruitless fig tree would be cut down; Israel would be cut off from God's blessing for refusing God's Son.

Jesus heals the handicapped woman

One Sabbath day as Jesus was teaching in a synagogue, he saw a woman who had been crippled by an evil spirit. She had been bent double for eighteen years and was unable to stand up straight. When Jesus saw her, he called her over and said, "Dear woman, you are healed of your sickness!" Then he touched her, and instantly she could stand straight. How she praised God!

But the leader in charge of the synagogue was indignant that Jesus had healed her on the Sabbath day. "There are six days of the week for working," he said to the crowd. "Come on those days to be healed, not on the Sabbath."

But the Lord replied, "You hypocrites! Each of you works on the Sabbath day! Don't you untie your ox or your donkey from its stall on the Sabbath and lead it out for water? This dear woman, a daughter of Abraham, has been held in bondage by Satan for eighteen years. Isn't it right that she be released, even on the Sabbath?"

This shamed his enemies, but all the people rejoiced at the wonderful things he did. LUKE 13:10-17

THE LETTER OF THE LAW

Why was healing considered work? The religious leaders saw healing as part of a doctor's profession, and practicing one's profession on the Sabbath was prohibited. The synagogue ruler could not see beyond the law to Jesus' compassion in healing this handicapped woman. Jesus shamed him and the other leaders by pointing out their hypocrisy. The Pharisees hid behind their own set of laws to avoid love's obligations. We, too, can use the letter of the law to rationalize away our obligation to care for others (for example, by tithing regularly and then refusing to help a needy neighbor). But people's needs are more important than rules and regulations. Take time to help others, even if doing so might compromise your public image.

In our fallen world, disease and disability are common. Their causes are many and often multiple—inadequate nutrition, contact with a source of infection, a lowered immune system, and even direct attack by Satan. Whatever the immediate cause of our illness, we can trace its original source to Satan, the author of all the evil in our world. The good news is that Jesus is more powerful than the devil or any disease.

Jesus teaches about the Kingdom of God

Then Jesus said, "What is the Kingdom of God like? How can I illustrate it? It is like a tiny mustard seed that a man planted in a garden; it grows and becomes a tree, and the birds make nests in its branches."

He also asked, "What else is the Kingdom of God like? It is like the yeast a woman used in making bread. Even though she put only a little yeast in three measures of flour, it permeated every part of the dough." LUKE 13:18-21

LET IT GROW

The general expectation among Jesus' hearers was that the Messiah would come as a great king and leader, freeing the nation from Rome and restoring Israel's former glory. But Jesus said his Kingdom was beginning quietly. Like the tiny mustard seed that grows into an enormous tree or the spoonful of yeast that makes bread dough double in size, the Kingdom of God would eventually push outward until the whole world was changed. You are a part of that Kingdom because people have continued to spread the gospel since the days of Christ. What are you doing to continue the growth of the Kingdom?

The mustard plant grows to be quite large; in fact, one of the largest plants in Palestine. And yet its seeds are the tiniest. Jesus' audience easily understood his illustration.

Jesus heals the man who was born blind

As Jesus was walking along, he saw a man who had been blind from birth. "Rabbi," his disciples asked him, "why was this man born blind? Was it because of his own sins or his parents' sins?"

"It was not because of his sins or his parents' sins," Jesus answered. "This happened so the power of God could be seen in him. We must quickly carry out the tasks assigned us by the one who sent us. The night is coming, and then no one can work. But while I am here in the world, I am the light of the world."

JOHN 9:1-5

SUFFERING

A common belief in Jewish culture was that calamity or suffering was the result of some great sin. But Christ used this man's suffering to teach about faith and to glorify God. We live in a fallen world where good behavior is not always rewarded and bad behavior is not always punished. Therefore, innocent people sometimes suffer. If God took suffering away whenever we asked, we would follow him for comfort and convenience, not out of love and devotion. Regardless of the reasons for our suffering, Jesus has the power to help us deal with it. When you suffer from a disease, tragedy, or disability, try not to ask why this happened to you. Instead, ask God to give you strength for the trial and a clearer perspective on what is happening.

In John 9, we see four different reactions to Jesus: The neighbors revealed surprise and skepticism; the Pharisees showed disbelief and prejudice; the parents believed but kept quiet for fear of excommunication; and the healed man showed consistent, growing faith.

Jesus heals the man who was born blind

Then he spit on the ground, made mud with the saliva, and spread the mud over the blind man's eyes. He told him, "Go wash yourself in the pool of Siloam" (Siloam means "sent"). So the man went and washed and came back seeing!

His neighbors and others who knew him as a blind beggar asked each other, "Isn't this the man who used to sit and beg?" Some said he was, and others said, "No, he just looks like him!"

But the beggar kept saying, "Yes, I am the same one!"

They asked, "Who healed you? What happened?"

He told them, "The man they call Jesus made mud and spread it over my eyes and told me, 'Go to the pool of Siloam and wash yourself.' So I went and washed, and now I can see!"

"Where is he now?" they asked.

"I don't know," he replied.   JOHN 9:6-12

STEPS OF FAITH

Jesus' miracles were meant to strengthen people's faith and lead them to believe in him as the Messiah. Christ's miracles were significant, not just because of their power but because of their purpose—to help, to heal, and to point people to God. This man's simple act of faith in going to wash, as Jesus instructed, resulted in his restored sight. Faith is a step between promise and assurance. Miracles seem so out of reach for our feeble faith. But every miracle, large or small, begins with an act of obedience. We may not see the solution until we take the first step of faith.

The pool of Siloam was built by Hezekiah (2 Kings 20:20; 2 Chronicles 32:30). His workers had constructed an underground tunnel from a spring outside the city walls to carry water into the city. Thus, the people could always get water without fear of being attacked. This was especially important during times of siege.

Religious leaders question the blind man

Then they took the man who had been blind to the Pharisees, because it was on the Sabbath that Jesus had made the mud and healed him. The Pharisees asked the man all about it. So he told them, "He put the mud over my eyes, and when I washed it away, I could see!"

Some of the Pharisees said, "This man Jesus is not from God, for he is working on the Sabbath." Others said, "But how could an ordinary sinner do such miraculous signs?" So there was a deep division of opinion among them.

Then the Pharisees again questioned the man who had been blind and demanded, "What's your opinion about this man who healed you?"

The man replied, "I think he must be a prophet."

The Jewish leaders still refused to believe the man had been blind and could now see, so they called in his parents. They asked them, "Is this your son? Was he born blind? If so, how can he now see?"

His parents replied, "We know this is our son and that he was born blind, but we don't know how he can see or who healed him. Ask him. He is old enough to speak for himself." His parents said this because they were afraid of the Jewish leaders, who had announced that anyone saying Jesus was the Messiah would be expelled from the synagogue. That's why they said, "He is old enough. Ask him." JOHN 9:13-23

SABBATH REST

The Jewish Sabbath, Saturday, was the weekly holy day of rest. The Pharisees had made a long list of specific dos and don'ts regarding the Sabbath. Kneading the clay and healing the man were considered work and therefore were forbidden. Jesus may have purposely made the clay in order to emphasize his teaching about the Sabbath—that it is right to care for others' needs even if it involves working on a day of rest. The Sabbath had two purposes: It was a time *to rest* and a time *to remember* what God had done. We need rest. Without time out from the bustle, life loses its meaning. In our day, as in Moses' day, taking time out is not easy. Your Sabbath rest may be different from others'; to you gardening might be restful, while someone else would consider it work. Don't get bogged down in laws and judging. God created a Sabbath for you. He reminds us that without Sabbaths we will forget the purpose for all our activity and lose the balance crucial to a faithful life. Make sure that your Sabbath provides a time of both refreshment and remembrance of God.

August 20

Religious leaders question the blind man

So for the second time they called in the man who had been blind and told him, "God should get the glory for this, because we know this man Jesus is a sinner."

"I don't know whether he is a sinner," the man replied. "But I know this: I was blind, and now I can see!"

"But what did he do?" they asked. "How did he heal you?"

"Look!" the man exclaimed. "I told you once. Didn't you listen? Why do you want to hear it again? Do you want to become his disciples, too?"

Then they cursed him and said, "You are his disciple, but we are disciples of Moses! We know God spoke to Moses, but we don't even know where this man comes from."

"Why, that's very strange!" the man replied. "He healed my eyes, and yet you don't know where he comes from? We know that God doesn't listen to sinners, but he is ready to hear those who worship him and do his will. Ever since the world began, no one has been able to open the eyes of someone born blind. If this man were not from God, he couldn't have done it."

"You were born a total sinner!" they answered. "Are you trying to teach us?" And they threw him out of the synagogue. JOHN 9:24-34

SPREAD THE NEWS

By now the man who had been blind had heard the same questions over and over. He did not know how or why he was healed, but he knew that his life had been miraculously changed, and he was not afraid to tell the truth. You don't need to know all the answers in order to share Christ with others. It is important to tell them how he has changed your life. Then trust that God will use your words to help others believe in him too.

The man's new faith was severely tested by some of the authorities. He was cursed and evicted from the synagogue—a horrible punishment for a Jew.

Jesus teaches about spiritual blindness

When Jesus heard what had happened, he found the man and asked, "Do you believe in the Son of Man?"

The man answered, "Who is he, sir? I want to believe in him."

"You have seen him," Jesus said, "and he is speaking to you!"

"Yes, Lord, I believe!" the man said. And he worshiped Jesus.

Then Jesus told him, "I entered this world to render judgment—to give sight to the blind and to show those who think they see that they are blind."

Some Pharisees who were standing nearby heard him and asked, "Are you saying we're blind?"

"If you were blind, you wouldn't be guilty," Jesus replied. "But you remain guilty because you claim you can see." JOHN 9:35-41

GETTING TO KNOW HIM

The longer this man experienced his new life in Christ, the more confident he became in the one who had healed him. He gained not only physical sight but also spiritual sight as he recognized Jesus, first as a prophet (John 9:17), then as his Lord. When you turn to Christ, you begin to see him differently. The longer you walk with him, the better you will understand who he is. Peter tells us to "grow in the grace and knowledge of our Lord and Savior Jesus Christ" (2 Peter 3:18). If you want to know more about Jesus, keep walking with him.

People lose a vital ability when they can no longer see their own sinfulness. The results are broken relationships, authority out of control, blindness to the needy, and forgetfulness toward God. Spiritual blindness is a matter of life and death.

August 22 READ JOHN 10:1-10

Jesus is the Good Shepherd

"I tell you the truth, anyone who sneaks over the wall of a sheepfold, rather than going through the gate, must surely be a thief and a robber! But the one who enters through the gate is the shepherd of the sheep. The gatekeeper opens the gate for him, and the sheep recognize his voice and come to him. He calls his own sheep by name and leads them out. After he has gathered his own flock, he walks ahead of them, and they follow him because they know his voice. They won't follow a stranger; they will run from him because they don't know his voice."

Those who heard Jesus use this illustration didn't understand what he meant, so he explained it to them: "I tell you the truth, I am the gate for the sheep. All who came before me were thieves and robbers. But the true sheep did not listen to them. Yes, I am the gate. Those who come in through me will be saved. They will come and go freely and will find good pastures. The thief's purpose is to steal and kill and destroy. My purpose is to give them a rich and satisfying life." JOHN 10:1-10

THE GOOD SHEPHERD

The New Testament calls Jesus the Good Shepherd (John 10:11) and the Great Shepherd (Hebrews 13:20; 1 Peter 5:4). Sheep are completely dependent on their shepherd for provision, guidance, and protection. As the Lord is the Good Shepherd, so we are his sheep—not frightened, passive animals, but obedient followers, wise enough to follow one who will lead us in the right places and in right ways. When we allow the Good Shepherd to guide us, we have contentment. When we choose to sin, however, we go our own way and cannot blame God for the environment we create for ourselves. Rebelling against the Shepherd's leading is actually rebelling against our own best interests. Remember this the next time you are tempted to go your own way rather than the Shepherd's way.

At night, sheep were often gathered into a sheepfold to protect them from thieves, weather, and wild animals. The sheepfolds were caves, sheds, or open areas surrounded by walls made of stones or branches. The shepherd often slept in the fold to protect the sheep.

Jesus is the Good Shepherd

"I am the good shepherd. The good shepherd sacrifices his life for the sheep. A hired hand will run when he sees a wolf coming. He will abandon the sheep because they don't belong to him and he isn't their shepherd. And so the wolf attacks them and scatters the flock. The hired hand runs away because he's working only for the money and doesn't really care about the sheep.

"I am the good shepherd; I know my own sheep, and they know me, just as my Father knows me and I know the Father. So I sacrifice my life for the sheep. I have other sheep, too, that are not in this sheepfold. I must bring them also. They will listen to my voice, and there will be one flock with one shepherd." JOHN 10:11-16

PAST, PRESENT, AND FUTURE

A hired man tends the sheep for money, while the shepherd does it for love. The shepherd owns the sheep and is committed to them. Jesus is not merely doing a job; he is committed to love us and even lay down his life for us. False teachers and false prophets do not have this commitment. Jesus *did* die for us. He has *once and for all* paid the penalty for our sins by his own sacrificial death, and he can be depended on to restore our broken relationship with God. We are released from sin's domination over us when we commit ourselves to Christ, trusting completely in what he has done for us. No one can add to what Jesus did to save us; our past, present, and future sins are all forgiven, and Jesus is with the Father as a sign that our sins are forgiven. If you are a Christian, remember that Christ has paid the price for your sins once and for all.

The "other sheep" were the non-Jews. Jesus came to save Gentiles as well as Jews. This is an insight into Christ's worldwide mission—to die for the sins of the world. People tend to want to restrict God's blessings to their own group, but Jesus refuses to be limited by the fences we build.

Jesus is the Good Shepherd

"The Father loves me because I sacrifice my life so I may take it back again. No one can take my life from me. I sacrifice it voluntarily. For I have the authority to lay it down when I want to and also to take it up again. For this is what my Father has commanded."

When he said these things, the people were again divided in their opinions about him. Some said, "He's demon possessed and out of his mind. Why listen to a man like that?" Others said, "This doesn't sound like a man possessed by a demon! Can a demon open the eyes of the blind?" JOHN 10:17-21

LAYING IT DOWN

Jesus is God; thus, he could say that he would both lay down his life *and* take it back again. Jesus' death and resurrection, as part of God's plan for the salvation of the world, were under God's full control. No one could kill Jesus without his consent. It was important that Jesus die on the cross to take the punishment for sin, but it was also important that he rise from the dead. The resurrection of Christ is the center of the Christian faith. Because Christ rose from the dead as he promised, we know that what he said is true—he is God. Because he rose, we have certainty that our sins are forgiven. Because he rose, he lives and represents us to God. Because he rose and defeated death, we know we will also be raised.

If Jesus had been merely a man, his claims to be God would have proved him insane. But his miracles proved his words true—he really is God. The Jewish leaders could not see beyond their own prejudices, and they looked at Jesus only from a human perspective—Jesus confined in a human box. But Jesus was not limited by their restricted vision.

People surround Jesus at the Temple

It was now winter, and Jesus was in Jerusalem at the time of Hanukkah, the Festival of Dedication. He was in the Temple, walking through the section known as Solomon's Colonnade. The people surrounded him and asked, "How long are you going to keep us in suspense? If you are the Messiah, tell us plainly."

Jesus replied, "I have already told you, and you don't believe me. The proof is the work I do in my Father's name. But you don't believe me because you are not my sheep. My sheep listen to my voice; I know them, and they follow me. I give them eternal life, and they will never perish. No one can snatch them away from me, for my Father has given them to me, and he is more powerful than anyone else. No one can snatch them from the Father's hand. The Father and I are one." JOHN 10:22-30

ON WHOSE TERMS?

The statement "the Father and I are one" is the clearest statement of Jesus' divinity he ever made. Jesus and his Father are not the same person, but they are one in essence and nature. Thus, Jesus was not merely a good teacher—he was God. His claim to be God was unmistakable. The religious leaders wanted to kill him because their laws said that anyone claiming to be God should die. Nothing could persuade them that Jesus' claim was true. Jesus tried to correct their mistaken ideas, but they clung to the wrong idea of what kind of Messiah God would send. Such blindness still keeps people away from Jesus. They want him on their own terms; they do not want him if it means changing their whole lives. Have you accepted Jesus on his terms?

Hanukkah (also called the Feast of Lights) commemorates the cleansing of the Temple under Judas Maccabeus in 165 BC after Antiochus Epiphanes had defiled it a few years earlier by sacrificing a pig on the altar of burnt offering. The feast is celebrated toward the end of December.

People surround Jesus at the Temple

Once again the people picked up stones to kill him. Jesus said, "At my Father's direction I have done many good works. For which one are you going to stone me?"

They replied, "We're stoning you not for any good work, but for blasphemy! You, a mere man, claim to be God."

Jesus replied, "It is written in your own Scriptures that God said to certain leaders of the people, 'I say, you are gods!' And you know that the Scriptures cannot be altered. So if those people who received God's message were called 'gods,' why do you call it blasphemy when I say, 'I am the Son of God'? After all, the Father set me apart and sent me into the world. Don't believe me unless I carry out my Father's work. But if I do his work, believe in the evidence of the miraculous works I have done, even if you don't believe me. Then you will know and understand that the Father is in me, and I am in the Father."

Once again they tried to arrest him, but he got away and left them. He went beyond the Jordan River near the place where John was first baptizing and stayed there awhile. And many followed him. "John didn't perform miraculous signs," they remarked to one another, "but everything he said about this man has come true." And many who were there believed in Jesus. JOHN 10:31-42

OUR ONLY SOURCE

"The Scriptures cannot be altered"—what the Bible says is true. If we accept Christ as Lord, we also must accept his testimony to the Bible as God's Word. The whole Bible is God's inspired Word. Because it is inspired and trustworthy, we should *read* it and *apply* it to our lives. The Bible is our standard for testing everything else that claims to be true. It is our safeguard against false teaching and our source of guidance for how we should live. It is our only source of knowledge about how we can be saved. God wants to show you what is true and equip you to live for him. How much time do you spend in God's Word? Read it regularly to discover God's truth and to become confident in your life and faith. Develop a plan for reading the whole Bible, not just the familiar passages.

The Jewish leaders attempted to carry out the directive found in Leviticus 24:16 regarding those who blaspheme (claim to be God). They intended to stone Jesus.

Jesus teaches about entering the Kingdom

Jesus went through the towns and villages, teaching as he went, always pressing on toward Jerusalem. Someone asked him, "Lord, will only a few be saved?"

He replied, "Work hard to enter the narrow door to God's Kingdom, for many will try to enter but will fail. When the master of the house has locked the door, it will be too late. You will stand outside knocking and pleading, 'Lord, open the door for us!' But he will reply, 'I don't know you or where you come from.' Then you will say, 'But we ate and drank with you, and you taught in our streets.' And he will reply, 'I tell you, I don't know you or where you come from. Get away from me, all you who do evil.'

"There will be weeping and gnashing of teeth, for you will see Abraham, Isaac, Jacob, and all the prophets in the Kingdom of God, but you will be thrown out. And people will come from all over the world—from east and west, north and south—to take their places in the Kingdom of God. And note this: Some who seem least important now will be the greatest then, and some who are the greatest now will be least important then." LUKE 13:22-30

THE FEAST

There will be many surprises in God's Kingdom. Some who are despised now will be greatly honored then; some influential people here will be left outside the gates. Many "great" people on this earth (in God's eyes) are virtually ignored by the rest of the world. What matters to God is not a person's earthly popularity, status, wealth, heritage, or power, but his or her commitment to Christ. How do your values match what the Bible tells you to value? Put God first in your life, and you will join people from all over the world who will take their places at the feast in the Kingdom of Heaven.

This is the second time Luke reminds us that Jesus was intentionally going to Jerusalem (the first is in Luke 9:51). Jesus knew he was on his way to die, but he continued preaching to large crowds. The prospect of death did not deter Jesus from carrying out his ministry.

August 28 READ LUKE 13:31-35

Jesus grieves over Jerusalem

At that time some Pharisees said to him, "Get away from here if you want to live! Herod Antipas wants to kill you!"

Jesus replied, "Go tell that fox that I will keep on casting out demons and healing people today and tomorrow; and the third day I will accomplish my purpose. Yes, today, tomorrow, and the next day I must proceed on my way. For it wouldn't do for a prophet of God to be killed except in Jerusalem!

"O Jerusalem, Jerusalem, the city that kills the prophets and stones God's messengers! How often I have wanted to gather your children together as a hen protects her chicks beneath her wings, but you wouldn't let me. And now, look, your house is abandoned. And you will never see me again until you say, 'Blessings on the one who comes in the name of the LORD!'" LUKE 13:31-35

GOD'S TIMING

The Pharisees weren't interested in protecting Jesus from danger—they were trying to trap him. The Pharisees urged Jesus to leave because they wanted to stop him from going to Jerusalem, not because they feared Herod. But Jesus' life, work, and death were not to be determined by Herod or the Pharisees. His life was planned and directed by God himself, and his mission would unfold in God's time and according to God's plan. When you are following God's will, you must do whatever he calls you to do without letting any obstacles get in your way. God will make sure that his will is accomplished.

Jerusalem, the city of God, symbolized the entire nation. It was Israel's largest city and the nation's spiritual and political capital. Jews from around the world visited it frequently. But Jerusalem had a history of rejecting God's prophets (1 Kings 19:10; 2 Chronicles 24:19; Jeremiah 2:30; 26:20-23), and it would reject the Messiah just as it had rejected his forerunners.

Jesus heals a man with dropsy

One Sabbath day Jesus went to eat dinner in the home of a leader of the Pharisees, and the people were watching him closely. There was a man there whose arms and legs were swollen. Jesus asked the Pharisees and experts in religious law, "Is it permitted in the law to heal people on the Sabbath day, or not?" When they refused to answer, Jesus touched the sick man and healed him and sent him away. Then he turned to them and said, "Which of you doesn't work on the Sabbath? If your son or your cow falls into a pit, don't you rush to get him out?" Again they could not answer. LUKE 14:1-6

UNAFRAID

Earlier Jesus had been invited to a Pharisee's home for discussion (Luke 7:36). This time a prominent Pharisee invited Jesus to his home specifically to trap him into saying or doing something for which he could be arrested. It may be surprising to see Jesus on the Pharisees' turf after he had denounced them so many times. But Jesus was not afraid to face the Pharisees, even though he knew that their purpose was to trick him into breaking their laws. Jesus was not afraid of confrontation; neither should his followers be. We can trust God to help us have the right words and to accomplish his will through us.

Luke, the physician, identified this man's disease—he was suffering from an abnormal accumulation of fluid in bodily tissues and cavities, sometimes called dropsy.

Jesus teaches about seeking honor

When Jesus noticed that all who had come to the dinner were trying to sit in the seats of honor near the head of the table, he gave them this advice: "When you are invited to a wedding feast, don't sit in the seat of honor. What if someone who is more distinguished than you has also been invited? The host will come and say, 'Give this person your seat.' Then you will be embarrassed, and you will have to take whatever seat is left at the foot of the table!

"Instead, take the lowest place at the foot of the table. Then when your host sees you, he will come and say, 'Friend, we have a better place for you!' Then you will be honored in front of all the other guests. For those who exalt themselves will be humbled, and those who humble themselves will be exalted."

Then he turned to his host. "When you put on a luncheon or a banquet," he said, "don't invite your friends, brothers, relatives, and rich neighbors. For they will invite you back, and that will be your only reward. Instead, invite the poor, the crippled, the lame, and the blind. Then at the resurrection of the righteous, God will reward you for inviting those who could not repay you." LUKE 14:7-14

REALISTIC EVALUATION

How can we humble ourselves? Some people try to give the appearance of humility in order to manipulate others. Others think that humility means putting themselves down. Truly humble people compare themselves only with Christ, realize their sinfulness, and understand their limitations. On the other hand, they also recognize their gifts and strengths and are willing to use them as Christ directs. Healthy self-esteem is important because some of us think too little of ourselves. On the other hand, some of us overestimate ourselves. The key to an honest and accurate evaluation is knowing the basis of our self-worth—our identity in Christ. Apart from him, we aren't capable of very much by eternal standards; in him, we are valuable and capable of worthy service. Evaluating yourself by the worldly standards of success and achievement can cause you to think too much about your worth in the eyes of others and thus miss your true value in God's eyes. Humility is not self-degradation; it is realistic assessment and commitment to serve.

Jesus taught two lessons here: First, he spoke to the guests, telling them not to seek places of honor. Service is more important in God's Kingdom than status. Second, he told the host not to be exclusive about whom he invites. God opens his Kingdom to everyone.

Jesus tells the parable of the great feast

Hearing this, a man sitting at the table with Jesus exclaimed, "What a blessing it will be to attend a banquet in the Kingdom of God!"

Jesus replied with this story: "A man prepared a great feast and sent out many invitations. When the banquet was ready, he sent his servant to tell the guests, 'Come, the banquet is ready.' But they all began making excuses. One said, 'I have just bought a field and must inspect it. Please excuse me.' Another said, 'I have just bought five pairs of oxen, and I want to try them out. Please excuse me.' Another said, 'I now have a wife, so I can't come.'

"The servant returned and told his master what they had said. His master was furious and said, 'Go quickly into the streets and alleys of the town and invite the poor, the crippled, the blind, and the lame.' After the servant had done this, he reported, 'There is still room for more.' So his master said, 'Go out into the country lanes and behind the hedges and urge anyone you find to come, so that the house will be full. For none of those I first invited will get even the smallest taste of my banquet.'" LUKE 14:15-24

ACCEPT THE INVITATION

It was customary to send two invitations to a party—the first to announce the event; the second to tell the guests that everything was ready. The guests in Jesus' story insulted the host by making excuses when they received the second invitation. In Jesus' story, many people turned down the invitation to the banquet because the timing was inconvenient. We, too, can resist or delay responding to God's invitation, and our excuses may sound reasonable—work duties, family responsibilities, financial needs, and so forth. Nevertheless, God's invitation is the most important event in our lives, no matter how inconveniently it may be timed. What are your favorite excuses? Jesus reminds us that the time will come when God will pull his invitation and offer it to others—then it will be too late to get into the banquet.

In Israel's history, God's first invitation came from Moses and the prophets; the second came from his Son. The religious leaders accepted the first invitation. They believed that God had called them to be his people, but they insulted God by refusing to accept his Son.

September 1 READ LUKE 14:25-27

Jesus teaches about the cost of being a disciple

A large crowd was following Jesus. He turned around and said to them, "If you want to be my disciple, you must hate everyone else by comparison—your father and mother, wife and children, brothers and sisters—yes, even your own life. Otherwise, you cannot be my disciple. And if you do not carry your own cross and follow me, you cannot be my disciple." LUKE 14:25-27

TOTAL SUBMISSION

Jesus' audience was well aware of what it meant to carry one's own cross. When the Romans led a criminal to his execution site, he was forced to carry the cross on which he would die. This showed his submission to Rome and warned observers that they had better submit too. Jesus spoke this teaching to get the crowds to think through their enthusiasm for him. He encouraged those whose commitment was superficial either to go deeper or to turn back. Following Christ means total submission to him—perhaps even to the point of death. Jesus wants more than enthusiasm—he wants total dedication. Have you dedicated your life to Jesus?

To love Jesus far more than even one's family means that, ultimately, Jesus is the focus of one's life. Loved ones should never be allowed to pull a person away from Christ.

Jesus teaches about the cost of being a disciple

"But don't begin until you count the cost. For who would begin construction of a building without first calculating the cost to see if there is enough money to finish it? Otherwise, you might complete only the foundation before running out of money, and then everyone would laugh at you. They would say, 'There's the person who started that building and couldn't afford to finish it!'

"Or what king would go to war against another king without first sitting down with his counselors to discuss whether his army of 10,000 could defeat the 20,000 soldiers marching against him? And if he can't, he will send a delegation to discuss terms of peace while the enemy is still far away. So you cannot become my disciple without giving up everything you own.

"Salt is good for seasoning. But if it loses its flavor, how do you make it salty again? Flavorless salt is good neither for the soil nor for the manure pile. It is thrown away. Anyone with ears to hear should listen and understand!"

LUKE 14:28-35

STAY SALTY

Salt can lose its flavor. When it gets wet and then dries, nothing is left but a tasteless residue. Many Christians blend into the world and avoid the cost of standing up for Christ. But Jesus says if Christians lose their distinctive saltiness, they become worthless. Just as salt flavors and preserves food, we are to preserve the good in the world, help keep it from spoiling, and bring new flavor to life. Being "salty" requires careful planning, willing sacrifice, and unswerving commitment to represent Christ in the world. How salty are you?

What are the costs of the Christian life? Christians may face loss of social status or wealth. They may have to give up control over their money, their time, or their careers. They may be hated, separated from their families, and even put to death. Following Christ does not mean a trouble-free life.

Jesus tells the parable of the lost sheep

Tax collectors and other notorious sinners often came to listen to Jesus teach. This made the Pharisees and teachers of religious law complain that he was associating with such sinful people—even eating with them!

So Jesus told them this story: "If a man has a hundred sheep and one of them gets lost, what will he do? Won't he leave the ninety-nine others in the wilderness and go to search for the one that is lost until he finds it? And when he has found it, he will joyfully carry it home on his shoulders. When he arrives, he will call together his friends and neighbors, saying, 'Rejoice with me because I have found my lost sheep.' In the same way, there is more joy in heaven over one lost sinner who repents and returns to God than over ninety-nine others who are righteous and haven't strayed away!" LUKE 15:1-7

GUILT BY ASSOCIATION

Why were the Pharisees and scribes bothered that Jesus associated with sinful people? Because the religious leaders were always careful to stay "clean" according to Old Testament law. In fact, they went well beyond the law in their avoidance of certain people and situations and in their ritual washings. By contrast, Jesus took their concept of "cleanness" lightly. He risked defilement by touching those who had leprosy and by neglecting to wash in the Pharisees' prescribed manner, and he showed complete disregard for their sanctions against associating with certain classes of people. He came to offer salvation to sinners, to show that God loves them. Jesus didn't worry about the accusations. Instead, he continued going to those who needed him, regardless of the effect on his reputation. What keeps you from people who need Christ? Jesus associated with sinners because he wanted to bring the gospel of God's Kingdom to the lost sheep—people considered beyond hope. Before you were a believer, God sought you, and his love is still seeking those who are yet lost.

It may seem foolish for the shepherd to leave ninety-nine sheep to go search for just one. But the shepherd knew that the ninety-nine would be safe in the sheepfold, whereas the lost sheep was in danger. God's love for each individual is so great that he seeks each one out and rejoices when he or she is "found."

READ LUKE 15:8-10 September 4

Jesus tells the parable of the lost coin

"Or suppose a woman has ten silver coins and loses one. Won't she light a lamp and sweep the entire house and search carefully until she finds it? And when she finds it, she will call in her friends and neighbors and say, 'Rejoice with me because I have found my lost coin.' In the same way, there is joy in the presence of God's angels when even one sinner repents." LUKE 15:8-10

EXTRAORDINARY LOVE

We may be able to understand a God who would forgive sinners who come to him for mercy. But a God who tenderly searches for sinners and then joyfully forgives them must possess an extraordinary love! That is what prompted Jesus to come to earth to search for lost people and save them. God has extraordinary love for you. If you feel far from God, don't despair. He is searching for you. Each individual is precious to God. He grieves over every loss and rejoices whenever one of the lost ones is found and brought into the Kingdom.

Palestinian women received ten silver coins as a wedding gift. Besides their monetary value, these coins held sentimental value like that of a wedding ring, and to lose one of these coins would be extremely distressing. Just as a woman would rejoice at finding her lost coin or ring, so the angels rejoice over a repentant sinner.

Jesus tells the parable of the lost son

To illustrate the point further, Jesus told them this story: "A man had two sons. The younger son told his father, 'I want my share of your estate now before you die.' So his father agreed to divide his wealth between his sons.

"A few days later this younger son packed all his belongings and moved to a distant land, and there he wasted all his money in wild living. About the time his money ran out, a great famine swept over the land, and he began to starve. He persuaded a local farmer to hire him, and the man sent him into his fields to feed the pigs. The young man became so hungry that even the pods he was feeding the pigs looked good to him. But no one gave him anything.

"When he finally came to his senses, he said to himself, 'At home even the hired servants have food enough to spare, and here I am dying of hunger! I will go home to my father and say, "Father, I have sinned against both heaven and you, and I am no longer worthy of being called your son. Please take me on as a hired servant."'

"So he returned home to his father. And while he was still a long way off, his father saw him coming. Filled with love and compassion, he ran to his son, embraced him, and kissed him. His son said to him, 'Father, I have sinned against both heaven and you, and I am no longer worthy of being called your son.'

"But his father said to the servants, 'Quick! Bring the finest robe in the house and put it on him. Get a ring for his finger and sandals for his feet. And kill the calf we have been fattening. We must celebrate with a feast, for this son of mine was dead and has now returned to life. He was lost, but now he is found.' So the party began." LUKE 15:11-24

BREAKING AWAY

The younger son, like many who are rebellious and immature, wanted to be free to live as he pleased, and he had to hit bottom before he came to his senses. It often takes great sorrow and tragedy to cause people to look to the only one who can help them. Are you trying to live life your own way, selfishly pushing aside any responsibility or commitment that gets in your way? Stop and look before you hit bottom. You will save yourself and your family much grief.

In the two preceding stories, the seeker actively looked for the coin and the sheep, which could not return by themselves. In this story, the father watched and waited. He was dealing with a human being with a will of his own, but he was ready to greet his son if he returned. In the same way, God's love is constant and patient and welcoming.

Jesus tells the parable of the lost son

"Meanwhile, the older son was in the fields working. When he returned home, he heard music and dancing in the house, and he asked one of the servants what was going on. 'Your brother is back,' he was told, 'and your father has killed the fattened calf. We are celebrating because of his safe return.'

"The older brother was angry and wouldn't go in. His father came out and begged him, but he replied, 'All these years I've slaved for you and never once refused to do a single thing you told me to. And in all that time you never gave me even one young goat for a feast with my friends. Yet when this son of yours comes back after squandering your money on prostitutes, you celebrate by killing the fattened calf!'

"His father said to him, 'Look, dear son, you have always stayed by me, and everything I have is yours. We had to celebrate this happy day. For your brother was dead and has come back to life! He was lost, but now he is found!'"

LUKE 15:25-32

JOY IN FORGIVING

In the story of the lost son, the father's response is contrasted with the older brother's. The father forgave because he was filled with love. The son refused to forgive because he was bitter about the injustice of the situation. His resentment rendered him just as lost to the father's love as his younger brother had been. Don't let anything keep you from forgiving others. If you are refusing to forgive people, you are missing a wonderful opportunity to experience joy and share it with others. Make your joy grow: Forgive somebody who has hurt you.

In Jesus' story the older brother represented the Pharisees, who were angry and resentful that sinners were being welcomed into God's Kingdom. How easy it is to resent God's gracious forgiveness of others whom we consider to be far worse sinners than we are.

Jesus tells the parable of the shrewd accountant

Jesus told this story to his disciples: "There was a certain rich man who had a manager handling his affairs. One day a report came that the manager was wasting his employer's money. So the employer called him in and said, 'What's this I hear about you? Get your report in order, because you are going to be fired.'

"The manager thought to himself, 'Now what? My boss has fired me. I don't have the strength to dig ditches, and I'm too proud to beg. Ah, I know how to ensure that I'll have plenty of friends who will give me a home when I am fired.'

"So he invited each person who owed money to his employer to come and discuss the situation. He asked the first one, 'How much do you owe him?' The man replied, 'I owe him 800 gallons of olive oil.' So the manager told him, 'Take the bill and quickly change it to 400 gallons.'

"'And how much do you owe my employer?' he asked the next man. 'I owe him 1,000 bushels of wheat,' was the reply. 'Here,' the manager said, 'take the bill and change it to 800 bushels.'

"The rich man had to admire the dishonest rascal for being so shrewd. And it is true that the children of this world are more shrewd in dealing with the world around them than are the children of the light. Here's the lesson: Use your worldly resources to benefit others and make friends. Then, when your earthly possessions are gone, they will welcome you to an eternal home.

"If you are faithful in little things, you will be faithful in large ones. But if you are dishonest in little things, you won't be honest with greater responsibilities. And if you are untrustworthy about worldly wealth, who will trust you with the true riches of heaven? And if you are not faithful with other people's things, why should you be trusted with things of your own?"

LUKE 16:1-12

MONEY MATTERS MATTER

Our use of money is a good test of the lordship of Christ in our lives: (1) Our resources belong to God, and not to us, so we should use them wisely. (2) Money can be used for good or evil; let us use ours for good. (3) Money has a lot of power, so we must use it carefully and thoughtfully. (4) We must use our material goods in a way that will foster faith and obedience (Luke 12:33-34). Our integrity often meets its match in money matters. God calls us to be honest in small details so that in time we can be trusted with greater responsibility and wealth. Heaven's riches are far more valuable than earthly wealth. But if we are not trustworthy with our money here (no matter how much or little we have), we will be unfit to handle the vast riches of God's Kingdom.

Jesus tells the parable of the shrewd accountant

"No one can serve two masters. For you will hate one and love the other; you will be devoted to one and despise the other. You cannot serve both God and money."

The Pharisees, who dearly loved their money, heard all this and scoffed at him. Then he said to them, "You like to appear righteous in public, but God knows your hearts. What this world honors is detestable in the sight of God.

"Until John the Baptist, the law of Moses and the messages of the prophets were your guides. But now the Good News of the Kingdom of God is preached, and everyone is eager to get in. But that doesn't mean that the law has lost its force. It is easier for heaven and earth to disappear than for the smallest point of God's law to be overturned.

"For example, a man who divorces his wife and marries someone else commits adultery. And anyone who marries a woman divorced from her husband commits adultery." LUKE 16:13-18

MASTER MONEY

Money has the power to take God's place in your life. It can become your master. How can you tell if you are a slave to money? (1) Do you think and worry about it frequently? (2) Do you give up doing what you should do or would like to do in order to make more money? (3) Do you spend a great deal of time caring for your possessions? (4) Is it difficult for you to give money away? (5) Are you in debt?

Money is a hard master and a deceptive one. Wealth promises power and control, but often it cannot deliver. Great fortunes can be made—and lost—overnight, and no amount of money can provide health, happiness, or eternal life. How much better it is to let God be your Master. His servants have peace of mind and security, both now and forever. Heaven's riches are far more valuable than earthly wealth.

John the Baptist's ministry was the dividing line between the Old and New Testaments (John 1:15-18). With the arrival of Jesus came the realization of all the prophets' hopes. Jesus emphasized that his Kingdom fulfilled the law (the Old Testament); it did not cancel it (Matthew 5:17). His was not a new system but the culmination of the old.

Jesus tells about the rich man and the beggar

Jesus said, "There was a certain rich man who was splendidly clothed in purple and fine linen and who lived each day in luxury. At his gate lay a poor man named Lazarus who was covered with sores. As Lazarus lay there longing for scraps from the rich man's table, the dogs would come and lick his open sores.

"Finally, the poor man died and was carried by the angels to be with Abraham. The rich man also died and was buried, and his soul went to the place of the dead. There, in torment, he saw Abraham in the far distance with Lazarus at his side.

"The rich man shouted, 'Father Abraham, have some pity! Send Lazarus over here to dip the tip of his finger in water and cool my tongue. I am in anguish in these flames.'

"But Abraham said to him, 'Son, remember that during your lifetime you had everything you wanted, and Lazarus had nothing. So now he is here being comforted, and you are in anguish. And besides, there is a great chasm separating us. No one can cross over to you from here, and no one can cross over to us from there.'

"Then the rich man said, 'Please, Father Abraham, at least send him to my father's home. For I have five brothers, and I want him to warn them so they don't end up in this place of torment.'

"But Abraham said, 'Moses and the prophets have warned them. Your brothers can read what they wrote.'

"The rich man replied, 'No, Father Abraham! But if someone is sent to them from the dead, then they will repent of their sins and turn to God.'

"But Abraham said, 'If they won't listen to Moses and the prophets, they won't listen even if someone rises from the dead.'" LUKE 16:19-31

HOARD OR HELP?

The Pharisees considered wealth to be a proof of a person's righteousness. Jesus startled them with this story, where a diseased beggar is rewarded and a rich man is punished. The rich man did not go to hell because of his wealth but because he was self-centered. He refused to feed Lazarus, to take him in, or to care for him. He was hard-hearted in spite of his great blessings. The amount of money we have is not as important as the way we use it. What is your attitude toward your money and possessions? Do you hoard them selfishly, or do you use them to help others?

Jesus tells about forgiveness and faith

One day Jesus said to his disciples, "There will always be temptations to sin, but what sorrow awaits the person who does the tempting! It would be better to be thrown into the sea with a millstone hung around your neck than to cause one of these little ones to fall into sin. So watch yourselves!

"If another believer sins, rebuke that person; then if there is repentance, forgive. Even if that person wrongs you seven times a day and each time turns again and asks forgiveness, you must forgive." LUKE 17:1-4

POINTING OUT SIN

To rebuke does not mean to point out every sin we see; it means to bring sin to a person's attention with the purpose of restoring him or her to God and to fellow humans. When you feel you must rebuke another Christian for a sin, check your attitudes before you speak. Do you love the person? Are you willing to forgive? Unless rebuke is tied to forgiveness, it will not help the sinning person. It's too easy to point out someone else's faults or sins. If we feel we must admonish someone, we should be sure we are confronting that person in love and forgiveness, not because we are annoyed, inconvenienced, or seeking to blame him or her.

Jesus may have been directing this warning at the religious leaders who taught their converts their own hypocritical ways (Matthew 23:15). They were perpetuating an evil system. A person who teaches others has a solemn responsibility (James 3:1).

Jesus tells about forgiveness and faith

The apostles said to the Lord, "Show us how to increase our faith."

The Lord answered, "If you had faith even as small as a mustard seed, you could say to this mulberry tree, 'May you be uprooted and thrown into the sea,' and it would obey you!

"When a servant comes in from plowing or taking care of sheep, does his master say, 'Come in and eat with me'? No, he says, 'Prepare my meal, put on your apron, and serve me while I eat. Then you can eat later.' And does the master thank the servant for doing what he was told to do? Of course not. In the same way, when you obey me you should say, 'We are unworthy servants who have simply done our duty.'"   LUKE 17:5-10

SEED FAITH

The disciples' request was genuine; they wanted the faith necessary for such radical forgiveness. But Jesus didn't directly answer their question, because the amount of faith is not as important as its genuineness. Faith is total dependence on God and a willingness to do his will. Faith is not something we use to put on a show for others; it is complete and humble obedience to God's will, readiness to do whatever he calls us to do. A mustard seed is small, but it is alive and growing. Like a tiny seed, a small amount of genuine faith in God will take root and grow. Almost invisible at first, it will begin to spread, first under the ground and then visibly. Although each change will be gradual and imperceptible, soon this faith will have produced major results that will uproot and destroy competing loyalties. We don't need more faith; a tiny seed of faith is enough, if it is alive and growing. The amount of faith isn't as important as the right kind of faith—faith in our all-powerful God. Ask God to give you the right kind of faith and the strength to act on the faith you have.

If we have obeyed God, we have only done our duty and should regard it as a privilege. Obedience is not something extra we do; it is our duty. However, Jesus is not rendering our service as meaningless or useless, nor is he doing away with rewards. He is attacking unwarranted self-esteem and spiritual pride.

Lazarus becomes ill and dies

A man named Lazarus was sick. He lived in Bethany with his sisters, Mary and Martha. This is the Mary who later poured the expensive perfume on the Lord's feet and wiped them with her hair. Her brother, Lazarus, was sick. So the two sisters sent a message to Jesus telling him, "Lord, your dear friend is very sick."

But when Jesus heard about it he said, "Lazarus's sickness will not end in death. No, it happened for the glory of God so that the Son of God will receive glory from this." So although Jesus loved Martha, Mary, and Lazarus, he stayed where he was for the next two days. Finally, he said to his disciples, "Let's go back to Judea."

But his disciples objected. "Rabbi," they said, "only a few days ago the people in Judea were trying to stone you. Are you going there again?"

Jesus replied, "There are twelve hours of daylight every day. During the day people can walk safely. They can see because they have the light of this world. But at night there is danger of stumbling because they have no light." Then he said, "Our friend Lazarus has fallen asleep, but now I will go and wake him up."

The disciples said, "Lord, if he is sleeping, he will soon get better!" They thought Jesus meant Lazarus was simply sleeping, but Jesus meant Lazarus had died.

So he told them plainly, "Lazarus is dead. And for your sakes, I'm glad I wasn't there, for now you will really believe. Come, let's go see him."

Thomas, nicknamed the Twin, said to his fellow disciples, "Let's go, too— and die with Jesus." JOHN 11:1-16

WAITING ON GOD

Jesus loved this family and often stayed with them. He knew their pain but did not respond immediately. His delay had a specific purpose. God's timing, especially his delays, may make us think he is not answering or is not answering the way we want. But he will meet all our needs according to his perfect schedule and purpose (Philippians 4:19). If Jesus had been with Lazarus during the final moments of Lazarus's sickness, Jesus might have healed Lazarus rather than let him die. But Lazarus died so that Jesus' power over death could be shown to his disciples and others. Any trial a believer faces can ultimately bring glory to God because God can bring good out of any bad situation (Genesis 50:20; Romans 8:28). When trouble comes, do you grumble, complain, and blame God, or do you see your problems as opportunities to honor him?

Jesus comforts Mary and Martha

When Jesus arrived at Bethany, he was told that Lazarus had already been in his grave for four days. Bethany was only a few miles down the road from Jerusalem, and many of the people had come to console Martha and Mary in their loss. When Martha got word that Jesus was coming, she went to meet him. But Mary stayed in the house. Martha said to Jesus, "Lord, if only you had been here, my brother would not have died. But even now I know that God will give you whatever you ask."

Jesus told her, "Your brother will rise again."

"Yes," Martha said, "he will rise when everyone else rises, at the last day."

Jesus told her, "I am the resurrection and the life. Anyone who believes in me will live, even after dying. Everyone who lives in me and believes in me will never ever die. Do you believe this, Martha?" JOHN 11:17-26

HIS AWESOME POWER

Their brother was growing very sick, so Mary and Martha called for Jesus to help. They believed in his ability to help because they had seen his miracles. We, too, know of Jesus' miracles, both from Scripture and through the changed lives we have seen. When we need extraordinary help, Jesus offers extraordinary resources. We should not hesitate to ask him for assistance. Jesus has power over life and death as well as power to forgive sins because he is the Creator of life (John 14:6). He who *is* life can surely restore life. And whoever believes in Christ has a spiritual life that death cannot conquer or diminish in any way. When we realize Christ's power and how wonderful his offer to us really is, how can we help but commit our lives to him? To those of us who believe, what wonderful assurance and certainty we have: "Since I live, you also will live" (John 14:19)!

The village of Bethany is located about two miles east of the city of Jerusalem on the road to Jericho. It was near enough to Jerusalem for Jesus and the disciples to be in danger, but far enough away so as not to attract attention prematurely.

Jesus comforts Mary and Martha

"Yes, Lord," she told him. "I have always believed you are the Messiah, the Son of God, the one who has come into the world from God." Then she returned to Mary. She called Mary aside from the mourners and told her, "The Teacher is here and wants to see you." So Mary immediately went to him.

Jesus had stayed outside the village, at the place where Martha met him. When the people who were at the house consoling Mary saw her leave so hastily, they assumed she was going to Lazarus's grave to weep. So they followed her there. When Mary arrived and saw Jesus, she fell at his feet and said, "Lord, if only you had been here, my brother would not have died."

When Jesus saw her weeping and saw the other people wailing with her, a deep anger welled up within him, and he was deeply troubled. "Where have you put him?" he asked them.

They told him, "Lord, come and see." Then Jesus wept. The people who were standing nearby said, "See how much he loved him!" JOHN 11:27-36

JESUS CARES

When Jesus saw the weeping and wailing, he, too, wept openly. Perhaps he empathized with their grief, or perhaps he was troubled at their unbelief. In either case, Jesus showed that he cares enough for us to weep with us in our sorrow. John stresses that we have a God who cares. This portrait contrasts with the popular Greek concept that God had no emotions and no messy involvement with humans. Here we see many of Jesus' emotions—compassion, indignation, sorrow, even frustration. He often expressed deep emotion, and we must never be afraid to reveal our true feelings to him. He understands them, for he experienced them. Be honest, and don't try to hide anything from your Savior. He cares.

Martha is best known for being too busy to sit down and talk with Jesus (Luke 10:38-42). But here we see her as a woman of deep faith. Her statement of faith is exactly the response that Jesus wants from us.

Jesus raises Lazarus from the dead

But some said, "This man healed a blind man. Couldn't he have kept Lazarus from dying?"

Jesus was still angry as he arrived at the tomb, a cave with a stone rolled across its entrance. "Roll the stone aside," Jesus told them.

But Martha, the dead man's sister, protested, "Lord, he has been dead for four days. The smell will be terrible."

Jesus responded, "Didn't I tell you that you would see God's glory if you believe?" So they rolled the stone aside. Then Jesus looked up to heaven and said, "Father, thank you for hearing me. You always hear me, but I said it out loud for the sake of all these people standing here, so that they will believe you sent me." Then Jesus shouted, "Lazarus, come out!" And the dead man came out, his hands and feet bound in graveclothes, his face wrapped in a headcloth. Jesus told them, "Unwrap him and let him go!" JOHN 11:37-44

TRAGEDIES INTO TRIUMPHS

Lazarus came back to life, but he would die again physically. Yet, because he believed in Jesus, he would be raised again to eternal life. We know this because Jesus Christ came back to life. All Christians, including those living when Christ returns, will live with Christ forever. Therefore, we need not despair when loved ones die or world events take a tragic turn. God will turn our tragedies to triumphs, our poverty to riches, our pain to glory, and our defeat to victory. All believers throughout history will stand reunited in God's very presence, safe and secure. Comfort and reassure one another with this great hope.

Tombs at this time were usually caves carved in the limestone rock of a hillside. A tomb was often large enough for people to walk inside. Several bodies would be placed in one tomb. After burial, a large stone would be rolled across the entrance to the tomb.

Religious leaders plot to kill Jesus

Many of the people who were with Mary believed in Jesus when they saw this happen. But some went to the Pharisees and told them what Jesus had done. Then the leading priests and Pharisees called the high council together. "What are we going to do?" they asked each other. "This man certainly performs many miraculous signs. If we allow him to go on like this, soon everyone will believe in him. Then the Roman army will come and destroy both our Temple and our nation."

Caiaphas, who was high priest at that time, said, "You don't know what you're talking about! You don't realize that it's better for you that one man should die for the people than for the whole nation to be destroyed."

He did not say this on his own; as high priest at that time he was led to prophesy that Jesus would die for the entire nation. And not only for that nation, but to bring together and unite all the children of God scattered around the world.

So from that time on, the Jewish leaders began to plot Jesus' death.

JOHN 11:45-53

HARD HEARTS

Even when confronted point-blank with the power of Jesus' deity, some refused to believe. These eyewitnesses not only rejected Jesus; they also plotted his murder. They were so hardened that they preferred to reject God's Son rather than admit they were wrong. When we judge others, we automatically consider ourselves to be better. Beware of pride. If allowed to grow, it can lead to enormous sin.

The Jewish leaders knew that if they didn't stop Jesus, the Romans would discipline them. Rome gave partial freedom to the Jews as long as they were quiet and obedient. Jesus' miracles often caused a disturbance. The leaders feared that Rome's displeasure would bring additional hardship to their nation.

September 17

Religious leaders plot to kill Jesus

As a result, Jesus stopped his public ministry among the people and left Jerusalem. He went to a place near the wilderness, to the village of Ephraim, and stayed there with his disciples.

It was now almost time for the Jewish Passover celebration, and many people from all over the country arrived in Jerusalem several days early so they could go through the purification ceremony before Passover began. They kept looking for Jesus, but as they stood around in the Temple, they said to each other, "What do you think? He won't come for Passover, will he?" Meanwhile, the leading priests and Pharisees had publicly ordered that anyone seeing Jesus must report it immediately so they could arrest him. JOHN 11:54-57

QUIET TIME

Lazarus's return to life became the last straw for the religious leaders who were bent on killing Jesus. So Jesus stopped his public ministry and took his disciples away from Jerusalem to Ephraim, a town several miles to the north. Jesus needed time to talk to his disciples and teach them many things before he died. He wanted to get away from the conflict in Jerusalem so the disciples could rest and concentrate on his words for them. At times all of us need to get away from the busyness of our daily routines, resting and listening to God. Set aside a certain time each day when you can quietly listen and talk to God.

Passover was a holiday designed to celebrate Israel's deliverance from Egypt and to remind the people what God had done. Many Jews came to Jerusalem to celebrate this holy day.

Jesus heals ten lepers

As Jesus continued on toward Jerusalem, he reached the border between Galilee and Samaria. As he entered a village there, ten lepers stood at a distance, crying out, "Jesus, Master, have mercy on us!"

He looked at them and said, "Go show yourselves to the priests." And as they went, they were cleansed of their leprosy.

One of them, when he saw that he was healed, came back to Jesus, shouting, "Praise God!" He fell to the ground at Jesus' feet, thanking him for what he had done. This man was a Samaritan.

Jesus asked, "Didn't I heal ten men? Where are the other nine? Has no one returned to give glory to God except this foreigner?" And Jesus said to the man, "Stand up and go. Your faith has healed you." LUKE 17:11-19

GRATEFUL BELIEVERS

Jesus healed all ten lepers, but only one returned to thank him. It is possible to receive God's great gifts with an ungrateful spirit—nine of the ten men did so. Only the thankful man, however, learned that his faith had played a role in his healing; and only grateful Christians grow in understanding God's grace. God does not demand that we thank him, but he is pleased when we do so. And he uses our responsiveness to teach us more about himself.

Not only was this man a leper, he was also a Samaritan—a race despised by the Jews as idolatrous half-breeds. Once again Luke is pointing out that God's grace is for everybody.

September 19 READ LUKE 17:20-21

Jesus teaches about the coming of the Kingdom of God

One day the Pharisees asked Jesus, "When will the Kingdom of God come?"

Jesus replied, "The Kingdom of God can't be detected by visible signs. You won't be able to say, 'Here it is!' or 'It's over there!' For the Kingdom of God is already among you." LUKE 17:20-21

THE KINGDOM WITHIN

The Pharisees asked when God's Kingdom would come, not knowing that it had already arrived. The Kingdom of God is not like an earthly kingdom with geographical boundaries. Instead, it begins with the work of God's Spirit in people's lives and in relationships. When Jesus ascended into heaven, God's Kingdom would remain in the hearts of all believers through the presence of the Holy Spirit. Still today, we must resist looking to institutions or programs for evidence of the progress of God's Kingdom. Instead, we should look for what God is doing in people's hearts.

Some versions say, "The Kingdom of God is within you." The Kingdom within emphasized that it would begin with inner spiritual change. Jesus emphasized that he, the King, was in their midst.

Jesus teaches about the coming of the Kingdom of God

Then he said to his disciples, "The time is coming when you will long to see the day when the Son of Man returns, but you won't see it. People will tell you, 'Look, there is the Son of Man,' or 'Here he is,' but don't go out and follow them. For as the lightning flashes and lights up the sky from one end to the other, so it will be on the day when the Son of Man comes. But first the Son of Man must suffer terribly and be rejected by this generation.

"When the Son of Man returns, it will be like it was in Noah's day. In those days, the people enjoyed banquets and parties and weddings right up to the time Noah entered his boat and the flood came and destroyed them all.

"And the world will be as it was in the days of Lot. People went about their daily business—eating and drinking, buying and selling, farming and building—until the morning Lot left Sodom. Then fire and burning sulfur rained down from heaven and destroyed them all. Yes, it will be 'business as usual' right up to the day when the Son of Man is revealed. On that day a person out on the deck of a roof must not go down into the house to pack. A person out in the field must not return home. Remember what happened to Lot's wife! If you cling to your life, you will lose it, and if you let your life go, you will save it. That night two people will be asleep in one bed; one will be taken, the other left. Two women will be grinding flour together at the mill; one will be taken, the other left."

"Where will this happen, Lord?" the disciples asked.

Jesus replied, "Just as the gathering of vultures shows there is a carcass nearby, so these signs indicate that the end is near." LUKE 17:22-37

IT MAY BE TODAY

Life will be going on as usual on the day Christ returns. There will be no warning. Most people will be going about their everyday tasks, indifferent to the demands of God. They will be as surprised by Christ's return as the people in Noah's day were by the Flood (Genesis 6–8) or the people in Lot's day were by the destruction of Sodom (Genesis 19). We don't know the time of Christ's return, but we do know that he is coming. He may come today, tomorrow, or centuries in the future. Whenever Christ returns, we must be morally and spiritually ready. Live as if Jesus were returning today.

Jesus tells the parable of the persistent widow

One day Jesus told his disciples a story to show that they should always pray and never give up. "There was a judge in a certain city," he said, "who neither feared God nor cared about people. A widow of that city came to him repeatedly, saying, 'Give me justice in this dispute with my enemy.' The judge ignored her for a while, but finally he said to himself, 'I don't fear God or care about people, but this woman is driving me crazy. I'm going to see that she gets justice, because she is wearing me out with her constant requests!'"

Then the Lord said, "Learn a lesson from this unjust judge. Even he rendered a just decision in the end. So don't you think God will surely give justice to his chosen people who cry out to him day and night? Will he keep putting them off? I tell you, he will grant justice to them quickly! But when the Son of Man returns, how many will he find on the earth who have faith?" LUKE 18:1-8

CONSTANT PRAYER

To repeat our prayers until the answer comes does not mean endless repetition or painfully long prayer sessions. Constant prayer means keeping our requests constantly before God as we live for him day by day, believing he will answer. When we live by faith, we are not to give up. God may delay answering, but his delays always have good reasons. As we persist in prayer, we grow in character, faith, and hope.

Widows and orphans were among the most vulnerable of all God's people, and both Old Testament prophets and New Testament apostles insisted that these needy people be properly cared for. See, for example, Exodus 22:22-24; Isaiah 1:17; 1 Timothy 5:3; James 1:27.

Jesus tells the parable of two men who prayed

Then Jesus told this story to some who had great confidence in their own righteousness and scorned everyone else: "Two men went to the Temple to pray. One was a Pharisee, and the other was a despised tax collector. The Pharisee stood by himself and prayed this prayer: 'I thank you, God, that I am not a sinner like everyone else. For I don't cheat, I don't sin, and I don't commit adultery. I'm certainly not like that tax collector! I fast twice a week, and I give you a tenth of my income.'

"But the tax collector stood at a distance and dared not even lift his eyes to heaven as he prayed. Instead, he beat his chest in sorrow, saying, 'O God, be merciful to me, for I am a sinner.' I tell you, this sinner, not the Pharisee, returned home justified before God. For those who exalt themselves will be humbled, and those who humble themselves will be exalted." LUKE 18:9-14

PRIDE'S TRAP

The Pharisee did not go to the Temple to pray to God but to announce to all within earshot how good he was. The tax collector went recognizing his sin and begging for mercy. Self-righteousness is dangerous. It leads to pride, causes a person to despise others, and prevents him or her from learning anything from God. The tax collector's prayer should be our prayer because we all need God's mercy every day. Don't let pride in your achievements cut you off from God.

The people who lived near Jerusalem often went to the Temple to pray. The Temple was the center of their worship.

Jesus teaches about marriage and divorce

When Jesus had finished saying these things, he left Galilee and went down to the region of Judea east of the Jordan River. Large crowds followed him there, and he healed their sick.

Some Pharisees came and tried to trap him with this question: "Should a man be allowed to divorce his wife for just any reason?"

"Haven't you read the Scriptures?" Jesus replied. "They record that from the beginning 'God made them male and female.' And he said, 'This explains why a man leaves his father and mother and is joined to his wife, and the two are united into one.' Since they are no longer two but one, let no one split apart what God has joined together."

"Then why did Moses say in the law that a man could give his wife a written notice of divorce and send her away?" they asked.

Jesus replied, "Moses permitted divorce only as a concession to your hard hearts, but it was not what God had originally intended. And I tell you this, whoever divorces his wife and marries someone else commits adultery—unless his wife has been unfaithful."

Jesus' disciples then said to him, "If this is the case, it is better not to marry!"

"Not everyone can accept this statement," Jesus said. "Only those whom God helps. Some are born as eunuchs, some have been made eunuchs by others, and some choose not to marry for the sake of the Kingdom of Heaven. Let anyone accept this who can." MATTHEW 19:1-12 *(see also Mark 10:1-12)*

COMMITTED TO PERMANENCE

God allowed divorce as a concession to people's sinfulness. Divorce was not approved, but it was instituted to protect the injured party in a bad situation. Unfortunately, the Pharisees used Deuteronomy 24:1 as a proof text for divorce. Jesus explained that this was not God's intent; instead, God wants married people to consider their marriage permanent. Don't enter marriage with the option of getting out. Your marriage is more likely to be happy if from the outset you are committed to permanence. Don't be hard-hearted like these Pharisees, but be hardheaded in your determination, with God's help, to stay together.

Women were often treated as property. Marriage and divorce were regarded as transactions similar to buying and selling land. But Jesus condemned this attitude, clarifying God's original intention— that marriage bring oneness (Genesis 2:24).

Jesus blesses little children

One day some parents brought their children to Jesus so he could touch and bless them. But the disciples scolded the parents for bothering him.

When Jesus saw what was happening, he was angry with his disciples. He said to them, "Let the children come to me. Don't stop them! For the Kingdom of God belongs to those who are like these children. I tell you the truth, anyone who doesn't receive the Kingdom of God like a child will never enter it." Then he took the children in his arms and placed his hands on their heads and blessed them. MARK 10:13-16 *(see also Matthew 19:13-15; Luke 18:15-17)*

WELCOME THE CHILDREN

It was customary for a mother to bring her children to a rabbi for a blessing, and that is why these mothers gathered around Jesus. The disciples, however, thought the children were unworthy of the Master's time—less important than whatever else he was doing. But Jesus welcomed them because little children have the kind of faith and trust needed to enter God's Kingdom. It is important that we introduce our children to Jesus and that we ourselves approach him with childlike attitudes of acceptance, faith, and trust.

Jesus didn't mean that heaven is only for children but that people need childlike attitudes of trust in God. The receptiveness of little children was a great contrast to the stubbornness of the religious leaders who let their education and sophistication stand in the way of the simple faith needed to believe in Jesus.

September 25

Jesus speaks to the rich young man

As Jesus was starting out on his way to Jerusalem, a man came running up to him, knelt down, and asked, "Good Teacher, what must I do to inherit eternal life?"

"Why do you call me good?" Jesus asked. "Only God is truly good. But to answer your question, you know the commandments: 'You must not murder. You must not commit adultery. You must not steal. You must not testify falsely. You must not cheat anyone. Honor your father and mother.'"

"Teacher," the man replied, "I've obeyed all these commandments since I was young."

Looking at the man, Jesus felt genuine love for him. "There is still one thing you haven't done," he told him. "Go and sell all your possessions and give the money to the poor, and you will have treasure in heaven. Then come, follow me."

At this the man's face fell, and he went away sad, for he had many possessions.

Jesus looked around and said to his disciples, "How hard it is for the rich to enter the Kingdom of God!" This amazed them. But Jesus said again, "Dear children, it is very hard to enter the Kingdom of God. In fact, it is easier for a camel to go through the eye of a needle than for a rich person to enter the Kingdom of God!"

The disciples were astounded. "Then who in the world can be saved?" they asked.

Jesus looked at them intently and said, "Humanly speaking, it is impossible. But not with God. Everything is possible with God."

Then Peter began to speak up. "We've given up everything to follow you," he said.

"Yes," Jesus replied, "and I assure you that everyone who has given up house or brothers or sisters or mother or father or children or property, for my sake and for the Good News, will receive now in return a hundred times as many houses, brothers, sisters, mothers, children, and property—along with persecution. And in the world to come that person will have eternal life. But many who are the greatest now will be least important then, and those who seem least important now will be the greatest then."

MARK 10:17-31 *(see also Matthew 19:16-30; Luke 18:18-30)*

GIVING, GAINING

Peter and the other disciples had paid a high price—leaving their homes and jobs—to follow Jesus. But Jesus reminded Peter that following him has its benefits as well as its sacrifices. Any believer who has had to give up something to follow Christ will be paid back in this life as well as in the next. For example, if you must give up a secure job, you will find that God offers a secure relationship with himself now and forever. If you must give up your family's approval, you will gain the love of the family of God. The disciples had begun to pay the price of following Jesus, and Jesus said they would be rewarded. Don't dwell on what you have given up; think about what you have gained, and give thanks for it. You can never outgive God.

Jesus does not ask that all believers sell everything they have. However, because money represents power, authority, and success, often it is difficult for wealthy people to realize their need and their powerlessness to save themselves. The rich in talent or intelligence suffer the same difficulty. The person who has everything on earth can still lack what is most important— eternal life.

Jesus tells the parable of the workers paid equally

"For the Kingdom of Heaven is like the landowner who went out early one morning to hire workers for his vineyard. He agreed to pay the normal daily wage and sent them out to work.

"At nine o'clock in the morning he was passing through the marketplace and saw some people standing around doing nothing. So he hired them, telling them he would pay them whatever was right at the end of the day. So they went to work in the vineyard. At noon and again at three o'clock he did the same thing.

"At five o'clock that afternoon he was in town again and saw some more people standing around. He asked them, 'Why haven't you been working today?'

"They replied, 'Because no one hired us.'

"The landowner told them, 'Then go out and join the others in my vineyard.'

"That evening he told the foreman to call the workers in and pay them, beginning with the last workers first. When those hired at five o'clock were paid, each received a full day's wage. When those hired first came to get their pay, they assumed they would receive more. But they, too, were paid a day's wage. When they received their pay, they protested to the owner, 'Those people worked only one hour, and yet you've paid them just as much as you paid us who worked all day in the scorching heat.'

"He answered one of them, 'Friend, I haven't been unfair! Didn't you agree to work all day for the usual wage? Take your money and go. I wanted to pay this last worker the same as you. Is it against the law for me to do what I want with my money? Should you be jealous because I am kind to others?'

"So those who are last now will be first then, and those who are first will be last."   MATTHEW 20:1-16

WHO DESERVES IT?

This parable is not about rewards but about salvation. It is strong teaching about *grace*, God's generosity. We shouldn't begrudge those who turn to God in the last moments of life because, in reality, *no one* deserves eternal life.

Many people we don't expect to see in the Kingdom will be there. The criminal who repented as he was dying (Luke 23:40-43) will be there along with people who have believed and served God for many years. Do you resent God's gracious acceptance of the despised, the outcast, and the sinners who have turned to him for forgiveness? Are you ever jealous of what God has given to another person? Instead, focus on God's gracious benefits to you, and be thankful for what you have.

Jesus predicts his death for the third time

Taking the twelve disciples aside, Jesus said, "Listen, we're going up to Jerusalem, where all the predictions of the prophets concerning the Son of Man will come true. He will be handed over to the Romans, and he will be mocked, treated shamefully, and spit upon. They will flog him with a whip and kill him, but on the third day he will rise again."

But they didn't understand any of this. The significance of his words was hidden from them, and they failed to grasp what he was talking about.

LUKE 18:31-34 *(see also Matthew 20:17-19; Mark 10:32-34)*

NO ACCIDENT

Jesus' death and resurrection should have come as no surprise to the disciples. Here he clearly explained to them what would happen to him. Unfortunately, they didn't really hear what he was saying. Jesus said he was the Messiah, but they thought the Messiah would be a conquering king. He spoke to them of resurrection, but they heard only his words about death. Because Jesus often spoke in parables, the disciples may have thought that his words on death and resurrection were another parable that they weren't astute enough to understand. The Gospels include Jesus' predictions of his death and resurrection to show that these events were God's plan from the beginning. We can trust that all other biblical predictions about the future for believers will also come true.

Some predictions about what would happen to Jesus are found in Psalm 41:9 (betrayal); Psalm 22:16-18 and Isaiah 53:4-7 (crucifixion); and Psalm 16:10 (resurrection). Even though Jesus spoke plainly, the disciples would not grasp the significance of his words until they saw the risen Christ face-to-face.

Jesus teaches about serving others

Then James and John, the sons of Zebedee, came over and spoke to him. "Teacher," they said, "we want you to do us a favor."

"What is your request?" he asked.

They replied, "When you sit on your glorious throne, we want to sit in places of honor next to you, one on your right and the other on your left."

But Jesus said to them, "You don't know what you are asking! Are you able to drink from the bitter cup of suffering I am about to drink? Are you able to be baptized with the baptism of suffering I must be baptized with?"

"Oh yes," they replied, "we are able!"

Then Jesus told them, "You will indeed drink from my bitter cup and be baptized with my baptism of suffering. But I have no right to say who will sit on my right or my left. God has prepared those places for the ones he has chosen."

When the ten other disciples heard what James and John had asked, they were indignant. So Jesus called them together and said, "You know that the rulers in this world lord it over their people, and officials flaunt their authority over those under them. But among you it will be different. Whoever wants to be a leader among you must be your servant, and whoever wants to be first among you must be the slave of everyone else. For even the Son of Man came not to be served but to serve others and to give his life as a ransom for many."

MARK 10:35-45 *(see also Matthew 20:20-28)*

TRUE LEADERS

James and John wanted the highest positions in Jesus' Kingdom, but Jesus told them that true greatness comes in serving others. Jesus described leadership from a new perspective. Instead of using people, we are to serve them. Jesus' mission was to serve others and to give his life away. A real leader has a servant's heart. Most businesses, organizations, and institutions measure greatness by high personal achievement. In Christ's Kingdom, however, service is the way to get ahead. The desire to be on top will hinder, not help. Rather than seeking to have your needs met, look for ways that you can minister to the needs of others. Servant leaders appreciate others' worth and realize that they're not above any job. If you see something that needs to be done, don't wait to be asked. Take the initiative, and do it like a faithful servant.

Jesus heals a blind beggar

Then they reached Jericho, and as Jesus and his disciples left town, a large crowd followed him. A blind beggar named Bartimaeus (son of Timaeus) was sitting beside the road. When Bartimaeus heard that Jesus of Nazareth was nearby, he began to shout, "Jesus, Son of David, have mercy on me!"

"Be quiet!" many of the people yelled at him.

But he only shouted louder, "Son of David, have mercy on me!"

When Jesus heard him, he stopped and said, "Tell him to come here."

So they called the blind man. "Cheer up," they said. "Come on, he's calling you!" Bartimaeus threw aside his coat, jumped up, and came to Jesus.

"What do you want me to do for you?" Jesus asked.

"My rabbi," the blind man said, "I want to see!"

And Jesus said to him, "Go, for your faith has healed you." Instantly the man could see, and he followed Jesus down the road.

MARK 10:46-52 *(see also Matthew 20:29-34; Luke 18:35-43)*

CALL OUT

Beggars often waited along the roads near cities because that was where they were able to be seen by the most people. Usually disabled in some way, beggars were unable to earn a living. Medical help was not available for their problems, and people tended to ignore their obligations to care for the needy (Leviticus 25:35-38). Thus, beggars had little hope of escaping their degrading way of life. But this blind beggar took hope in the Messiah. He shamelessly cried out for Jesus' attention, and Jesus said that his faith had healed him. No matter how desperate your situation may seem, if you call out to Jesus in faith, he will help you.

The blind man called Jesus "Son of David," a title for the Messiah (Isaiah 11:1-3). This means that he understood Jesus to be the long-awaited Messiah. A poor and blind beggar could see that Jesus was the Messiah, while the religious leaders who saw his miracles were blinded to his identity and refused to recognize him as the Messiah.

Jesus brings salvation to Zacchaeus's home

Jesus entered Jericho and made his way through the town. There was a man there named Zacchaeus. He was the chief tax collector in the region, and he had become very rich. He tried to get a look at Jesus, but he was too short to see over the crowd. So he ran ahead and climbed a sycamore-fig tree beside the road, for Jesus was going to pass that way.

When Jesus came by, he looked up at Zacchaeus and called him by name. "Zacchaeus!" he said. "Quick, come down! I must be a guest in your home today."

Zacchaeus quickly climbed down and took Jesus to his house in great excitement and joy. But the people were displeased. "He has gone to be the guest of a notorious sinner," they grumbled. LUKE 19:1-7

LOVING THE UNLOVABLE

Tax collectors were among the most unpopular people in Israel. Jews by birth, they chose to work for Rome and were considered traitors. Besides, it was common knowledge that tax collectors were making themselves rich by gouging their fellow Jews. No wonder the people muttered when Jesus went home with the tax collector Zacchaeus. But despite the fact that Zacchaeus was both a cheater and a turncoat, Jesus loved him; and in response, the little tax collector was converted. In every society certain groups of people are considered "untouchable" because of their political views, their immoral behavior, or their lifestyle. We should not give in to social pressure to avoid these people. Jesus loves them, and they need to hear the Good News.

To finance their great world empire, the Romans levied heavy taxes on all nations under their control. The Jews opposed these taxes because they went to support a secular government and its heathen gods, but they were still forced to pay.

Jesus brings salvation to Zacchaeus's home

Meanwhile, Zacchaeus stood before the Lord and said, "I will give half my wealth to the poor, Lord, and if I have cheated people on their taxes, I will give them back four times as much!"

Jesus responded, "Salvation has come to this home today, for this man has shown himself to be a true son of Abraham. For the Son of Man came to seek and save those who are lost." LUKE 19:8-10

A CHANGED LIFE

Judging from the crowd's reaction to him, Zacchaeus must have been a very crooked tax collector. But after he met Jesus, he realized that his life needed straightening out. By giving to the poor and making restitution—with generous interest—to those he had cheated, Zacchaeus demonstrated inward change by outward action. It is not enough to follow Jesus in your head or heart alone. Intellectual assent—agreement with a set of Christian teachings—is incomplete faith. True faith transforms our lives. If our lives remain unchanged, we don't truly believe the truths we claim to believe. You must show your faith by changed behavior. Has your faith resulted in action? What changes do you need to make?

———————————•••————————————

When Jesus said Zacchaeus was a son of Abraham and yet was lost, he must have shocked his hearers in at least two ways. They would not have liked to acknowledge that this unpopular tax collector was a fellow son of Abraham, and they would not have wished to admit that sons of Abraham could be lost. But a person is not saved by a good heritage or condemned by a bad one; faith is more important than genealogy.

———————————•••————————————

Jesus tells the parable of the king's ten servants

The crowd was listening to everything Jesus said. And because he was nearing Jerusalem, he told them a story to correct the impression that the Kingdom of God would begin right away. He said, "A nobleman was called away to a distant empire to be crowned king and then return. Before he left, he called together ten of his servants and divided among them ten pounds of silver, saying, 'Invest this for me while I am gone.' But his people hated him and sent a delegation after him to say, 'We do not want him to be our king.'

"After he was crowned king, he returned and called in the servants to whom he had given the money. He wanted to find out what their profits were. The first servant reported, 'Master, I invested your money and made ten times the original amount!'

"'Well done!' the king exclaimed. 'You are a good servant. You have been faithful with the little I entrusted to you, so you will be governor of ten cities as your reward.'

"The next servant reported, 'Master, I invested your money and made five times the original amount.'

"'Well done!' the king said. 'You will be governor over five cities.'

"But the third servant brought back only the original amount of money and said, 'Master, I hid your money and kept it safe. I was afraid because you are a hard man to deal with, taking what isn't yours and harvesting crops you didn't plant.'

"'You wicked servant!' the king roared. 'Your own words condemn you. If you knew that I'm a hard man who takes what isn't mine and harvests crops I didn't plant, why didn't you deposit my money in the bank? At least I could have gotten some interest on it.'

"Then, turning to the others standing nearby, the king ordered, 'Take the money from this servant, and give it to the one who has ten pounds.'

"'But, master,' they said, 'he already has ten pounds!'

"'Yes,' the king replied, 'and to those who use well what they are given, even more will be given. But from those who do nothing, even what little they have will be taken away. And as for these enemies of mine who didn't want me to be their king—bring them in and execute them right here in front of me.'"

LUKE 19:11-27

UNTIL HE COMES

This story showed Jesus' followers what they were to do during the time between Jesus' departure and his second coming. Because we live in that time period, it applies directly to us. We have been given excellent resources to build and expand God's Kingdom. Jesus expects us to use these talents so that they multiply and the Kingdom grows. He asks each of us to account for what we do with his gifts. While awaiting the coming of the Kingdom of God in glory, we must do Christ's work. Like the king in this story, God has given you gifts to use for the benefit of his Kingdom. Do you want the Kingdom to grow? Do you trust God to govern it fairly? Are you as concerned for others' welfare as you are for your own? Are you willing to use faithfully what he has entrusted to you?

———————◆◆●◆———————

The king punished the one man because (1) he didn't share his master's interest in the kingdom, (2) he didn't trust his master's intentions, (3) his only concern was for himself, and (4) he did nothing to use the money. Some people on earth are loyal to God, while others refuse to acknowledge his lordship. Each will receive rewards or punishment.

———————◆◆●◆———————

October 3 READ MARK 14:3-9

A woman anoints Jesus with perfume

Meanwhile, Jesus was in Bethany at the home of Simon, a man who had previously had leprosy. While he was eating, a woman came in with a beautiful alabaster jar of expensive perfume made from essence of nard. She broke open the jar and poured the perfume over his head.

Some of those at the table were indignant. "Why waste such expensive perfume?" they asked. "It could have been sold for a year's wages and the money given to the poor!" So they scolded her harshly.

But Jesus replied, "Leave her alone. Why criticize her for doing such a good thing to me? You will always have the poor among you, and you can help them whenever you want to. But you will not always have me. She has done what she could and has anointed my body for burial ahead of time. I tell you the truth, wherever the Good News is preached throughout the world, this woman's deed will be remembered and discussed."

MARK 14:3-9 *(see also Matthew 26:6-13; John 12:1-11)*

TRUE WORSHIP

This perfume was made from pure nard, a fragrant ointment imported from the mountains of India. The amount Mary used was worth a year's wages. This act and Jesus' response to it do not teach us to ignore the poor so we can spend money extravagantly for Christ. This was a unique act for a specific occasion—an anointing that anticipated Jesus' burial and a public declaration of faith in him as Messiah. Jesus was praising Mary for her unselfish act of worship. The essence of worshiping Christ is to regard him with the utmost love, respect, and devotion and to be willing to sacrifice to him what is most precious.

John mentions that Judas was indignant (John 12:4-5). Judas's indignation over Mary's act of worship was based not on concern for the poor but on greed. Because Judas was the treasurer of Jesus' ministry and had embezzled funds (John 12:6), he no doubt wanted the perfume sold so that he could benefit from the proceeds.

Jesus rides into Jerusalem on a donkey

After telling this story, Jesus went on toward Jerusalem, walking ahead of his disciples. As he came to the towns of Bethphage and Bethany on the Mount of Olives, he sent two disciples ahead. "Go into that village over there," he told them. "As you enter it, you will see a young donkey tied there that no one has ever ridden. Untie it and bring it here. If anyone asks, 'Why are you untying that colt?' just say, 'The Lord needs it.'"

So they went and found the colt, just as Jesus had said. And sure enough, as they were untying it, the owners asked them, "Why are you untying that colt?"

And the disciples simply replied, "The Lord needs it." So they brought the colt to Jesus and threw their garments over it for him to ride on.

LUKE 19:28-35 *(see also Matthew 21:1-7; Mark 11:1-7; John 12:12-19)*

PEACEABLE KING

Jesus came, not as a warring king on a horse or in a chariot, but as a gentle and peaceable king on a donkey's colt, just as Zechariah 9:9 had predicted. After Jesus' resurrection, the disciples would understand for the first time many of the prophecies that they had missed along the way. Jesus' words and actions would take on new meaning and make more sense. In retrospect, the disciples saw how Jesus had led them into a deeper and better understanding of his truth. Reflect on the events leading up to where you are now spiritually. How has God led you to this point? As you grow older, you will look back and see God's involvement more clearly than you do now. Stop right now and thank God for what he has done for you and how he led you to himself.

Jesus began his last week on earth by riding into Jerusalem on a donkey under a canopy of palm branches, with crowds hailing him as their king. The great Passover festival was about to begin, and Jews had come to Jerusalem from all over the Roman world during this weeklong celebration. On Palm Sunday we celebrate Jesus' triumphal entry into Jerusalem.

October 5 READ MATTHEW 21:8-11

Jesus rides into Jerusalem on a donkey

Most of the crowd spread their garments on the road ahead of him, and others cut branches from the trees and spread them on the road. Jesus was in the center of the procession, and the people all around him were shouting, "Praise God for the Son of David! Blessings on the one who comes in the name of the LORD! Praise God in highest heaven!"

The entire city of Jerusalem was in an uproar as he entered. "Who is this?" they asked.

And the crowds replied, "It's Jesus, the prophet from Nazareth in Galilee."

MATTHEW 21:8-11 *(see also Mark 11:8-11; Luke 19:36-44)*

THE WRONG IDEA

The people who were praising God for giving them a king had the wrong idea about Jesus. They expected him to be a national leader who would restore their nation to its former glory, and thus they were deaf to the words of their prophets and blind to Jesus' real mission. When it became apparent that Jesus was not going to fulfill their hopes, many people turned against him. The Jewish leaders rejected their King (Luke 19:47). They rejected God's offer of salvation in Jesus Christ when they were visited by God himself, and soon their nation would suffer. God did not turn away from the Jewish people who obeyed him, however, and he continues to offer salvation to the people he loves, both Jews and Gentiles. Eternal life is within your reach—accept it while the opportunity is still offered.

Upon approaching Jerusalem, Jesus wept and prophesied the city's destruction due to its rejection of him (Luke 19:41-44). About forty years after Jesus made this prediction, his words came true. In AD 66, the Jews revolted against Roman control. Three years later Titus, son of the emperor Vespasian, was sent to crush the rebellion. Roman soldiers laid siege to Jerusalem, and in AD 70 they entered the city and burned it. Six hundred thousand Jews were killed during Titus's onslaught.

Jesus clears the Temple again

The next morning as they were leaving Bethany, Jesus was hungry. He noticed a fig tree in full leaf a little way off, so he went over to see if he could find any figs. But there were only leaves because it was too early in the season for fruit. Then Jesus said to the tree, "May no one ever eat your fruit again!" And the disciples heard him say it.

When they arrived back in Jerusalem, Jesus entered the Temple and began to drive out the people buying and selling animals for sacrifices. He knocked over the tables of the money changers and the chairs of those selling doves, and he stopped everyone from using the Temple as a marketplace. He said to them, "The Scriptures declare, 'My Temple will be called a house of prayer for all nations,' but you have turned it into a den of thieves."

When the leading priests and teachers of religious law heard what Jesus had done, they began planning how to kill him. But they were afraid of him because the people were so amazed at his teaching.

That evening Jesus and the disciples left the city.

MARK 11:12-19 *(see also Matthew 21:12-13; Luke 19:45-48)*

WHEN TO GET ANGRY

This is the second time Jesus cleared the Temple (John 2:13-17). Merchants and money changers had set up their booths in the court of the Gentiles in the Temple, crowding out the Gentiles who had come from all over the civilized world to worship God. The merchants sold sacrificial animals at high prices, taking advantage of those who had come long distances. The money changers exchanged all international currency for the special Temple coins—the only money the merchants would accept. They often deceived foreigners who didn't know the exchange rates. Their commercialism in God's house frustrated people's attempts at worship. This, of course, greatly angered Jesus, but he did not sin in his anger. Christians should be upset about sin and injustice and should take a stand against them. Unfortunately, believers are often passive about these important issues and get angry instead over personal insults and petty irritations.

The leaders had several reasons for wanting to get rid of Jesus, mostly the fact that he had damaged their business in the Temple by driving the merchants out, preaching against injustice, and favoring the poor over the rich. Also, his great popularity was in danger of attracting Rome's attention.

Jesus explains why he must die

Some Greeks who had come to Jerusalem for the Passover celebration paid a visit to Philip, who was from Bethsaida in Galilee. They said, "Sir, we want to meet Jesus." Philip told Andrew about it, and they went together to ask Jesus.

Jesus replied, "Now the time has come for the Son of Man to enter into his glory. I tell you the truth, unless a kernel of wheat is planted in the soil and dies, it remains alone. But its death will produce many new kernels—a plentiful harvest of new lives. Those who love their life in this world will lose it. Those who care nothing for their life in this world will keep it for eternity."

JOHN 12:20-25

LOVE AND HATE

This is a beautiful picture of the necessary sacrifice of Jesus. Unless a grain of wheat is buried in the ground, it will not become a blade of wheat producing many more seeds. Jesus had to die to pay the penalty for our sin, but also to show his power over death. Jesus calls us to be so committed to living for God that we "hate" our lives by comparison. This does not mean that we long to die or that we are careless or destructive with the life God has given but that we are willing to die if doing so will glorify Christ. We must disown the tyrannical rule of our own self-centeredness. By laying aside our striving for advantage, security, and pleasure, we can serve God lovingly and freely. Releasing control of our lives and transferring that control to Christ bring eternal life and genuine joy.

These Greeks probably were converts to the Jewish faith. They may have gone to Philip because, though he was a Jew, he had a Greek name.

Jesus explains why he must die

"Anyone who wants to be my disciple must follow me, because my servants must be where I am. And the Father will honor anyone who serves me.

"Now my soul is deeply troubled. Should I pray, 'Father, save me from this hour'? But this is the very reason I came! Father, bring glory to your name."

Then a voice spoke from heaven, saying, "I have already brought glory to my name, and I will do so again." When the crowd heard the voice, some thought it was thunder, while others declared an angel had spoken to him.

Then Jesus told them, "The voice was for your benefit, not mine. The time for judging this world has come, when Satan, the ruler of this world, will be cast out. And when I am lifted up from the earth, I will draw everyone to myself." He said this to indicate how he was going to die.

The crowd responded, "We understood from Scripture that the Messiah would live forever. How can you say the Son of Man will die? Just who is this Son of Man, anyway?"

Jesus replied, "My light will shine for you just a little longer. Walk in the light while you can, so the darkness will not overtake you. Those who walk in the darkness cannot see where they are going. Put your trust in the light while there is still time; then you will become children of the light."

After saying these things, Jesus went away and was hidden from them.

JOHN 12:26-36

WHOM DO YOU SEEK?

The crowd could not believe what Jesus was saying about the Messiah. They were waving palm branches for a victorious leader who would set up a political, earthly kingdom that would never end. From their reading of certain Scriptures, they thought the Messiah would never die (Psalms 89:35-36; 110:4; Isaiah 9:7). Other passages, however, showed that he would (Isaiah 53:5-9). Jesus' words did not mesh with the crowd's concept of the Messiah! First he had to suffer and die—then he would one day set up his eternal Kingdom. What kind of Messiah, or Savior, are *you* seeking? Beware of trying to force Jesus into your own mold—he won't fit.

The ruler of this world is Satan, an angel who rebelled against God. Satan is real, not symbolic, and is constantly working against God and those who obey him. Satan has great power, but people can be delivered from his reign of spiritual darkness because of Christ's victory on the cross. Satan is powerful, but Jesus is much more powerful.

October 9 READ JOHN 12:37-43

Most of the people do not believe in Jesus

But despite all the miraculous signs Jesus had done, most of the people still did not believe in him. This is exactly what Isaiah the prophet had predicted: "LORD, who has believed our message? To whom has the LORD revealed his powerful arm?" But the people couldn't believe, for as Isaiah also said, "The Lord has blinded their eyes and hardened their hearts—so that their eyes cannot see, and their hearts cannot understand, and they cannot turn to me and have me heal them." Isaiah was referring to Jesus when he said this, because he saw the future and spoke of the Messiah's glory. Many people did believe in him, however, including some of the Jewish leaders. But they wouldn't admit it for fear that the Pharisees would expel them from the synagogue. For they loved human praise more than the praise of God. JOHN 12:37-43*

TEMPORARY PRAISE

Along with those who refused to believe, many believed but refused to admit it. This is just as bad, and Jesus had strong words for such people (Matthew 10:32-33). People who will not take a stand for Jesus are afraid of rejection or ridicule. Many Jewish leaders wouldn't admit to faith in Jesus because they feared excommunication from the synagogue (which was their livelihood) and loss of their prestigious place in the community. But the praise of others is fickle and short-lived. We should be much more concerned about God's eternal acceptance than about the temporary approval of other people.

People in Jesus' time, like those in the time of Isaiah, would not believe despite the evidence (John 12:37). As a result, God hardened their hearts. Does that mean God intentionally prevented these people from believing in him? No, he simply confirmed their own choices. For such people, it is virtually impossible to come to God.

Jesus summarizes his message

Jesus shouted to the crowds, "If you trust me, you are trusting not only me, but also God who sent me. For when you see me, you are seeing the one who sent me. I have come as a light to shine in this dark world, so that all who put their trust in me will no longer remain in the dark. I will not judge those who hear me but don't obey me, for I have come to save the world and not to judge it. But all who reject me and my message will be judged on the day of judgment by the truth I have spoken. I don't speak on my own authority. The Father who sent me has commanded me what to say and how to say it. And I know his commands lead to eternal life; so I say whatever the Father tells me to say."   JOHN 12:44-50

DECISION TIME

The purpose of Jesus' first mission on earth was not to judge people but to show them the way to find salvation and eternal life. When he comes again, one of his main purposes will be to judge people for how they lived on earth. Christ's words we would *not* accept and obey will condemn us. On the Day of Judgment, those who have accepted Jesus and have lived his way will be raised to eternal life (1 Corinthians 15:51-57; 1 Thessalonians 4:15-18; Revelation 21:1-7), and those who have rejected Jesus and have lived any way they pleased will face eternal punishment (Revelation 21:8). Decide now which side you'll be on, for the consequences of your decision last forever.

We often wonder what God is like. How can we know the Creator when he doesn't make himself visible? Jesus said plainly that those who see him see God because he is God. If you want to know what God is like, study the person and words of Jesus Christ.

Jesus says the disciples can pray for anything

The next morning as they passed by the fig tree he had cursed, the disciples noticed it had withered from the roots up. Peter remembered what Jesus had said to the tree on the previous day and exclaimed, "Look, Rabbi! The fig tree you cursed has withered and died!"

Then Jesus said to the disciples, "Have faith in God. I tell you the truth, you can say to this mountain, 'May you be lifted up and thrown into the sea,' and it will happen. But you must really believe it will happen and have no doubt in your heart. I tell you, you can pray for anything, and if you believe that you've received it, it will be yours. But when you are praying, first forgive anyone you are holding a grudge against, so that your Father in heaven will forgive your sins, too." MARK 11:20-25 *(see also Matthew 21:18-22)*

THE PRAYER OF FAITH

The kind of prayer that moves mountains is prayer for the fruitfulness of God's Kingdom. It would seem impossible to move a mountain into the sea, so Jesus used that picture to say that God can do anything. God will answer your prayers, but not as a result of your positive mental attitude. Other conditions must be met: (1) You must be a believer; (2) you must not hold a grudge against another person; (3) you must not pray with selfish motives; and (4) your request must be for the good of God's Kingdom. To pray effectively, you need faith in *God*, not faith in the object of your request. If you focus only on your request, you will be left with nothing when your request is refused. Be a person of prayer, and watch God move mountains.

Jesus' judgment on the fig tree occurred early in the spring fig season when the leaves usually would begin to bud. The figs normally grow as the leaves fill out, but this tree, though full of leaves, had no fruit. The tree looked promising but offered no figs. Jesus' harsh words to the fig tree could be applied to the nation of Israel. Fruitful in appearance only, Israel was spiritually barren.

Religious leaders challenge Jesus' authority

Again they entered Jerusalem. As Jesus was walking through the Temple area, the leading priests, the teachers of religious law, and the elders came up to him. They demanded, "By what authority are you doing all these things? Who gave you the right to do them?"

"I'll tell you by what authority I do these things if you answer one question," Jesus replied. "Did John's authority to baptize come from heaven, or was it merely human? Answer me!"

They talked it over among themselves. "If we say it was from heaven, he will ask why we didn't believe John. But do we dare say it was merely human?" For they were afraid of what the people would do, because everyone believed that John was a prophet. So they finally replied, "We don't know."

And Jesus responded, "Then I won't tell you by what authority I do these things." MARK 11:27-33 *(see also Matthew 21:23-27; Luke 20:1-8)*

TRUE MOTIVES

The religious leaders asked Jesus who had given him the authority to chase away the merchants and money changers. Their question was a trap. If Jesus said his authority was from God, they would accuse him of blasphemy; if he said his authority was his own, they would dismiss him as a fanatic. To expose their real motives, Jesus countered their question with a question about John the Baptist. The leaders' silence proved that they were not interested in the truth. They simply wanted to get rid of Jesus because he was undermining their authority. Sometimes people will ask questions about your faith to try to trip you up or make fun of you. Others will ask questions sincerely looking for answers. Spend your time with those who really want answers.

Jesus took the Jewish leaders' trap and turned it back on them. How exasperated they must have been that they were unable to get Jesus to say anything that they could use against him!

Jesus tells the parable of the two sons

"But what do you think about this? A man with two sons told the older boy, 'Son, go out and work in the vineyard today.' The son answered, 'No, I won't go,' but later he changed his mind and went anyway. Then the father told the other son, 'You go,' and he said, 'Yes, sir, I will.' But he didn't go.

"Which of the two obeyed his father?"

They replied, "The first."

Then Jesus explained his meaning: "I tell you the truth, corrupt tax collectors and prostitutes will get into the Kingdom of God before you do. For John the Baptist came and showed you the right way to live, but you didn't believe him, while tax collectors and prostitutes did. And even when you saw this happening, you refused to believe him and repent of your sins."

MATTHEW 21:28-32

PHONIES

The son who said he would obey and then didn't represented the nation of Israel in Jesus' day. The people said they wanted to do God's will, but they constantly disobeyed. They were phony, just going through the motions. It is dangerous to pretend to obey God when our hearts are far from him because God knows our true intentions. Our actions must match our words. *Knowing* God's will is not the same as *doing* it. Don't just go through the motions.

———————————————●●———————————————

This indictment surely made the Jewish leaders furious. That such people as evil men and prostitutes could be in heaven and not the pious leaders was absurd. But Jesus turns the world's values upside down.

———————————————●●———————————————

Jesus tells the parable of the wicked farmers

"Now listen to another story. A certain landowner planted a vineyard, built a wall around it, dug a pit for pressing out the grape juice, and built a lookout tower. Then he leased the vineyard to tenant farmers and moved to another country. At the time of the grape harvest, he sent his servants to collect his share of the crop. But the farmers grabbed his servants, beat one, killed one, and stoned another. So the landowner sent a larger group of his servants to collect for him, but the results were the same.

"Finally, the owner sent his son, thinking, 'Surely they will respect my son.'

"But when the tenant farmers saw his son coming, they said to one another, 'Here comes the heir to this estate. Come on, let's kill him and get the estate for ourselves!' So they grabbed him, dragged him out of the vineyard, and murdered him.

"When the owner of the vineyard returns," Jesus asked, "what do you think he will do to those farmers?"

The religious leaders replied, "He will put the wicked men to a horrible death and lease the vineyard to others who will give him his share of the crop after each harvest."

Then Jesus asked them, "Didn't you ever read this in the Scriptures? 'The stone that the builders rejected has now become the cornerstone. This is the LORD's doing, and it is wonderful to see.' I tell you, the Kingdom of God will be taken away from you and given to a nation that will produce the proper fruit. Anyone who stumbles over that stone will be broken to pieces, and it will crush anyone it falls on."

When the leading priests and Pharisees heard this parable, they realized he was telling the story against them—they were the wicked farmers. They wanted to arrest him, but they were afraid of the crowds, who considered Jesus to be a prophet. MATTHEW 21:33-46 *(see also Mark 12:1-12; Luke 20:9-19)*

STUMBLING STONE

The characters in this story are easily identified. Even the religious leaders got the point. The owner of the vineyard is God; the vineyard is Israel; the vinedressers are the religious leaders; the servants are the prophets and priests God sent to Israel; the son is the Messiah, Jesus; and the others are the Gentiles. Jesus' parable indirectly answered the religious leaders' question about his authority; it also showed them that he knew about their plan to kill him. There is no difference between those who ignore Christ and those who refuse to believe. All who stumble over Jesus, the Cornerstone, will be judged in the end. When sharing your faith, keep the focus on Christ. He's the only one who really matters.

Jesus tells the parable of the wedding feast

Jesus also told them other parables. He said, "The Kingdom of Heaven can be illustrated by the story of a king who prepared a great wedding feast for his son. When the banquet was ready, he sent his servants to notify those who were invited. But they all refused to come!

"So he sent other servants to tell them, 'The feast has been prepared. The bulls and fattened cattle have been killed, and everything is ready. Come to the banquet!' But the guests he had invited ignored them and went their own way, one to his farm, another to his business. Others seized his messengers and insulted them and killed them.

"The king was furious, and he sent out his army to destroy the murderers and burn their town. And he said to his servants, 'The wedding feast is ready, and the guests I invited aren't worthy of the honor. Now go out to the street corners and invite everyone you see.' So the servants brought in everyone they could find, good and bad alike, and the banquet hall was filled with guests.

"But when the king came in to meet the guests, he noticed a man who wasn't wearing the proper clothes for a wedding. 'Friend,' he asked, 'how is it that you are here without wedding clothes?' But the man had no reply. Then the king said to his aides, 'Bind his hands and feet and throw him into the outer darkness, where there will be weeping and gnashing of teeth.'

"For many are called, but few are chosen." MATTHEW 22:1-14

R.S.V.P.

In this culture, two invitations were expected when wedding dinners were given. The first invitation asked the guests to attend; the second one announced that all was ready. In this story the king invited his guests three times, and each time they rejected his invitation. God wants us to join him at his banquet, which will last for eternity. That's why he sends us invitations again and again. What should you do to accept his invitation?

———————————●●●————————————

It was customary for wedding guests to be given special clothes to wear to the dinner. It was unthinkable to refuse to wear them. That would insult the host, who could assume only that guests were arrogant and thought they didn't need them or that they didn't want to take part in the wedding celebration. The wedding clothes picture the righteousness needed to enter God's Kingdom.

———————————●●●————————————

Religious leaders question Jesus about taxes

*Later the leaders sent some Pharisees and supporters of Herod to trap Jesus
into saying something for which he could be arrested. "Teacher," they said, "we
know how honest you are. You are impartial and don't play favorites. You teach
the way of God truthfully. Now tell us—is it right to pay taxes to Caesar or not?
Should we pay them, or shouldn't we?"*

*Jesus saw through their hypocrisy and said, "Why are you trying to trap me?
Show me a Roman coin, and I'll tell you." When they handed it to him, he asked,
"Whose picture and title are stamped on it?"*

"Caesar's," they replied.

*"Well, then," Jesus said, "give to Caesar what belongs to Caesar, and give to
God what belongs to God."*

His reply completely amazed them.

MARK 12:13-17 *(see also Matthew 22:15-22; Luke 20:20-26)*

WHOSE IMAGE?

Anyone who avoided paying taxes faced harsh penalties. The Jews hated to pay
taxes to Rome because the money supported their oppressors and symbolized their
subjection. Much of the tax money also went to maintain the heathen temples and
luxurious lifestyles of Rome's upper class. The Pharisees and Herodians hoped to
trap Jesus with this tax question. A yes would mean that he supported Rome—this
would turn the people against him. A no would bring accusations of treason and
rebellion against Rome and could lead to civil penalties. Jesus answered wisely,
saying that the coin bearing the emperor's image should be given to the emperor.
But human lives, which bear God's image, belong to God. Are you giving God all
that is rightfully his? Give your life to God—you bear his image.

---

*The Pharisees were primarily a religious group concerned for ritual
purity; the Herodians were a Jewish political group that approved
of Herod's compromises with Rome. Normally the two groups
totally avoided each other.*

Religious leaders question Jesus about the Resurrection

Then Jesus was approached by some Sadducees—religious leaders who say there is no resurrection from the dead. They posed this question: "Teacher, Moses gave us a law that if a man dies, leaving a wife without children, his brother should marry the widow and have a child who will carry on the brother's name. Well, suppose there were seven brothers. The oldest one married and then died without children. So the second brother married the widow, but he also died without children. Then the third brother married her. This continued with all seven of them, and still there were no children. Last of all, the woman also died. So tell us, whose wife will she be in the resurrection? For all seven were married to her."

Jesus replied, "Your mistake is that you don't know the Scriptures, and you don't know the power of God. For when the dead rise, they will neither marry nor be given in marriage. In this respect they will be like the angels in heaven.

"But now, as to whether the dead will be raised—haven't you ever read about this in the writings of Moses, in the story of the burning bush? Long after Abraham, Isaac, and Jacob had died, God said to Moses, 'I am the God of Abraham, the God of Isaac, and the God of Jacob.' So he is the God of the living, not the dead. You have made a serious error."

MARK 12:18-27 *(see also Matthew 22:23-32; Luke 20:27-40)*

FUTURE LIFE

What life will be like after the Resurrection is far beyond our ability to understand or imagine (Isaiah 64:4; 1 Corinthians 2:9). We need not be afraid of eternal life because of the unknowns, however. Jesus' statement does not mean that people won't recognize their partners in the coming Kingdom. It simply means that God's new order will not be an extension of this life and that the same physical and natural rules won't apply. Instead of wondering what God's coming Kingdom will be like, we should concentrate on our relationship with Christ right now, because in the new Kingdom we will be with him. If we learn to love and trust Christ *now*, we will not be afraid of the future.

The Sadducees' real question was not about marriage but about the doctrine of resurrection. Because the Sadducees followed only the Pentateuch (Genesis through Deuteronomy), Jesus quoted from Exodus 3:6 to prove that there is life after death. God spoke of Abraham, Isaac, and Jacob years after their deaths as if they still lived. God's covenant with people exists beyond death.

Religious leaders question Jesus about the greatest commandment

One of the teachers of religious law was standing there listening to the debate. He realized that Jesus had answered well, so he asked, "Of all the commandments, which is the most important?"

Jesus replied, "The most important commandment is this: 'Listen, O Israel! The LORD our God is the one and only LORD. And you must love the LORD your God with all your heart, all your soul, all your mind, and all your strength.' The second is equally important: 'Love your neighbor as yourself.' No other commandment is greater than these."

The teacher of religious law replied, "Well said, Teacher. You have spoken the truth by saying that there is only one God and no other. And I know it is important to love him with all my heart and all my understanding and all my strength, and to love my neighbor as myself. This is more important than to offer all of the burnt offerings and sacrifices required in the law."

Realizing how much the man understood, Jesus said to him, "You are not far from the Kingdom of God." And after that, no one dared to ask him any more questions. MARK 12:28-34 *(see also Matthew 22:33-40)*

LAW OF LOVE

God's laws are not burdensome. They can be reduced to two simple principles: (1) Love God, and (2) love others. These commands are from the Old Testament (Deuteronomy 6:5; Leviticus 19:18). When you love God completely and care for others as you care for yourself, then you have fulfilled the intent of the Ten Commandments and the other Old Testament laws. According to Jesus, these two commandments summarize all God's laws. Let them rule your thoughts, decisions, and actions. When you are uncertain about what to do, ask yourself which course of action best demonstrates love for God and love for others.

The Pharisees, who had classified over six hundred laws, often tried to distinguish the more important from the less important. But they failed to see that all the commands in the Old Testament lead to Christ.

Religious leaders cannot answer Jesus' question

Then, surrounded by the Pharisees, Jesus asked them a question: "What do you think about the Messiah? Whose son is he?"

They replied, "He is the son of David."

Jesus responded, "Then why does David, speaking under the inspiration of the Spirit, call the Messiah 'my Lord'? For David said, 'The LORD said to my Lord, Sit in the place of honor at my right hand until I humble your enemies beneath your feet.' Since David called the Messiah 'my Lord,' how can the Messiah be his son?"

No one could answer him. And after that, no one dared to ask him any more questions.   MATTHEW 22:41-46 *(see also Mark 12:35-37; Luke 20:41-44)*

THE MOST IMPORTANT QUESTION

The Pharisees and Sadducees had asked their questions. Then Jesus turned the tables and asked them a question that went right to the heart of the matter—what they thought about the Messiah's identity. The Pharisees knew that the Messiah would be a descendant of David, but they did not understand that he would be more than a human descendant—he would be God in the flesh. Jesus quoted from Psalm 110:1 to show that David had known that the Messiah would be both human and divine. The Pharisees expected only a human ruler to restore Israel's greatness as in the days of David and Solomon. The central issue of life is what we believe about Jesus. Other spiritual questions are irrelevant unless we first believe that Jesus is who he said.

The Jewish religious leaders should have been the first to recognize Jesus as the promised Messiah, rejoice over his arrival, and lead the nation to follow him. Instead, they refused to believe.

Jesus warns against the religious leaders

Then Jesus said to the crowds and to his disciples, "The teachers of religious law and the Pharisees are the official interpreters of the law of Moses. So practice and obey whatever they tell you, but don't follow their example. For they don't practice what they teach. They crush people with unbearable religious demands and never lift a finger to ease the burden.

"Everything they do is for show. On their arms they wear extra wide prayer boxes with Scripture verses inside, and they wear robes with extra long tassels. And they love to sit at the head table at banquets and in the seats of honor in the synagogues. They love to receive respectful greetings as they walk in the marketplaces, and to be called 'Rabbi.'

"Don't let anyone call you 'Rabbi,' for you have only one teacher, and all of you are equal as brothers and sisters. And don't address anyone here on earth as 'Father,' for only God in heaven is your spiritual Father. And don't let anyone call you 'Teacher,' for you have only one teacher, the Messiah. The greatest among you must be a servant. But those who exalt themselves will be humbled, and those who humble themselves will be exalted."

MATTHEW 23:1-12 *(see also Mark 12:38-40; Luke 20:45-47)*

MAKE SURE THEY MATCH

Jesus again exposed the hypocritical attitudes of the religious leaders who knew the Scriptures but did not live by them. The Pharisees' traditions and their interpretations and applications of the laws had become as important to them as God's law itself. Their laws were not all bad—some were beneficial. Usually Jesus did not condemn what the Pharisees taught but who they *were*—hypocrites. They didn't care about *being* holy but just about *looking* holy in order to receive the people's admiration and praise. Today many people, like the Pharisees, know the Bible but do not let it change their lives. They say they follow Jesus, but they don't live by his standards of love. Make sure that your actions match your beliefs.

The little prayer boxes, called phylacteries, contained Scripture verses. Very religious people wore these boxes on their foreheads and arms in order to obey Deuteronomy 6:8 and Exodus 13:9, 16. But the prayer boxes had become more important for the status they gave than for the truth they contained.

Jesus condemns the religious leaders

"What sorrow awaits you teachers of religious law and you Pharisees. Hypocrites! For you shut the door of the Kingdom of Heaven in people's faces. You won't go in yourselves, and you don't let others enter either.

"What sorrow awaits you teachers of religious law and you Pharisees. Hypocrites! For you cross land and sea to make one convert, and then you turn that person into twice the child of hell you yourselves are!

"Blind guides! What sorrow awaits you! For you say that it means nothing to swear 'by God's Temple,' but that it is binding to swear 'by the gold in the Temple.' Blind fools! Which is more important—the gold or the Temple that makes the gold sacred? And you say that to swear 'by the altar' is not binding, but to swear 'by the gifts on the altar' is binding. How blind! For which is more important— the gift on the altar or the altar that makes the gift sacred? When you swear 'by the altar,' you are swearing by it and by everything on it. And when you swear 'by the Temple,' you are swearing by it and by God, who lives in it. And when you swear 'by heaven,' you are swearing by the throne of God and by God, who sits on the throne.

"What sorrow awaits you teachers of religious law and you Pharisees. Hypocrites! For you are careful to tithe even the tiniest income from your herb gardens, but you ignore the more important aspects of the law—justice, mercy, and faith. You should tithe, yes, but do not neglect the more important things. Blind guides! You strain your water so you won't accidentally swallow a gnat, but you swallow a camel!

"What sorrow awaits you teachers of religious law and you Pharisees. Hypocrites! For you are so careful to clean the outside of the cup and the dish, but inside you are filthy—full of greed and self-indulgence! You blind Pharisee! First wash the inside of the cup and the dish, and then the outside will become clean, too.

"What sorrow awaits you teachers of religious law and you Pharisees. Hypocrites! For you are like whitewashed tombs—beautiful on the outside but filled on the inside with dead people's bones and all sorts of impurity. Outwardly you look like righteous people, but inwardly your hearts are filled with hypocrisy and lawlessness.

"What sorrow awaits you teachers of religious law and you Pharisees. Hypocrites! For you build tombs for the prophets your ancestors killed, and you decorate the monuments of the godly people your ancestors destroyed. Then you say, 'If we had lived in the days of our ancestors, we would never have joined them in killing the prophets.'

"But in saying that, you testify against yourselves that you are indeed the descendants of those who murdered the prophets. Go ahead and finish what your ancestors started. Snakes! Sons of vipers! How will you escape the judgment of hell?

"Therefore, I am sending you prophets and wise men and teachers of religious law. But you will kill some by crucifixion, and you will flog others with whips in your synagogues, chasing them from city to city. As a result, you will be held responsible for the murder of all godly people of all time—from the murder of righteous Abel to the murder of Zechariah son of Barachiah, whom you killed in the Temple between the sanctuary and the altar. I tell you the truth, this judgment will fall on this very generation." MATTHEW 23:13-36

DON'T SWALLOW A CAMEL!

The Pharisees strained their water so they wouldn't accidentally swallow a gnat—an unclean insect according to the law. Meticulous about the details of ceremonial cleanliness, they nevertheless had lost their perspective on inner purity. Ceremonially clean on the outside, they had corrupt hearts. It's possible to obey the details of the law but still be disobedient in our general behavior. Jesus condemned the Pharisees and religious leaders for *appearing* saintly and holy but inwardly remaining full of corruption and greed. Living our Christianity merely as a show for others is like washing a cup on the outside only. When we are clean on the inside, our cleanliness on the outside won't be a sham.

Being a religious leader in Jerusalem was very different from being a pastor in a secular society today. Israel's history, culture, and daily life centered around its relationship with God. The religious leaders were the best known, most powerful, and most respected of all leaders. Jesus made these stinging accusations because the leaders' hunger for more power, money, and status had made them lose sight of God and their blindness was spreading to the whole nation.

Jesus grieves over Jerusalem again

"O Jerusalem, Jerusalem, the city that kills the prophets and stones God's messengers! How often I have wanted to gather your children together as a hen protects her chicks beneath her wings, but you wouldn't let me. And now, look, your house is abandoned and desolate. For I tell you this, you will never see me again until you say, 'Blessings on the one who comes in the name of the LORD!'"

MATTHEW 23:37-39

PROTECTION

Here we see the depth of Jesus' feelings for lost people and for his beloved city, which would soon be destroyed. Jesus wanted to gather his people together as a hen protects her chicks under her wings, but they wouldn't let him. Jesus also wants to protect us, if we will just come to him. Many times we hurt and don't know where to turn. We reject Christ's help because we don't think he can give us what we need. But who knows our needs better than our Creator? Those who turn to Jesus will find that he helps and comforts as no one else can.

―――――――――――――――●●――――――――――――――――

Jerusalem was the capital city of God's chosen people; the home of David, Israel's greatest king; and the location of the Temple, the earthly dwelling place of God. It was intended to be the center of worship of the true God and a symbol of justice to all people. But Jerusalem had become blind to God and insensitive to human need.

―――――――――――――――●●――――――――――――――――

A poor widow gives all she has

Jesus sat down near the collection box in the Temple and watched as the crowds dropped in their money. Many rich people put in large amounts. Then a poor widow came and dropped in two small coins.

Jesus called his disciples to him and said, "I tell you the truth, this poor widow has given more than all the others who are making contributions. For they gave a tiny part of their surplus, but she, poor as she is, has given everything she had to live on."   MARK 12:41-44 *(see also Luke 21:1-4)*

GIFTS THAT COUNT

In the Lord's eyes, this poor widow had given more than all the others put together, although her gift was by far the smallest. She had given all she had to live on, in contrast to the way most of us handle our money. When we consider giving a certain percentage of our income a great accomplishment, we resemble those who had given "a tiny part of their surplus." Here, Jesus was extolling generous and sacrificial giving. Not only was she poor, but as a widow she had few resources for making money. Her small gift was a sacrifice, but she gave it willingly. As believers, we should consider increasing our giving—whether of money, time, or talents—to a point beyond convenience or safety.

Jesus was in the area of the Temple called the Court of Women. The treasury was located there or in an adjoining walkway. In this area were seven boxes in which worshipers could deposit their Temple tax and six boxes for freewill offerings like the one given by this woman.

October 24

Jesus tells about the future

As Jesus was leaving the Temple that day, one of his disciples said, "Teacher, look at these magnificent buildings! Look at the impressive stones in the walls."

Jesus replied, "Yes, look at these great buildings. But they will be completely demolished. Not one stone will be left on top of another!"

Later, Jesus sat on the Mount of Olives across the valley from the Temple. Peter, James, John, and Andrew came to him privately and asked him, "Tell us, when will all this happen? What sign will show us that these things are about to be fulfilled?" MARK 13:1-4 *(see also Matthew 24:1-3; Luke 21:5-7)*

BE READY

The disciples wanted to know when the Temple would be destroyed. Jesus gave them a prophetic picture of that time, including events leading up to it. He also talked about future events connected with his return to earth to judge all people. Jesus predicted both near and distant events without putting them in chronological order. Some of the disciples lived to see the destruction of Jerusalem in AD 70. This event would assure them that everything else Jesus predicted would also happen. Jesus warned his followers about the future so that they could learn how to live in the present. Many predictions Jesus made in this chapter have not yet been fulfilled. He did not make them so that we would guess when they might be fulfilled, but to help us remain spiritually alert and prepared at all times as we wait for his return. What changes would you make if you knew that Jesus would return one of these days? Be ready for his second coming.

The Mount of Olives rises above Jerusalem to the east. From its slopes a person can look down into the city and see the Temple. Zechariah 14:1-4 predicts that the Messiah will stand on this very mountain when he returns to set up his eternal Kingdom.

Jesus tells about the future

Jesus replied, "Don't let anyone mislead you, for many will come in my name, claiming, 'I am the Messiah.' They will deceive many. And you will hear of wars and threats of wars, but don't panic. Yes, these things must take place, but the end won't follow immediately. Nation will go to war against nation, and kingdom against kingdom. There will be earthquakes in many parts of the world, as well as famines. But this is only the first of the birth pains, with more to come.

"When these things begin to happen, watch out! You will be handed over to the local councils and beaten in the synagogues. You will stand trial before governors and kings because you are my followers. But this will be your opportunity to tell them about me. For the Good News must first be preached to all nations. But when you are arrested and stand trial, don't worry in advance about what to say. Just say what God tells you at that time, for it is not you who will be speaking, but the Holy Spirit.

"A brother will betray his brother to death, a father will betray his own child, and children will rebel against their parents and cause them to be killed. And everyone will hate you because you are my followers. But the one who endures to the end will be saved." MARK 13:5-13 *(see also Matthew 24:4-14; Luke 21:8-19)*

END SIGNS

What are the signs of the end times? There have been people in every generation since Christ's resurrection claiming to know exactly when Jesus will return. No one has been right yet, however, because Christ will return on God's timetable, not ours. Jesus predicted that before his return, many believers would be misled by false teachers claiming to have revelations from God.

According to Scripture, the one clear sign of Christ's return will be his unmistakable appearance in the clouds, which will be seen by all people (Mark 13:26; Revelation 1:7). In other words, you do not have to wonder whether a certain person is the Messiah or whether these are the "end times." When Jesus returns, *you will know* beyond a doubt because it will be evident to all true believers. Beware of groups who claim special knowledge of the last days, because no one knows when that time will be (Mark 13:32). Be cautious about saying, "This is it!" but be bold in your total commitment to have your heart and life ready for Christ's return.

October 26 READ MATTHEW 24:15-22

Jesus tells about the future

*"The day is coming when you will see what Daniel the prophet spoke about—
the sacrilegious object that causes desecration standing in the Holy Place."
(Reader, pay attention!) "Then those in Judea must flee to the hills. A person out
on the deck of a roof must not go down into the house to pack. A person out in
the field must not return even to get a coat. How terrible it will be for pregnant
women and for nursing mothers in those days. And pray that your flight will
not be in winter or on the Sabbath. For there will be greater anguish than at any
time since the world began. And it will never be so great again. In fact, unless
that time of calamity is shortened, not a single person will survive. But it will be
shortened for the sake of God's chosen ones."*

MATTHEW 24:15-22 *(see also Mark 13:14-20; Luke 21:20-24)*

NEEDED KNOWLEDGE

Jesus was talking about the desecration of the Temple by God's enemies. This has
happened repeatedly in Israel's history: in 597 BC, when Nebuchadnezzar looted
the Temple and took Judean captives to Babylon (2 Chronicles 36); in 168 BC,
when Antiochus Epiphanes sacrificed a pig to Zeus on the sacred Temple altar
(Daniel 9:27; 11:30-31); and in AD 70, when the Roman general Titus placed an
idol on the site of the burned-out Temple after the destruction of Jerusalem. Just a
few years after Jesus gave this warning, the emperor Caligula made plans to put a
statue of himself in the Temple, but he died before this could be carried out. Talking about the end times, Jesus telescoped near future and far future events, as did
the Old Testament prophets. Many of these persecutions have already occurred;
more are yet to come. But God is in control of even the length of each persecution. He will not forget his people. This is all we need to know about the future to
motivate us to live rightly now.

*While this desecration of the Temple has specific applications in
history, it also can be seen as any deliberate attempt to mock and
deny the reality of God's presence.*

Jesus tells about his return

"Then if anyone tells you, 'Look, here is the Messiah,' or 'There he is,' don't believe it. For false messiahs and false prophets will rise up and perform great signs and wonders so as to deceive, if possible, even God's chosen ones. See, I have warned you about this ahead of time.

"So if someone tells you, 'Look, the Messiah is out in the desert,' don't bother to go and look. Or, 'Look, he is hiding here,' don't believe it! For as the lightning flashes in the east and shines to the west, so it will be when the Son of Man comes. Just as the gathering of vultures shows there is a carcass nearby, so these signs indicate that the end is near."

MATTHEW 24:23-28 *(see also Mark 13:21-23)*

DECEPTIONS

Is it possible for Christians to be deceived? Yes. So convincing will be the arguments and proofs from deceivers in the end times that it will be difficult *not* to fall away from Christ. If we are prepared, Jesus says, we can remain faithful. But if we are not prepared, we will turn away. To penetrate the disguises of false teachers, we can ask, (1) Have their predictions come true, or do they have to revise them to fit what's already happened? (2) Does any teaching utilize a small section of the Bible to the neglect of the whole? (3) Does the teaching contradict what the Bible says about God? (4) Are the practices meant to glorify the teacher or Christ? (5) Do the teachings promote hostility toward other Christians?

Jesus' warnings about false teachers still hold true. Upon close examination we can see that many nice-sounding messages don't agree with God's message in the Bible. Only a solid foundation in God's Word can equip believers to perceive the errors and distortions in false teaching.

Jesus tells about his return

"Immediately after the anguish of those days, the sun will be darkened, the moon will give no light, the stars will fall from the sky, and the powers in the heavens will be shaken.

"And then at last, the sign that the Son of Man is coming will appear in the heavens, and there will be deep mourning among all the peoples of the earth. And they will see the Son of Man coming on the clouds of heaven with power and great glory. And he will send out his angels with the mighty blast of a trumpet, and they will gather his chosen ones from all over the world—from the farthest ends of the earth and heaven.

"Now learn a lesson from the fig tree. When its branches bud and its leaves begin to sprout, you know that summer is near. In the same way, when you see all these things, you can know his return is very near, right at the door. I tell you the truth, this generation will not pass from the scene until all these things take place. Heaven and earth will disappear, but my words will never disappear."

MATTHEW 24:29-35 *(see also Mark 13:24-31; Luke 21:25-33)*

ETERNAL TRUTH

In Jesus' day the world seemed concrete, dependable, and permanent. These days many people fear its destruction by nuclear war. Jesus tells us, however, that even if the earth should pass away, the truth of his words will never be changed or abolished. God and his Word provide the only stability in our unstable world. How shortsighted people are who spend their time learning about this temporary world and accumulating its possessions while neglecting the Bible and its eternal truths!

The nations of the earth will mourn because unbelievers will suddenly realize that they have chosen the wrong side. Everything they have mocked will be happening, and it will be too late for them.

Jesus tells about remaining watchful

"However, no one knows the day or hour when these things will happen, not even the angels in heaven or the Son himself. Only the Father knows.

"When the Son of Man returns, it will be like it was in Noah's day. In those days before the flood, the people were enjoying banquets and parties and weddings right up to the time Noah entered his boat. People didn't realize what was going to happen until the flood came and swept them all away. That is the way it will be when the Son of Man comes.

"Two men will be working together in the field; one will be taken, the other left. Two women will be grinding flour at the mill; one will be taken, the other left.

"So you, too, must keep watch! For you don't know what day your Lord is coming. Understand this: If a homeowner knew exactly when a burglar was coming, he would keep watch and not permit his house to be broken into. You also must be ready all the time, for the Son of Man will come when least expected.

"A faithful, sensible servant is one to whom the master can give the responsibility of managing his other household servants and feeding them. If the master returns and finds that the servant has done a good job, there will be a reward. I tell you the truth, the master will put that servant in charge of all he owns. But what if the servant is evil and thinks, 'My master won't be back for a while,' and he begins beating the other servants, partying, and getting drunk? The master will return unannounced and unexpected, and he will cut the servant to pieces and assign him a place with the hypocrites. In that place there will be weeping and gnashing of teeth."

MATTHEW 24:36-51 *(see also Mark 13:32-37; Luke 21:34-38)*

WHILE WAITING . . .

Jesus' words here tell us how to live while we wait for his return: (1) We are not to be misled by confusing claims or speculative interpretations of what will happen. (2) We should not be afraid to tell people about Christ, despite what they might say or do to us. (3) We must stand firm by faith and not be surprised by persecution. (4) We must be morally alert, obedient to the commands for living found in God's Word. Jesus didn't want to promote discussions on prophetic timetables. We're not supposed to "figure out" when he's coming back. Instead, it is good that we *don't* know exactly when Christ will return. If we knew the precise date, we might be tempted to be lazy in our work for Christ. Worse yet, we might plan to keep sinning and then turn to God right at the end. Heaven is not our only goal; we have work to do here. And we must keep on doing it until death or until we see the unmistakable return of our Savior.

Jesus tells the parable of the ten bridesmaids

"Then the Kingdom of Heaven will be like ten bridesmaids who took their lamps and went to meet the bridegroom. Five of them were foolish, and five were wise. The five who were foolish didn't take enough olive oil for their lamps, but the other five were wise enough to take along extra oil. When the bridegroom was delayed, they all became drowsy and fell asleep.

"At midnight they were roused by the shout, 'Look, the bridegroom is coming! Come out and meet him!'

"All the bridesmaids got up and prepared their lamps. Then the five foolish ones asked the others, 'Please give us some of your oil because our lamps are going out.'

"But the others replied, 'We don't have enough for all of us. Go to a shop and buy some for yourselves.'

"But while they were gone to buy oil, the bridegroom came. Then those who were ready went in with him to the marriage feast, and the door was locked. Later, when the other five bridesmaids returned, they stood outside, calling, 'Lord! Lord! Open the door for us!'

"But he called back, 'Believe me, I don't know you!'

"So you, too, must keep watch! For you do not know the day or hour of my return." MATTHEW 25:1-13

DON'T BE OUT SHOPPING

These ten virgins were waiting to join the bride and groom in their wedding procession, and they hoped to take part in the wedding banquet. But when the groom didn't come at the expected time, five of them were out of lamp oil. By the time they had purchased extra oil, it was too late to join the feast. When Jesus returns to take his people to heaven, we must be ready. Spiritual preparation cannot be bought or borrowed at the last minute. Our relationship with God must be our own. Christ's second coming will be swift and sudden. There will be no opportunity for last-minute repentance or bargaining. The choice we have already made will determine our eternal destiny.

This parable is about a wedding. On the wedding day the bridegroom would go to the bride's house for the ceremony; then the bride and groom, along with a great procession, would return to the groom's house for a great feast, often lasting a week.

Jesus tells the parable of the loaned money

"Again, the Kingdom of Heaven can be illustrated by the story of a man going on a long trip. He called together his servants and entrusted his money to them while he was gone. He gave five bags of silver to one, two bags of silver to another, and one bag of silver to the last—dividing it in proportion to their abilities. He then left on his trip.

"The servant who received the five bags of silver began to invest the money and earned five more. The servant with two bags of silver also went to work and earned two more. But the servant who received the one bag of silver dug a hole in the ground and hid the master's money.

"After a long time their master returned from his trip and called them to give an account of how they had used his money. The servant to whom he had entrusted the five bags of silver came forward with five more and said, 'Master, you gave me five bags of silver to invest, and I have earned five more.'

"The master was full of praise. 'Well done, my good and faithful servant. You have been faithful in handling this small amount, so now I will give you many more responsibilities. Let's celebrate together!'

"The servant who had received the two bags of silver came forward and said, 'Master, you gave me two bags of silver to invest, and I have earned two more.'

"The master said, 'Well done, my good and faithful servant. You have been faithful in handling this small amount, so now I will give you many more responsibilities. Let's celebrate together!'

"Then the servant with the one bag of silver came and said, 'Master, I knew you were a harsh man, harvesting crops you didn't plant and gathering crops you didn't cultivate. I was afraid I would lose your money, so I hid it in the earth. Look, here is your money back.'

"But the master replied, 'You wicked and lazy servant! If you knew I harvested crops I didn't plant and gathered crops I didn't cultivate, why didn't you deposit my money in the bank? At least I could have gotten some interest on it.'

"Then he ordered, 'Take the money from this servant, and give it to the one with the ten bags of silver. To those who use well what they are given, even more will be given, and they will have an abundance. But from those who do nothing, even what little they have will be taken away. Now throw this useless servant into outer darkness, where there will be weeping and gnashing of teeth.'"

MATTHEW 25:14-30

A GOOD INVESTMENT

The master divided the money among his servants according to their abilities. No one received more or less than he could handle. If he failed in his assignment, his excuse could not be that he was overwhelmed. Failure could come only from laziness or hatred toward the master. "Bags of silver" represents any kind of resource we are given. God gives us time, gifts, and other resources according to our abilities, and he expects us to invest them wisely until he returns. Our time, abilities, and money aren't ours in the first place—we are caretakers, not owners. We are responsible to use well what God has given us. The issue is not how much we have but how well we use what we have.

This last man was thinking only of himself. He hoped to play it safe and protect himself from his hard master; thus, he was judged for his self-centeredness. We must not make excuses to avoid doing what God calls us to do.

Jesus tells about the final judgment

"But when the Son of Man comes in his glory, and all the angels with him, then he will sit upon his glorious throne. All the nations will be gathered in his presence, and he will separate the people as a shepherd separates the sheep from the goats. He will place the sheep at his right hand and the goats at his left.

"Then the King will say to those on his right, 'Come, you who are blessed by my Father, inherit the Kingdom prepared for you from the creation of the world. For I was hungry, and you fed me. I was thirsty, and you gave me a drink. I was a stranger, and you invited me into your home. I was naked, and you gave me clothing. I was sick, and you cared for me. I was in prison, and you visited me.'

"Then these righteous ones will reply, 'Lord, when did we ever see you hungry and feed you? Or thirsty and give you something to drink? Or a stranger and show you hospitality? Or naked and give you clothing? When did we ever see you sick or in prison and visit you?'

"And the King will say, 'I tell you the truth, when you did it to one of the least of these my brothers and sisters, you were doing it to me!'

"Then the King will turn to those on the left and say, 'Away with you, you cursed ones, into the eternal fire prepared for the devil and his demons. For I was hungry, and you didn't feed me. I was thirsty, and you didn't give me a drink. I was a stranger, and you didn't invite me into your home. I was naked, and you didn't give me clothing. I was sick and in prison, and you didn't visit me.'

"Then they will reply, 'Lord, when did we ever see you hungry or thirsty or a stranger or naked or sick or in prison, and not help you?'

"And he will answer, 'I tell you the truth, when you refused to help the least of these my brothers and sisters, you were refusing to help me.'

"And they will go away into eternal punishment, but the righteous will go into eternal life." MATTHEW 25:31-46

THE GREAT PRETENDERS

God will separate his obedient followers from pretenders and unbelievers. The real evidence of our belief is the way we act. To treat all persons we encounter as if they were Jesus is no easy task. What we do for others demonstrates what we really think about Jesus' words to us—feed the hungry, give the homeless a place to stay, look after the sick. These acts do not depend on wealth, ability, or intelligence; they are simple acts freely given and freely received. We have no excuse to neglect those who have deep needs, and we cannot hand over this responsibility to the church or the government. Jesus demands our personal involvement in caring for others' needs (Isaiah 58:7). How well do your actions separate you from pretenders and unbelievers?

Religious leaders plot to kill Jesus

When Jesus had finished saying all these things, he said to his disciples, "As you know, Passover begins in two days, and the Son of Man will be handed over to be crucified."

At that same time the leading priests and elders were meeting at the residence of Caiaphas, the high priest, plotting how to capture Jesus secretly and kill him. "But not during the Passover celebration," they agreed, "or the people may riot."   MATTHEW 26:1-5 *(see also Mark 14:1-2; Luke 22:1-2)*

EASY TO JUSTIFY

Caiaphas was the ruling high priest during Jesus' ministry. He was the son-in-law of Annas, a previous high priest. The Roman government had taken over the process of appointing all political and religious leaders. Caiaphas served for eighteen years, longer than most high priests, which suggests that he was gifted at cooperating with the Romans. He was the first to recommend Jesus' death in order to "save" the nation (John 11:49-50). This was a deliberate plot to kill Jesus. Without this plot there would have been no groundswell of popular opinion against him. In fact, because of Jesus' popularity, the religious leaders were afraid to arrest him during the Passover; they did not want their actions to incite a riot. So these religious leaders, very pious in their self-righteousness and law keeping, were at the high priest's house planning murder. We can criticize these leaders (rightfully), but we should admit that we find it easy to justify our own sinful actions! Be honest about sin—don't rationalize it.

All Jewish males over the age of twelve were required to go to Jerusalem for the Passover feast, followed by a seven-day festival called the Festival of Unleavened Bread. For these feasts, Jews from all over the Roman Empire converged on Jerusalem to celebrate one of the most important events in their history.

Judas agrees to betray Jesus

Then Satan entered into Judas Iscariot, who was one of the twelve disciples, and he went to the leading priests and captains of the Temple guard to discuss the best way to betray Jesus to them. They were delighted, and they promised to give him money. So he agreed and began looking for an opportunity to betray Jesus so they could arrest him when the crowds weren't around.

LUKE 22:3-6 *(see also Matthew 26:14-16; Mark 14:10-11)*

WEAK SPOTS

Why would Judas want to betray Jesus? Judas, like the other disciples, expected Jesus to start a political rebellion and overthrow Rome. As treasurer, Judas certainly assumed that he would be given an important position in Jesus' new government. However, Judas finally realized that Jesus' Kingdom was not physical or political, but spiritual. Judas's greedy desire for money and status could not be realized if he followed Jesus, so he betrayed Jesus in exchange for money and favor from the religious leaders. Judas allowed his desires to put him in a position where Satan could manipulate him. Satan is good at finding our weak spots and trying to use them for his purposes. That's why it's so important to yield every part of your life to Christ. Recognize your weak spots and yield them to Jesus' power.

Satan's part in the betrayal of Jesus does not remove any of the responsibility from Judas. Disillusioned because Jesus had been talking about dying rather than about setting up his Kingdom, Judas may have been trying to force Jesus' hand and make him use his power to prove he was the Messiah.

November 4 READ LUKE 22:7-13

Disciples prepare for the Passover

Now the Festival of Unleavened Bread arrived, when the Passover lamb is sacrificed. Jesus sent Peter and John ahead and said, "Go and prepare the Passover meal, so we can eat it together."

"Where do you want us to prepare it?" they asked him.

He replied, "As soon as you enter Jerusalem, a man carrying a pitcher of water will meet you. Follow him. At the house he enters, say to the owner, 'The Teacher asks: Where is the guest room where I can eat the Passover meal with my disciples?' He will take you upstairs to a large room that is already set up. That is where you should prepare our meal." They went off to the city and found everything just as Jesus had said, and they prepared the Passover meal there.

LUKE 22:7-13 *(see also Matthew 26:17-19; Mark 14:12-16)*

REMEMBERING

Passover became an annual remembrance of how God had delivered the Hebrews from Egypt. Each year the people would pause to remember the day when the destroyer (God's angel of death) had passed over their homes (Exodus 12). They would give thanks to God for saving them from death and bringing them out of a land of slavery and sin. Believers today have experienced a day of deliverance as well—the day we were delivered from spiritual death and slavery to sin. The Lord's Supper is our Passover remembrance of our new life and freedom from sin. The next time struggles and trials come, remember how God has delivered you in the past and focus on his promise of new life with him.

The Passover meal included the sacrifice of a lamb because of the association with the Exodus from Egypt. When the Jews were getting ready to leave, God told them to kill a lamb and paint its blood on the doorposts of their houses. They then were to prepare the meat for food. Peter and John had to buy and prepare the lamb as well as the unleavened bread, herbs, wine, and other ceremonial food.

Jesus washes the disciples' feet

Before the Passover celebration, Jesus knew that his hour had come to leave this world and return to his Father. He had loved his disciples during his ministry on earth, and now he loved them to the very end. It was time for supper, and the devil had already prompted Judas, son of Simon Iscariot, to betray Jesus. Jesus knew that the Father had given him authority over everything and that he had come from God and would return to God. So he got up from the table, took off his robe, wrapped a towel around his waist, and poured water into a basin. Then he began to wash the disciples' feet, drying them with the towel he had around him.

When Jesus came to Simon Peter, Peter said to him, "Lord, are you going to wash my feet?"

Jesus replied, "You don't understand now what I am doing, but someday you will."

"No," Peter protested, "you will never ever wash my feet!"

Jesus replied, "Unless I wash you, you won't belong to me."

Simon Peter exclaimed, "Then wash my hands and head as well, Lord, not just my feet!"

Jesus replied, "A person who has bathed all over does not need to wash, except for the feet, to be entirely clean. And you disciples are clean, but not all of you." For Jesus knew who would betray him. That is what he meant when he said, "Not all of you are clean." JOHN 13:1-11

TRUE LEADERS

Imagine being Peter and watching Jesus wash the others' feet, all the while moving closer to you. Seeing his Master behave like a slave must have confused Peter. He still did not understand Jesus' teaching that to be a leader, a person must be a servant. This is not a comfortable passage for leaders who find it difficult to serve those beneath them. The world's system of leadership is very different from leadership in God's Kingdom. Worldly leaders are often selfish and arrogant as they claw their way to the top. (Some kings in the ancient world gave themselves the title "Benefactor.") But among Christians, the leader is to be the one who *serves* best. There are different styles of leadership—some lead through public speaking, some through administering, some through relationships—but every Christian leader needs a servant's heart. How do you treat those who work under you (whether children, employees, or volunteers)? Ask the people you lead how you can serve them better.

Jesus washes the disciples' feet

After washing their feet, he put on his robe again and sat down and asked, "Do you understand what I was doing? You call me 'Teacher' and 'Lord,' and you are right, because that's what I am. And since I, your Lord and Teacher, have washed your feet, you ought to wash each other's feet. I have given you an example to follow. Do as I have done to you. I tell you the truth, slaves are not greater than their master. Nor is the messenger more important than the one who sends the message. Now that you know these things, God will bless you for doing them.

"I am not saying these things to all of you; I know the ones I have chosen. But this fulfills the Scripture that says, 'The one who eats my food has turned against me.' I tell you this beforehand, so that when it happens you will believe that I AM the Messiah. I tell you the truth, anyone who welcomes my messenger is welcoming me, and anyone who welcomes me is welcoming the Father who sent me."   JOHN 13:12-20

FOLLOW THROUGH

Jesus was the model servant, and he showed his servant attitude to his disciples. Washing guests' feet was a job for a household servant to carry out when guests arrived. But Jesus wrapped a towel around his waist, as the lowliest slave would do, and washed and dried his disciples' feet. If even he, God in the flesh, is willing to serve, we, his followers, must also be servants, willing to serve in any way that glorifies God. Are you willing to follow Christ's example of serving? Whom can you serve today? There is a special blessing for those who not only agree that humble service is Christ's way but also follow through and do it (John 13:17).

Jesus did not wash his disciples' feet just to get them to be nice to one another. His far greater goal for them was to extend his mission on earth after he had left them. These men were to move into the world, serving God, one another, and all people to whom they took the message of salvation.

Jesus and his disciples have the Last Supper

Now Jesus was deeply troubled, and he exclaimed, "I tell you the truth, one of you will betray me!"

The disciples looked at each other, wondering whom he could mean. The disciple Jesus loved was sitting next to Jesus at the table. Simon Peter motioned to him to ask, "Who's he talking about?" So that disciple leaned over to Jesus and asked, "Lord, who is it?"

Jesus responded, "It is the one to whom I give the bread I dip in the bowl." And when he had dipped it, he gave it to Judas, son of Simon Iscariot. When Judas had eaten the bread, Satan entered into him. Then Jesus told him, "Hurry and do what you're going to do." None of the others at the table knew what Jesus meant. Since Judas was their treasurer, some thought Jesus was telling him to go and pay for the food or to give some money to the poor. So Judas left at once, going out into the night.

JOHN 13:21-30 *(see also Matthew 26:20-29; Mark 14:17-25; Luke 22:14-30*

MATCHING WORDS AND ACTIONS

Judas, the man who would betray Jesus, was at the table with the others. Judas had already determined to betray Jesus, but in cold-blooded hypocrisy, he shared the fellowship of this meal. It is easy to become enraged or shocked by what Judas did; yet professing commitment to Christ and then denying him with one's life is also betraying him. It is denying Christ's love to disobey him; it is denying his truth to distrust him; it is denying his deity to reject his authority. Do your words and actions match? If not, consider a change of mind and heart that will protect you from making a terrible mistake.

The honored guest at a meal would be singled out by the host by giving him or her a piece of bread dipped in sauce.

Jesus predicts Peter's denial

As soon as Judas left the room, Jesus said, "The time has come for the Son of Man to enter into his glory, and God will be glorified because of him. And since God receives glory because of the Son, he will soon give glory to the Son. Dear children, I will be with you only a little longer. And as I told the Jewish leaders, you will search for me, but you can't come where I am going. So now I am giving you a new commandment: Love each other. Just as I have loved you, you should love each other. Your love for one another will prove to the world that you are my disciples."

Simon Peter asked, "Lord, where are you going?"

And Jesus replied, "You can't go with me now, but you will follow me later."

"But why can't I come now, Lord?" he asked. "I'm ready to die for you."

Jesus answered, "Die for me? I tell you the truth, Peter—before the rooster crows tomorrow morning, you will deny three times that you even know me."

JOHN 13:31-38 *(see also Luke 22:31-34)*

LOVING AS CHRIST LOVED

Love is more than simply warm feelings; it is an attitude that reveals itself in action. To love others was not a new commandment (Leviticus 19:18), but to love others as much as Christ loved others was revolutionary. Now we are to love others based on Jesus' sacrificial love for us. Not only will such love bring unbelievers to Christ; it will also keep believers strong and united in a world hostile to God. Jesus was a living example of God's love, as we are to be living examples of Jesus' love. How can we love others as Jesus loves us? By helping when it's not convenient, by giving when it hurts, by devoting energy to others' welfare rather than our own, by absorbing hurts from others without complaining or fighting back. This kind of loving is difficult to do. That is why people notice when you do it and know you are empowered by a supernatural source.

Peter proudly told Jesus that he was ready to die for him. But Jesus corrected him. Jesus knew Peter would deny that he knew Jesus that very night to protect himself (John 18:17, 25-27).

Jesus is the way to the Father

"Don't let your hearts be troubled. Trust in God, and trust also in me. There is more than enough room in my Father's home. If this were not so, would I have told you that I am going to prepare a place for you? When everything is ready, I will come and get you, so that you will always be with me where I am. And you know the way to where I am going."

"No, we don't know, Lord," Thomas said. "We have no idea where you are going, so how can we know the way?"

Jesus told him, "I am the way, the truth, and the life. No one can come to the Father except through me. If you had really known me, you would know who my Father is. From now on, you do know him and have seen him!" JOHN 14:1-7

ONE WAY

Jesus says he is the *only* way to God the Father. This is one of the most basic and important passages in Scripture. How can we know the way to God? Only through Jesus. Some people may argue that this way is too narrow. In reality, it is wide enough for the whole world, if the world chooses to accept it. Instead of worrying about how limited it sounds to have only one way, we should be saying, "Thank you, God, for providing a sure way to get to you!" Jesus is the Way because he is both God and man. By uniting our lives with his, we are united with God. Trust Jesus to take you to the Father, and all the benefits of being God's child will be yours.

As the Way, Jesus is our path to the Father. As the Truth, he is the reality of all God's promises. As the Life, he joins his divine life to ours, both now and eternally.

November 10 READ JOHN 14:8-14

Jesus is the way to the Father

Philip said, "Lord, show us the Father, and we will be satisfied."

Jesus replied, "Have I been with you all this time, Philip, and yet you still don't know who I am? Anyone who has seen me has seen the Father! So why are you asking me to show him to you? Don't you believe that I am in the Father and the Father is in me? The words I speak are not my own, but my Father who lives in me does his work through me. Just believe that I am in the Father and the Father is in me. Or at least believe because of the work you have seen me do.

"I tell you the truth, anyone who believes in me will do the same works I have done, and even greater works, because I am going to be with the Father. You can ask for anything in my name, and I will do it, so that the Son can bring glory to the Father. Yes, ask me for anything in my name, and I will do it!" JOHN 14:8-14

ASKING IN FAITH

When Jesus says we can ask for anything, we must remember that our asking must be in his name—that is, according to God's character and will. God will not grant requests contrary to his nature or his will, and we cannot use his name as a magic formula to fulfill our selfish desires. If we are sincerely following God and seeking to do his will, then our requests will be in line with what he wants and he will grant them.

Jesus is the visible, tangible image of the invisible God. He is the complete revelation of what God is like. Jesus explained to Philip, who wanted to see the Father, that to know Jesus is to know God. The search for God, for truth and reality, ends in Christ.

Jesus promises to send the Holy Spirit

"If you love me, obey my commandments. And I will ask the Father, and he will give you another Advocate, who will never leave you. He is the Holy Spirit, who leads into all truth. The world cannot receive him, because it isn't looking for him and doesn't recognize him. But you know him, because he lives with you now and later will be in you. No, I will not abandon you as orphans—I will come to you. Soon the world will no longer see me, but you will see me. Since I live, you also will live. When I am raised to life again, you will know that I am in my Father, and you are in me, and I am in you. Those who accept my commandments and obey them are the ones who love me. And because they love me, my Father will love them. And I will love them and reveal myself to each of them." JOHN 14:15-21

GOD KNOWS THE FUTURE

Sometimes people wish they knew the future so they could prepare for it. God has chosen not to give us this knowledge. He alone knows what will happen, but he tells us all we need to know to *prepare* for the future. When we live by his standards, he will not leave us; he will come to us, he will be in us, and he will show himself to us. God knows what will happen, and because he will be with us through it all, we need not fear. We don't have to know the future to have faith in God; we have to have faith in God to be secure about the future.

Jesus was soon going to leave the disciples, but he would remain with them. How could this be? The Helper—the Spirit of God himself—would come after Jesus was gone to care for and guide the disciples. The Holy Spirit is the very presence of God within us and all believers, helping us live as God wants and building Christ's church on earth.

Jesus promises to send the Holy Spirit

Judas (not Judas Iscariot, but the other disciple with that name) said to him, "Lord, why are you going to reveal yourself only to us and not to the world at large?"

Jesus replied, "All who love me will do what I say. My Father will love them, and we will come and make our home with each of them. Anyone who doesn't love me will not obey me. And remember, my words are not my own. What I am telling you is from the Father who sent me. I am telling you these things now while I am still with you. But when the Father sends the Advocate as my representative—that is, the Holy Spirit—he will teach you everything and will remind you of everything I have told you." JOHN 14:22-26

CONFIDENT IN THE WORD

Jesus promised the disciples that the Holy Spirit would help them remember what he had been teaching them. This promise ensures the validity of the New Testament. The disciples were eyewitnesses of Jesus' life and teachings, and the Holy Spirit helped them remember what they had seen and heard without taking away their individual perspectives. We can be confident that the Gospels are accurate records of what Jesus taught and did (1 Corinthians 2:10-14). The Holy Spirit can also help us. As we study the Bible, we can trust him to plant truth in our minds, convince us of God's will, and remind us when we stray from it.

Because the disciples were still expecting Jesus to establish an earthly kingdom and overthrow Rome, they found it hard to understand why he did not tell the world at large that he was the Messiah. But ever since Pentecost, the gospel of the Kingdom has been proclaimed in the whole world.

Jesus promises to send the Holy Spirit

"I am leaving you with a gift—peace of mind and heart. And the peace I give is a gift the world cannot give. So don't be troubled or afraid. Remember what I told you: I am going away, but I will come back to you again. If you really loved me, you would be happy that I am going to the Father, who is greater than I am. I have told you these things before they happen so that when they do happen, you will believe.

"I don't have much more time to talk to you, because the ruler of this world approaches. He has no power over me, but I will do what the Father requires of me, so that the world will know that I love the Father. Come, let's be going." JOHN 14:27-31

THE PEACE OF GOD

Sin, fear, uncertainty, doubt, and numerous other forces are at war within us. The peace of God comes into our hearts, helping to restrain these hostile forces and offering comfort in place of conflict. Jesus says he will give us that peace if we are willing to accept it from him.

The end result of the Holy Spirit's work in our lives is deep and lasting peace. Unlike worldly peace, which is usually defined as the absence of conflict, this peace is confident assurance in any circumstance; with Christ's peace, we have no need to fear the present or the future. If your life is full of stress, allow the Holy Spirit to fill you with Christ's peace.

As God the Son, Jesus willingly submits to God the Father. On earth, Jesus also submitted to many of the physical limitations of his humanity (John 14:31; Philippians 2:6-7).

November 14 READ JOHN 15:1-4

Jesus teaches about the vine and the branches

"I am the true grapevine, and my Father is the gardener. He cuts off every branch of mine that doesn't produce fruit, and he prunes the branches that do bear fruit so they will produce even more. You have already been pruned and purified by the message I have given you. Remain in me, and I will remain in you. For a branch cannot produce fruit if it is severed from the vine, and you cannot be fruitful unless you remain in me." JOHN 15:1-4

VINE AND BRANCHES

Christ is the vine, and God is the gardener who cares for the branches to make them fruitful. The branches are all those who claim to be followers of Christ. The fruitful branches are true believers who by their living union with Christ produce much fruit. But those who become unproductive—those who turn back from following Christ after making a superficial commitment—will be separated from the vine. Unproductive followers are as good as dead and will be cut off and tossed aside. Those who won't bear fruit for God or who try to block the efforts of God's followers will be cut off from the divine flow of life. Keep your focus on Christ, the vine—that is your only source of strength and life.

The grapevine is a prolific plant; a single vine bears many grapes. In the Old Testament, grapes symbolized Israel's fruitfulness in doing God's work on the earth (Psalm 80:8; Isaiah 5:1-7; Ezekiel 19:10-14). In the Passover meal, the fruit of the vine symbolized God's goodness to his people.

Jesus teaches about the vine and the branches

"Yes, I am the vine; you are the branches. Those who remain in me, and I in them, will produce much fruit. For apart from me you can do nothing. Anyone who does not remain in me is thrown away like a useless branch and withers. Such branches are gathered into a pile to be burned. But if you remain in me and my words remain in you, you may ask for anything you want, and it will be granted! When you produce much fruit, you are my true disciples. This brings great glory to my Father." JOHN 15:5-8

LIFE IN CHRIST

Many people try to be good, honest people who do what is right. But Jesus says that the only way to live a truly good life is to stay close to him, like a branch attached to the vine. Apart from Christ our efforts are unfruitful. Living in Christ means (1) believing that he is God's Son (1 John 4:15); (2) receiving him as Savior and Lord (John 1:12); (3) doing what God says (1 John 3:24); (4) continuing to believe the gospel (1 John 2:24); and (5) relating in love to the community of believers, Christ's body (John 15:12). Are you receiving the nourishment and life offered by Christ, the vine? If not, you are missing a special gift he has for you.

Fruit is not limited to soul winning. In this chapter, answered prayer, joy, and love are mentioned as fruit (John 15:7, 11-12). Galatians 5:22-23 and 2 Peter 1:5-8 describe additional fruit: qualities of Christian character.

Jesus teaches about the vine and the branches

"I have loved you even as the Father has loved me. Remain in my love. When you obey my commandments, you remain in my love, just as I obey my Father's commandments and remain in his love. I have told you these things so that you will be filled with my joy. Yes, your joy will overflow! This is my commandment: Love each other in the same way I have loved you. There is no greater love than to lay down one's life for one's friends. You are my friends if you do what I command. I no longer call you slaves, because a master doesn't confide in his slaves. Now you are my friends, since I have told you everything the Father told me. You didn't choose me. I chose you. I appointed you to go and produce lasting fruit, so that the Father will give you whatever you ask for, using my name." JOHN 15:9-16

HIGHS AND LOWS

When things are going well, we are elated. When hardships come, we can sink into depression. But true joy transcends the rolling waves of circumstance. Joy comes from a consistent relationship with Jesus Christ. When our lives are intertwined with his, he will help us to walk through adversity without sinking into debilitating lows and to manage prosperity without moving into deceptive highs. The joy of living with Jesus Christ daily will keep us levelheaded, no matter how high or low our circumstances.

Jesus made the first choice—to live and to die for us, to invite us to live with him forever. We make the next choice—to accept or to reject his offer. Without his choice, we would have no choice to make.

Jesus warns about the world's hatred

"This is my command: Love each other.

"If the world hates you, remember that it hated me first. The world would love you as one of its own if you belonged to it, but you are no longer part of the world. I chose you to come out of the world, so it hates you. Do you remember what I told you? 'A slave is not greater than the master.' Since they persecuted me, naturally they will persecute you. And if they had listened to me, they would listen to you. They will do all this to you because of me, for they have rejected the one who sent me. They would not be guilty if I had not come and spoken to them. But now they have no excuse for their sin. Anyone who hates me also hates my Father. If I hadn't done such miraculous signs among them that no one else could do, they would not be guilty. But as it is, they have seen everything I did, yet they still hate me and my Father. This fulfills what is written in their Scriptures: 'They hated me without cause.'" JOHN 15:17-25

COMMANDED TO LOVE

Jesus offers hope. The Holy Spirit gives strength to endure the unreasonable hatred and evil in our world and the hostility many have toward Christ. This is especially comforting for those facing persecution. But all Christians should expect to be the target of hatred from the world. Thus, it's important to give one another love and support. Do you allow small problems to get in the way of loving other believers? Jesus commands you to love them, and he will give you the strength to do it.

Because Jesus Christ is Lord and Master, he should call us servants; instead, he calls us friends. How comforting and reassuring to be chosen as Christ's friends. Because he is Lord and Master, we owe him our unqualified obedience. But most important, Jesus asks us to obey him because we love him.

Jesus warns about the world's hatred

"But I will send you the Advocate—the Spirit of truth. He will come to you from the Father and will testify all about me. And you must also testify about me because you have been with me from the beginning of my ministry.

"I have told you these things so that you won't abandon your faith. For you will be expelled from the synagogues, and the time is coming when those who kill you will think they are doing a holy service for God. This is because they have never known the Father or me. Yes, I'm telling you these things now, so that when they happen, you will remember my warning. I didn't tell you earlier because I was going to be with you for a while longer." JOHN 15:26–16:4

NEVER ALONE

In his last moments with his disciples, Jesus (1) warned them about further persecution; (2) told them where, when, and why he was going; and (3) assured them that they would not be left alone but that the Spirit would come. Jesus knew what lay ahead, and he did not want the disciples' faith shaken or destroyed. God wants you to know that you are not alone. You have the Holy Spirit to comfort you, teach you truth, and help you.

Jesus uses two names for the Holy Spirit—Advocate and Spirit of truth. The word Advocate conveys the protecting, encouraging, and counseling work of the Spirit. Spirit of truth points to the teaching, illuminating, and reminding work of the Spirit.

Jesus teaches about the Holy Spirit

"But now I am going away to the one who sent me, and not one of you is asking where I am going. Instead, you grieve because of what I've told you. But in fact, it is best for you that I go away, because if I don't, the Advocate won't come. If I do go away, then I will send him to you. And when he comes, he will convict the world of its sin, and of God's righteousness, and of the coming judgment. The world's sin is that it refuses to believe in me. Righteousness is available because I go to the Father, and you will see me no more. Judgment will come because the ruler of this world has already been judged." JOHN 16:5-11

THE SPIRIT

If Jesus had not done what he came to do, there would be no gospel. If he had not died, he could not have removed our sins; he could not have risen again and defeated death. If he had not gone back to the Father, the Holy Spirit would not have come. Christ's presence on earth was limited to one place at a time. His leaving meant that he could be present to the whole world through the Holy Spirit. God wants you to know you are not alone.

Three important tasks of the Holy Spirit are (1) convicting the world of its sin and calling it to repentance; (2) revealing the standard of God's righteousness to anyone who believes, because Christ would no longer be physically present on earth; and (3) demonstrating Christ's judgment over Satan.

November 20

Jesus teaches about the Holy Spirit

"There is so much more I want to tell you, but you can't bear it now. When the Spirit of truth comes, he will guide you into all truth. He will not speak on his own but will tell you what he has heard. He will tell you about the future. He will bring me glory by telling you whatever he receives from me. All that belongs to the Father is mine; this is why I said, 'The Spirit will tell you whatever he receives from me.'

"In a little while you won't see me anymore. But a little while after that, you will see me again." JOHN 16:12-16

THE PATHFINDER

The Holy Spirit is our guide, navigator, and pathfinder. Jesus also gave us a reliable map when he gave us his Word. These essential resources help us find our way as his disciples. The disciples could not absorb all Jesus taught them. Jesus said the Holy Spirit would tell them "about the future"—the nature of their mission, the opposition they would face, and the final outcome of their efforts. They didn't fully understand these promises until the Holy Spirit had come after Jesus' death and resurrection. Some steps of discipleship cannot even be comprehended until we have taken steps of obedience. Our knowledge of the way and the future will always be limited. But as we trust Christ and read his Word, the Holy Spirit will guide and direct our steps.

When Jesus said that in just a little while the disciples wouldn't see him anymore, he was referring to his death, now only a few hours away. But they would see him again after his resurrection three days later.

Jesus teaches about using his name in prayer

Some of the disciples asked each other, "What does he mean when he says, 'In a little while you won't see me, but then you will see me,' and 'I am going to the Father'? And what does he mean by 'a little while'? We don't understand."

Jesus realized they wanted to ask him about it, so he said, "Are you asking yourselves what I meant? I said in a little while you won't see me, but a little while after that you will see me again. I tell you the truth, you will weep and mourn over what is going to happen to me, but the world will rejoice. You will grieve, but your grief will suddenly turn to wonderful joy. It will be like a woman suffering the pains of labor. When her child is born, her anguish gives way to joy because she has brought a new baby into the world. So you have sorrow now, but I will see you again; then you will rejoice, and no one can rob you of that joy. At that time you won't need to ask me for anything. I tell you the truth, you will ask the Father directly, and he will grant your request because you use my name. You haven't done this before. Ask, using my name, and you will receive, and you will have abundant joy.

"I have spoken of these matters in figures of speech, but soon I will stop speaking figuratively and will tell you plainly all about the Father. Then you will ask in my name. I'm not saying I will ask the Father on your behalf, for the Father himself loves you dearly because you love me and believe that I came from God. Yes, I came from the Father into the world, and now I will leave the world and return to the Father." JOHN 16:17-28

A NEW DAY

Jesus is talking about a new relationship between the believer and God. Previously, people had approached God through priests. After Jesus' resurrection, any believer could approach God directly. A new day has dawned, and now all believers, as priests, can talk with God personally and directly (Hebrews 10:19-23). We can now approach God, not because of our own merit, but because Jesus, our great High Priest, has made us acceptable to God.

———————————◆◆◆———————————

What a contrast between the disciples and the world! The world rejoiced as the disciples wept, but the disciples would see him again (in three days) and rejoice. The world's values are often the opposite of God's values.

———————————◆◆◆———————————

Jesus teaches about using his name in prayer

Then his disciples said, "At last you are speaking plainly and not figuratively. Now we understand that you know everything, and there's no need to question you. From this we believe that you came from God."

Jesus asked, "Do you finally believe? But the time is coming—indeed it's here now—when you will be scattered, each one going his own way, leaving me alone. Yet I am not alone because the Father is with me. I have told you all this so that you may have peace in me. Here on earth you will have many trials and sorrows. But take heart, because I have overcome the world."   JOHN 16:29-33

THE OVERCOMER

With these words, Jesus told his disciples to take courage. In spite of the inevitable struggles they would face, they could take courage that Jesus had "overcome the world." In the book of Revelation, Jesus is called "the Alpha and the Omega—the beginning and the end" (Revelation 1:8). Jesus is the eternal Lord and Ruler of the past, present, and future (Revelation 4:8; Isaiah 44:6; 48:12-13). Without him you have nothing that is eternal, nothing that can change your life, nothing that can save you from sin. Is the Lord your reason for living—the beginning and the end of your life? Honor the one who is the beginning and the end of all existence, wisdom, and power.

The disciples believed Jesus' words because they were convinced that he knew everything. But their belief was only a first step toward the great faith they would receive when the Holy Spirit would come to live in them.

Jesus prays for himself

After saying all these things, Jesus looked up to heaven and said, "Father, the hour has come. Glorify your Son so he can give glory back to you. For you have given him authority over everyone. He gives eternal life to each one you have given him. And this is the way to have eternal life—to know you, the only true God, and Jesus Christ, the one you sent to earth. I brought glory to you here on earth by completing the work you gave me to do. Now, Father, bring me into the glory we shared before the world began." JOHN 17:1-5

KNOWING GOD

Jesus explained that knowing God is the essence of having eternal life. Eternal life is a gift we receive when we enter into a personal relationship with God in Jesus Christ. We cannot know God unless we have eternal life, and at the core of eternal life is intimate knowledge of God.

Eternal life gives us the capacity for intimacy with others who have eternal life. Jesus is the source of eternal life. Our first step toward eternal life includes realizing that we don't have it. That sense of separation, rebellion, lostness, or inadequacy before God is defined as "sin" in the Bible. When we admit our sin, turn away from it, and then turn to Christ, Christ's love lives in us through the Holy Spirit. Eternal life is not just being around forever; for believers it means eternity with God, their loving Father.

Before Jesus came to earth, he was one with God. At this point, when his mission on earth was almost finished, Jesus was asking his Father to restore him to his original place of honor and authority. Jesus' resurrection and ascension—and Stephen's dying exclamation (Acts 7:56)—attest that Jesus did return to his exalted position at the right hand of God.

Jesus prays for his disciples

"I have revealed you to the ones you gave me from this world. They were always yours. You gave them to me, and they have kept your word. Now they know that everything I have is a gift from you, for I have passed on to them the message you gave me. They accepted it and know that I came from you, and they believe you sent me.

"My prayer is not for the world, but for those you have given me, because they belong to you. All who are mine belong to you, and you have given them to me, so they bring me glory. Now I am departing from the world; they are staying in this world, but I am coming to you. Holy Father, you have given me your name; now protect them by the power of your name so that they will be united just as we are. During my time here, I protected them by the power of the name you gave me. I guarded them so that not one was lost, except the one headed for destruction, as the Scriptures foretold." JOHN 17:6-12

IN THE WORLD

Like Jesus' original disciples, we still live in the world. "The world" is a system of values typified by Satan himself, centered on power, deceit, and self-will. While we're in the world, Satan wants to neutralize or destroy us. As Jesus' disciples today, we are on a collision course with the world's values; therefore, we need God's protection. The fact that we are *in* the world does not grant us license to become *of* the world. We must not betray Jesus by loving the world. We must be sure that we allow Christ—not the media and the world around us—to define who we are.

Judas was "the one headed for destruction," who was lost because he betrayed Jesus (Psalm 41:9).

Jesus prays for his disciples

"Now I am coming to you. I told them many things while I was with them in this world so they would be filled with my joy. I have given them your word. And the world hates them because they do not belong to the world, just as I do not belong to the world. I'm not asking you to take them out of the world, but to keep them safe from the evil one. They do not belong to this world any more than I do. Make them holy by your truth; teach them your word, which is truth. Just as you sent me into the world, I am sending them into the world. And I give myself as a holy sacrifice for them so they can be made holy by your truth." JOHN 17:13-19

SENT ONES

The world hates Christians because Christians' values differ from the world's. Because Christ's followers don't cooperate with the world by joining in its sin, they are living accusations against the world's immorality. The world follows Satan's agenda, and Satan is the avowed enemy of Jesus and his people. Yet Jesus asked God not to take believers *out* of the world but to use them *in* the world. Because Jesus sends us into the world, we should not try to escape from the world, nor should we avoid all relationships with non-Christians. We are called to be salt and light (Matthew 5:13-16), and we are to do the work that God sent us to do.

A follower of Christ becomes pure and holy through believing and obeying the Word of God (Hebrews 4:12). He or she has already accepted forgiveness through Christ's sacrificial death. But daily application of God's Word has a purifying effect on our minds and hearts.

November 26 READ JOHN 17:20-21

Jesus prays for future believers

"I am praying not only for these disciples but also for all who will ever believe in me through their message. I pray that they will all be one, just as you and I are one—as you are in me, Father, and I am in you. And may they be in us so that the world will believe you sent me." JOHN 17:20-21

ON HIS MIND

When Jesus prayed for all who would believe through the apostles' testimony, he was praying for every future believer. In a sense, everyone who has become a Christian has done so through the apostles' message because they wrote the New Testament and were the founders of the Christian church. Jesus prayed for you and others you know, that you would have unity (John 17:11), protection from Satan (John 17:15), and holiness (John 17:17). Realizing that Jesus was praying for you should give you great comfort during times of discouragement and confidence as you work for his Kingdom. Jesus had you in mind as he prepared for the Cross.

The pattern of Jesus' prayer provides a helpful outline for us. He prayed for himself, for those close to him, and for those beyond his immediate sphere who would be affected by the ministry of his friends.

Jesus prays for future believers

*"I have given them the glory you gave me, so they may be one as we are one.
I am in them and you are in me. May they experience such perfect unity that the
world will know that you sent me and that you love them as much as you love
me. Father, I want these whom you have given me to be with me where I am.
Then they can see all the glory you gave me because you loved me even before
the world began!*

*"O righteous Father, the world doesn't know you, but I do; and these disciples
know you sent me. I have revealed you to them, and I will continue to do so.
Then your love for me will be in them, and I will be in them."* JOHN 17:22-26

THE WITNESS OF UNITY

Jesus' great desire for his disciples was that they would become one. He wanted
them unified as a powerful witness to the reality of God's love. Christian unity
provides an environment for the gospel message to make its clearest impact; lack
of unity among Christians frequently drives people away. Are you helping to unify
the body of Christ, the church? You can pray for other Christians, avoid gossip,
build others up, work together in humility, give your time and money, exalt Christ,
and refuse to get sidetracked into arguing over divisive matters.

*Jesus asked that the Father's love would be in believers and
that he himself (Jesus) would be in them. This expresses the
Father's desire, and because it is his desire, he will make sure it
is accomplished.*

Jesus again predicts Peter's denial

Then they sang a hymn and went out to the Mount of Olives.

On the way, Jesus told them, "All of you will desert me. For the Scriptures say, 'God will strike the Shepherd, and the sheep will be scattered.' But after I am raised from the dead, I will go ahead of you to Galilee and meet you there."

Peter said to him, "Even if everyone else deserts you, I never will."

Jesus replied, "I tell you the truth, Peter—this very night, before the rooster crows twice, you will deny three times that you even know me."

"No!" Peter declared emphatically. "Even if I have to die with you, I will never deny you!" And all the others vowed the same.

MARK 14:26-31 *(see also Matthew 26:30-35)*

FAITH IN A CRUCIBLE

This was the second time that evening that Jesus predicted his disciples would desert him (Luke 22:31-34; John 13:31-38 for the first prediction). And for a second time, all the disciples declared that they would die before deserting Jesus. A few hours later, however, they all would scatter. Talk is cheap. It is easy to say we are devoted to Christ, but our claims are meaningful only when they are tested in the crucible of persecution. How strong is your faith? Is it strong enough to stand up under intense trial?

It's easy to think that Satan temporarily gained the upper hand in this drama about Jesus' death. But we see later that God was in control, even in the death of his Son. Satan gained no victory—everything occurred exactly as God had planned.

Jesus agonizes in the garden

They went to the olive grove called Gethsemane, and Jesus said, "Sit here while I go and pray." He took Peter, James, and John with him, and he became deeply troubled and distressed. He told them, "My soul is crushed with grief to the point of death. Stay here and keep watch with me."

He went on a little farther and fell to the ground. He prayed that, if it were possible, the awful hour awaiting him might pass him by. "Abba, Father," he cried out, "everything is possible for you. Please take this cup of suffering away from me. Yet I want your will to be done, not mine."

Then he returned and found the disciples asleep. He said to Peter, "Simon, are you asleep? Couldn't you watch with me even one hour? Keep watch and pray, so that you will not give in to temptation. For the spirit is willing, but the body is weak."

Then Jesus left them again and prayed the same prayer as before. When he returned to them again, he found them sleeping, for they couldn't keep their eyes open. And they didn't know what to say.

When he returned to them the third time, he said, "Go ahead and sleep. Have your rest. But no—the time has come. The Son of Man is betrayed into the hands of sinners. Up, let's be going. Look, my betrayer is here!"

MARK 14:32-42 *(see also Matthew 26:36-46; Luke 22:39-46)*

WANTING GOD'S WILL

Was Jesus trying to get out of his task? Jesus expressed his true feelings, but he did not deny or rebel against God's will. He reaffirmed his desire to do what God wanted. Jesus' prayer highlights the terrible suffering he had to endure—an agony so much more magnified because he had to take on the sins of the whole world. This "cup" was the agony of alienation from God, his Father, at the cross (Hebrews 5:7-9). The sinless Son of God took on our sins and was separated for a while from God so that we could be eternally saved. While praying, Jesus was aware of what doing the Father's will would cost him. He understood the suffering he was about to encounter, and he did not want to have to endure the horrible experience. But Jesus prayed, "I want your will to be done, not mine." Anything worth having costs something. What does your commitment to God cost you? Be willing to pay the price to gain something worthwhile in the end.

Jesus is betrayed and arrested

After saying these things, Jesus crossed the Kidron Valley with his disciples and entered a grove of olive trees. Judas, the betrayer, knew this place, because Jesus had often gone there with his disciples. The leading priests and Pharisees had given Judas a contingent of Roman soldiers and Temple guards to accompany him. Now with blazing torches, lanterns, and weapons, they arrived at the olive grove.

Jesus fully realized all that was going to happen to him, so he stepped forward to meet them. "Who are you looking for?" he asked.

"Jesus the Nazarene," they replied.

"I AM he," Jesus said. (Judas, who betrayed him, was standing with them.) As Jesus said "I AM he," they all drew back and fell to the ground! Once more he asked them, "Who are you looking for?"

And again they replied, "Jesus the Nazarene."

"I told you that I AM he," Jesus said. "And since I am the one you want, let these others go." He did this to fulfill his own statement: "I did not lose a single one of those you have given me."

JOHN 18:1-9 *(see also Matthew 26:47; Mark 14:43; Luke 22:47)*

DON'T RUN AWAY

John does not record Judas's kiss of greeting (Matthew 26:49; Mark 14:45; Luke 22:47-48), but Judas's kiss marked a turning point for the disciples. With Jesus' arrest, each one's life would be radically different. For the first time, Judas openly betrayed Jesus before the other disciples. For the first time, Jesus' loyal disciples ran away from him (Matthew 26:56). The band of disciples would undergo severe testing before they were transformed from hesitant followers to dynamic leaders. You may have made big mistakes in your life, committed sins you're ashamed to remember. Yet nothing is beyond Jesus' forgiveness. He can help you become the person he wants you to become, but you must allow him to forgive you and work in your life. He did it for these disciples—and they changed the world!

Judas was given a contingent of police and soldiers in order to seize Jesus and bring him before the religious court for trial. The religious leaders had issued the warrant for Jesus' arrest, and Judas was acting as Jesus' official accuser.

Jesus is betrayed and arrested

The traitor, Judas, had given them a prearranged signal: "You will know which one to arrest when I greet him with a kiss." So Judas came straight to Jesus. "Greetings, Rabbi!" he exclaimed and gave him the kiss.

Jesus said, "My friend, go ahead and do what you have come for."

Then the others grabbed Jesus and arrested him. But one of the men with Jesus pulled out his sword and struck the high priest's slave, slashing off his ear.

"Put away your sword," Jesus told him. "Those who use the sword will die by the sword. Don't you realize that I could ask my Father for thousands of angels to protect us, and he would send them instantly? But if I did, how would the Scriptures be fulfilled that describe what must happen now?"

Then Jesus said to the crowd, "Am I some dangerous revolutionary, that you come with swords and clubs to arrest me? Why didn't you arrest me in the Temple? I was there teaching every day. But this is all happening to fulfill the words of the prophets as recorded in the Scriptures." At that point, all the disciples deserted him and fled.

MATTHEW 26:48-56 *(see also Mark 14:44-52; Luke 22:48-53; John 18:10-11)*

FORCING THE ISSUE

The religious leaders had not arrested Jesus in the Temple, because they were afraid of a riot. Instead, they came secretly at night, under the influence of the prince of darkness, Satan himself. Although it looked as though Satan were getting the upper hand, everything was proceeding according to God's plan. It was time for Jesus to die. Still not understanding this and wanting to protect Jesus, one of the disciples (Peter, see John 18:10) pulled out a sword and wounded the high priest's servant. But Jesus told Peter to put away his sword and allow God's plan to unfold. At times it is tempting to take matters into our own hands, to force some issue. Usually such moves lead to sin. Instead, we must trust God to work out his plan.

Judas had told the crowd to arrest the man he kissed. This was not an arrest by Roman soldiers under Roman law but an arrest instigated by the religious leaders. Judas pointed Jesus out, not because Jesus was hard to recognize, but because Judas had agreed to be the formal accuser in case a trial was called.

December 2 READ JOHN 18:12-24

Annas questions Jesus

So the soldiers, their commanding officer, and the Temple guards arrested Jesus and tied him up. First they took him to Annas, the father-in-law of Caiaphas, the high priest at that time. Caiaphas was the one who had told the other Jewish leaders, "It's better that one man should die for the people."

Simon Peter followed Jesus, as did another of the disciples. That other disciple was acquainted with the high priest, so he was allowed to enter the high priest's courtyard with Jesus. Peter had to stay outside the gate. Then the disciple who knew the high priest spoke to the woman watching at the gate, and she let Peter in. The woman asked Peter, "You're not one of that man's disciples, are you?"

"No," he said, "I am not."

Because it was cold, the household servants and the guards had made a charcoal fire. They stood around it, warming themselves, and Peter stood with them, warming himself.

Inside, the high priest began asking Jesus about his followers and what he had been teaching them. Jesus replied, "Everyone knows what I teach. I have preached regularly in the synagogues and the Temple, where the people gather. I have not spoken in secret. Why are you asking me this question? Ask those who heard me. They know what I said."

Then one of the Temple guards standing nearby slapped Jesus across the face. "Is that the way to answer the high priest?" he demanded.

Jesus replied, "If I said anything wrong, you must prove it. But if I'm speaking the truth, why are you beating me?"

Then Annas bound Jesus and sent him to Caiaphas, the high priest.

JOHN 18:12-24

POINTING FINGERS

We can easily get angry at the Jewish religious leaders for their injustice toward Jesus, but we must remember that Peter and the rest of the disciples also contributed to Jesus' pain by deserting and denying him (Matthew 26:56, 75). Only hours earlier, these disciples had vowed never to leave Jesus (Matthew 26:35). While most of us are not like the religious leaders, we are all like the disciples, for all of us have been guilty of denying that Christ is Lord in vital areas of our lives or of keeping secret our identity as believers in times of pressure. Don't excuse yourself by pointing at others whose sins seem worse than yours. Instead, admit your guilt and come to Jesus for forgiveness and healing.

Caiaphas questions Jesus

They took Jesus to the high priest's home where the leading priests, the elders, and the teachers of religious law had gathered. Meanwhile, Peter followed him at a distance and went right into the high priest's courtyard. There he sat with the guards, warming himself by the fire.

Inside, the leading priests and the entire high council were trying to find evidence against Jesus, so they could put him to death. But they couldn't find any. Many false witnesses spoke against him, but they contradicted each other. Finally, some men stood up and gave this false testimony: "We heard him say, 'I will destroy this Temple made with human hands, and in three days I will build another, made without human hands.'" But even then they didn't get their stories straight!

Then the high priest stood up before the others and asked Jesus, "Well, aren't you going to answer these charges? What do you have to say for yourself?" But Jesus was silent and made no reply. Then the high priest asked him, "Are you the Messiah, the Son of the Blessed One?"

Jesus said, "I AM. And you will see the Son of Man seated in the place of power at God's right hand and coming on the clouds of heaven."

Then the high priest tore his clothing to show his horror and said, "Why do we need other witnesses? You have all heard his blasphemy. What is your verdict?"

"Guilty!" they all cried. "He deserves to die!"

Then some of them began to spit at him, and they blindfolded him and beat him with their fists. "Prophesy to us," they jeered. And the guards slapped him as they took him away. MARK 14:53-65 *(see also Matthew 26:57-68)*

YOU MUST DECIDE

Jesus made no reply to the first question because it was based on confusing and erroneous evidence. Not answering was wiser than trying to clarify the fabricated accusations. But if Jesus had refused to answer the second question, it could have been taken as a denial of his mission. Jesus declared, in no uncertain terms, that he was the Messiah. The high priest accused Jesus of blasphemy—calling himself God. To the Jews, this was a great crime, punishable by death (Leviticus 24:16). The religious leaders refused even to consider that Jesus' words might be true. They had decided against Jesus and in so doing had sealed their own fate as well as his. Like the members of the council, you must decide whether Jesus' words are blasphemy or truth. Your decision has eternal implications.

Peter denies knowing Jesus

Meanwhile, Peter was in the courtyard below. One of the servant girls who worked for the high priest came by and noticed Peter warming himself at the fire. She looked at him closely and said, "You were one of those with Jesus of Nazareth."

But Peter denied it. "I don't know what you're talking about," he said, and he went out into the entryway. Just then, a rooster crowed.

When the servant girl saw him standing there, she began telling the others, "This man is definitely one of them!" But Peter denied it again.

A little later some of the other bystanders confronted Peter and said, "You must be one of them, because you are a Galilean."

Peter swore, "A curse on me if I'm lying—I don't know this man you're talking about!" And immediately the rooster crowed the second time.

Suddenly, Jesus' words flashed through Peter's mind: "Before the rooster crows twice, you will deny three times that you even know me." And he broke down and wept.

MARK 14:66-72 *(see also Matthew 26:69-75; Luke 22:54-62; John 18:25-27)*

STAGES OF DENIAL

There were three stages to Peter's denial. First, he acted confused and tried to divert attention from himself by changing the subject. Second, using an oath, he denied that he knew Jesus. Third, he began to curse and swear. Believers who deny Christ often begin doing so subtly by pretending not to know him. When opportunities to discuss religious issues come up, they walk away or pretend they don't know the answers. With only a little more pressure, they can be induced to deny flatly their relationship with Christ. If you find yourself subtly diverting conversations so you don't have to talk about Christ, watch out. You may be on the road to denying him.

Peter's curse was more than just a common swear word. He was making the strongest denial he could think of by denying with an oath that he knew Jesus. He was saying, in effect, "May God strike me dead if I'm lying."

The council of religious leaders condemns Jesus

At daybreak all the elders of the people assembled, including the leading priests and the teachers of religious law. Jesus was led before this high council, and they said, "Tell us, are you the Messiah?"

But he replied, "If I tell you, you won't believe me. And if I ask you a question, you won't answer. But from now on the Son of Man will be seated in the place of power at God's right hand."

They all shouted, "So, are you claiming to be the Son of God?"

And he replied, "You say that I am."

"Why do we need other witnesses?" they said. "We ourselves heard him say it."

LUKE 22:66-71 *(see also Matthew 27:1-2; Mark 15:1)*

I AM

Jesus agreed with the high priest's words that Jesus was the Son of God by saying, in effect, "Yes, I am." Jesus identified himself with God by using a familiar title for God found in the Old Testament: "I AM" (Exodus 3:14). The high priest recognized Jesus' claim and accused him of blasphemy. For any other human this claim would have been blasphemy, but in this case it was true. Blasphemy, the sin of claiming to be God or of attacking God's authority and majesty in any way, was punishable by death. The Jewish leaders had the evidence they wanted. The one man in all of history for whom they had been looking and waiting stood in their midst and told them who he was, and they chose to kill him. Jesus is standing with us today; he is the answer to what all humanity needs and desires. Unfortunately, many decide to crucify him rather than fall to their knees in worship. Have you taken Jesus at his word? Have you believed in him as your Messiah?

These leaders tried Jesus for religious offenses, such as calling himself the Son of God, which, according to law, was blasphemy. The trial was fixed: These religious leaders had already decided to kill Jesus (Luke 22:2).

Judas kills himself

When Judas, who had betrayed him, realized that Jesus had been condemned to die, he was filled with remorse. So he took the thirty pieces of silver back to the leading priests and the elders. "I have sinned," he declared, "for I have betrayed an innocent man."

"What do we care?" they retorted. "That's your problem."

Then Judas threw the silver coins down in the Temple and went out and hanged himself.

The leading priests picked up the coins. "It wouldn't be right to put this money in the Temple treasury," they said, "since it was payment for murder." After some discussion they finally decided to buy the potter's field, and they made it into a cemetery for foreigners. That is why the field is still called the Field of Blood. This fulfilled the prophecy of Jeremiah that says, "They took the thirty pieces of silver—the price at which he was valued by the people of Israel, and purchased the potter's field, as the LORD directed." MATTHEW 27:3-10

TOO LATE

Jesus' accuser wanted to drop his charges, but the religious leaders refused to halt the trial. When Judas betrayed Jesus, perhaps he was trying to force Jesus' hand and get him to lead a revolt against Rome. This did not work, of course. Whatever his reason, Judas changed his mind, but it was too late. Many of the plans we set into motion cannot be reversed. It is best to think of the potential consequences before we launch into an action we may later regret.

These chief priests felt no guilt in giving Judas money to betray an innocent man, but when Judas returned the money, the priests couldn't accept it because it was wrong to accept money paid for murder! Their hatred for Jesus had caused them to lose all sense of justice.

Jesus stands trial before Pilate

Jesus' trial before Caiaphas ended in the early hours of the morning. Then he was taken to the headquarters of the Roman governor. His accusers didn't go inside because it would defile them, and they wouldn't be allowed to celebrate the Passover. So Pilate, the governor, went out to them and asked, "What is your charge against this man?"

"We wouldn't have handed him over to you if he weren't a criminal!" they retorted.

"Then take him away and judge him by your own law," Pilate told them.

"Only the Romans are permitted to execute someone," the Jewish leaders replied. (This fulfilled Jesus' prediction about the way he would die.)

Then Pilate went back into his headquarters and called for Jesus to be brought to him. "Are you the king of the Jews?" he asked him.

Jesus replied, "Is this your own question, or did others tell you about me?"

"Am I a Jew?" Pilate retorted. "Your own people and their leading priests brought you to me for trial. Why? What have you done?"

Jesus answered, "My Kingdom is not an earthly kingdom. If it were, my followers would fight to keep me from being handed over to the Jewish leaders. But my Kingdom is not of this world."

Pilate said, "So you are a king?"

Jesus responded, "You say I am a king. Actually, I was born and came into the world to testify to the truth. All who love the truth recognize that what I say is true."

"What is truth?" Pilate asked. Then he went out again to the people and told them, "He is not guilty of any crime."

JOHN 18:28-38 *(see also Matthew 27:11-14; Mark 15:2-5; Luke 23:1-5)*

THE TRUTH

Some people today try to say that if only they could talk to Jesus, question him, and spend time with him personally, they would believe. Pilate had that chance. Pilate asked Jesus a straightforward question, and Jesus answered clearly. Jesus is a king, but one whose Kingdom is not of this world. There seems to have been no question in Pilate's mind that Jesus spoke the truth and was innocent of any crime. It also seems apparent that, while recognizing the truth, Pilate chose to reject it. It is a tragedy when we fail to recognize the truth. It is a greater tragedy when we recognize the truth but fail to heed it.

Jesus stands trial before Herod

"Oh, is he a Galilean?" Pilate asked. When they said that he was, Pilate sent him to Herod Antipas, because Galilee was under Herod's jurisdiction, and Herod happened to be in Jerusalem at the time.

Herod was delighted at the opportunity to see Jesus, because he had heard about him and had been hoping for a long time to see him perform a miracle. He asked Jesus question after question, but Jesus refused to answer. Meanwhile, the leading priests and the teachers of religious law stood there shouting their accusations. Then Herod and his soldiers began mocking and ridiculing Jesus. Finally, they put a royal robe on him and sent him back to Pilate. (Herod and Pilate, who had been enemies before, became friends that day.) LUKE 23:6-12

"NOT GUILTY"

Herod, also called Herod Antipas, was in Jerusalem that weekend for the Passover celebration. (This was the Herod who had killed John the Baptist.) Pilate hoped to pass Jesus off onto Herod because he knew that Jesus had lived and worked in Galilee. Herod Antipas had two advantages over Pilate: He came from a hereditary, part-Jewish monarchy, and he had held his position much longer. But Pilate had two advantages over Herod: He was a Roman citizen and an envoy of the emperor, and his position had been created to replace Herod's ineffective half brother. It is not surprising that the two men were uneasy around each other. Jesus' trial, however, brought them together. Because Pilate had recognized Herod's authority over Galilee, Herod had stopped feeling threatened by the Roman politician. And because neither man knew what to do in this predicament, their common problem united them. When Herod sent Jesus back to Pilate, it was with the verdict "not guilty." How unfortunate that these two leaders were unable to save an innocent man! If you had been in their position, how would you have decided? When you face a tough decision, you can take the easy way out, or you can stand for what is right, regardless of the cost. If we know to do right and don't do it, it is sin (James 4:17).

Herod was the part-Jewish ruler of Galilee and Perea. Pilate was the Roman governor of Judea and Samaria. Those four provinces had been united under Herod the Great. But when Herod died in 4 BC, the kingdom was divided among his sons. Archelaus, the son who had received Judea and Samaria, was removed from office within ten years, and his provinces were then ruled by a succession of Roman governors, of whom Pilate was the fifth.

Pilate hands Jesus over to be crucified

"What is truth?" Pilate asked. Then he went out again to the people and told them, "He is not guilty of any crime. But you have a custom of asking me to release one prisoner each year at Passover. Would you like me to release this 'King of the Jews'?"

But they shouted back, "No! Not this man. We want Barabbas!" (Barabbas was a revolutionary.)

Then Pilate had Jesus flogged with a lead-tipped whip. The soldiers wove a crown of thorns and put it on his head, and they put a purple robe on him. "Hail! King of the Jews!" they mocked, as they slapped him across the face.

Pilate went outside again and said to the people, "I am going to bring him out to you now, but understand clearly that I find him not guilty." Then Jesus came out wearing the crown of thorns and the purple robe. And Pilate said, "Look, here is the man!"

When they saw him, the leading priests and Temple guards began shouting, "Crucify him! Crucify him!"

"Take him yourselves and crucify him," Pilate said. "I find him not guilty."

The Jewish leaders replied, "By our law he ought to die because he called himself the Son of God."

When Pilate heard this, he was more frightened than ever. He took Jesus back into the headquarters again and asked him, "Where are you from?" But Jesus gave no answer. "Why don't you talk to me?" Pilate demanded. "Don't you realize that I have the power to release you or crucify you?"

Then Jesus said, "You would have no power over me at all unless it were given to you from above. So the one who handed me over to you has the greater sin."

Then Pilate tried to release him, but the Jewish leaders shouted, "If you release this man, you are no 'friend of Caesar.' Anyone who declares himself a king is a rebel against Caesar."

When they said this, Pilate brought Jesus out to them again. Then Pilate sat down on the judgment seat on the platform that is called the Stone Pavement (in Hebrew, Gabbatha*). It was now about noon on the day of preparation for the Passover. And Pilate said to the people, "Look, here is your king!"*

"Away with him," they yelled. "Away with him! Crucify him!"

"What? Crucify your king?" Pilate asked.

"We have no king but Caesar," the leading priests shouted back.

Then Pilate turned Jesus over to them to be crucified. So they took Jesus away.

JOHN 18:38–19:16 *(see also Matthew 27:15-26; Mark 15:6-15; Luke 23:13-25)*

WHO'S IN CONTROL?

Throughout the trial we see that Jesus was in control, not Pilate or the religious leaders. Pilate vacillated, the Jewish leaders reacted out of hatred and anger, but

Jesus remained composed. He knew the truth, he knew God's plan, and he knew the reason for his trial. Despite the pressure and persecution, Jesus remained unmoved. It was really Pilate and the religious leaders who were on trial, not Jesus. When you are questioned or ridiculed because of your faith, remember that while you may be on trial before your accusers, they are on trial before God.

Scourging could have killed Jesus. The usual procedure was to bare the upper half of the victim's body and tie his hands to a pillar before whipping him with a three-pronged whip. The number of lashes was determined by the severity of the crime; up to forty were permitted under Jewish law (Deuteronomy 25:3).

Roman soldiers mock Jesus

The soldiers took Jesus into the courtyard of the governor's headquarters (called the Praetorium) and called out the entire regiment. They dressed him in a purple robe, and they wove thorn branches into a crown and put it on his head. Then they saluted him and taunted, "Hail! King of the Jews!" And they struck him on the head with a reed stick, spit on him, and dropped to their knees in mock worship. When they were finally tired of mocking him, they took off the purple robe and put his own clothes on him again. Then they led him away to be crucified. MARK 15:16-20 *(see also Matthew 27:27-31)*

ALONE BUT UNAFRAID

These Roman soldiers were merciless in their torture of Jesus. Yet Jesus had already been deserted by all his disciples when they ran from the garden in terror. One of his closest friends, Peter, denied that he ever knew Jesus. Another disciple, Judas, had betrayed him. The crowds who had followed Jesus stood by and did nothing. Two influential leaders, Pilate and Herod, refused to do anything. The religious leaders, who should have been the first to recognize the Messiah, actively promoted Jesus' death. Jesus took all this for our sakes so that he could go to the cross and carry out the plan of salvation. When people don't understand your faith or they make fun of it, remember what Jesus went through for you and remain strong.

Crucifixion was the Roman penalty for rebellion. Only slaves or those who were not Roman citizens could be crucified. If Jesus died by crucifixion, he would die the death of a rebel and slave. Crucifixion also put the responsibility for killing Jesus on the Romans, and thus the crowds could not blame the religious leaders.

December 11 READ LUKE 23:26-31

Jesus is led away to be crucified

As they led Jesus away, a man named Simon, who was from Cyrene, happened to be coming in from the countryside. The soldiers seized him and put the cross on him and made him carry it behind Jesus. A large crowd trailed behind, including many grief-stricken women. But Jesus turned and said to them, "Daughters of Jerusalem, don't weep for me, but weep for yourselves and for your children. For the days are coming when they will say, 'Fortunate indeed are the women who are childless, the wombs that have not borne a child and the breasts that have never nursed.' People will beg the mountains, 'Fall on us,' and plead with the hills, 'Bury us.' For if these things are done when the tree is green, what will happen when it is dry?"

LUKE 23:26-31 *(see also Matthew 27:32-34; Mark 15:21-23; John 19:17)*

SIMON'S SERVICE

Colonies of Jews existed outside Judea. Simon had made a Passover pilgrimage to Jerusalem all the way from Cyrene in North Africa. Simon certainly never expected to carry a condemned man's cross to the execution site, yet the Roman soldiers forced him to do so. Simon is remembered only for this particular act of service—carrying the crossbeam after Jesus, in his beaten humanity, was unable to do so. Small acts can have big effects. Simon could not save Jesus' life, but he did help carry the cross. At some point, it seems that Simon also came to believe in this condemned man as his Savior, for the Bible records that his sons, Alexander and Rufus, became well known later in the early church (Mark 15:21). Never discount the long-reaching effects of small acts of help and service.

Luke alone mentions the tears of the Jewish women while Jesus was being led through the streets to his execution. Jesus told them not to weep for him but to weep for themselves. He knew that in only about forty years, Jerusalem and the Temple would be destroyed by the Romans.

Jesus is placed on the cross

After they had nailed him to the cross, the soldiers gambled for his clothes by throwing dice. Then they sat around and kept guard as he hung there. A sign was fastened above Jesus' head, announcing the charge against him. It read: "This is Jesus, the King of the Jews." Two revolutionaries were crucified with him, one on his right and one on his left.

The people passing by shouted abuse, shaking their heads in mockery. "Look at you now!" they yelled at him. "You said you were going to destroy the Temple and rebuild it in three days. Well then, if you are the Son of God, save yourself and come down from the cross!"

The leading priests, the teachers of religious law, and the elders also mocked Jesus. "He saved others," they scoffed, "but he can't save himself! So he is the King of Israel, is he? Let him come down from the cross right now, and we will believe in him! He trusted God, so let God rescue him now if he wants him! For he said, 'I am the Son of God.'" Even the revolutionaries who were crucified with him ridiculed him in the same way.

MATTHEW 27:35-44 *(see also Mark 15:24-32; Luke 23:32-43; John 19:18-24)*

THE WAY OF THE CROSS

When James and John asked Jesus for the places of honor next to him in his Kingdom, he told them they didn't know what they were asking (Mark 10:35-39). Here, as Jesus was preparing to inaugurate his Kingdom through his death, the places on his right and on his left were taken by dying men—criminals. As Jesus explained to his two position-conscious disciples, a person who wants to be close to Jesus must be prepared to suffer and die. The way to the Kingdom is the way of the Cross. Taking a stand for Christ may invite suffering and pain, but Jesus will be there with you, through it all.

Jesus was the Son of God, but the people who mocked him didn't believe it—they assumed that the Son of God would save himself. They didn't understand that Jesus' purpose was to save others, not to save himself.

December 13

Jesus dies on the cross

At noon, darkness fell across the whole land until three o'clock. At about three o'clock, Jesus called out with a loud voice, "Eli, Eli, lema sabachthani?" which means "My God, my God, why have you abandoned me?"

Some of the bystanders misunderstood and thought he was calling for the prophet Elijah. One of them ran and filled a sponge with sour wine, holding it up to him on a reed stick so he could drink. But the rest said, "Wait! Let's see whether Elijah comes to save him."

Then Jesus shouted out again, and he released his spirit.

MATTHEW 27:45-50 *(see also Mark 15:33-37; Luke 23:44-46; John 19:28-30)*

THE CUP

Jesus was not questioning God; he was quoting the first line of Psalm 22—a deep expression of the anguish he was feeling as he was taking on the sins of the world, which caused him to be separated from his Father. *This* was what Jesus had dreaded as he had prayed to God in the garden to take the cup from him (Matthew 26:39). The physical agony was horrible; even worse was the period of spiritual separation from his Father. Jesus suffered this double death so that we would never have to experience eternal separation from God. Jesus has gone through so much for you. What can you do for him?

We do not know how this darkness occurred, but it is clear that God caused it. Nature testified to the gravity of Jesus' death, while Jesus' friends and enemies alike fell silent in the encircling gloom. The darkness on that Friday afternoon was both physical and spiritual.

Jesus dies on the cross

At that moment the curtain in the sanctuary of the Temple was torn in two, from top to bottom. The earth shook, rocks split apart, and tombs opened. The bodies of many godly men and women who had died were raised from the dead. They left the cemetery after Jesus' resurrection, went into the holy city of Jerusalem, and appeared to many people.

The Roman officer and the other soldiers at the crucifixion were terrified by the earthquake and all that had happened. They said, "This man truly was the Son of God!"

And many women who had come from Galilee with Jesus to care for him were watching from a distance. Among them were Mary Magdalene, Mary (the mother of James and Joseph), and the mother of James and John, the sons of Zebedee. MATTHEW 27:51-56 *(see also Mark 15:38-41; Luke 23:47-49; John 19:31-37)*

DIRECT ACCESS

The tearing of the Temple curtain symbolized Christ's work on the cross. The Temple had three parts: the courts for all the people; the Holy Place, where only priests could enter; and the Most Holy Place, where the high priest alone could enter once a year to atone for the sins of the people. It was in the Most Holy Place that the Ark of the Covenant, and God's presence with it, rested. The curtain that was torn had closed off the Most Holy Place from view. At Christ's death, the barrier between God and man was split in two. Now all people can approach God directly through Christ (Hebrews 9:1-14; 10:19-22). Because of Christ's ultimate sacrifice, we have direct access to God. You can talk to God about anything, at any time. Stay close to him.

Christ's death was accompanied by at least four miraculous events: darkness, the tearing in two of the veil in the Temple, an earthquake, and dead people rising from their tombs. Jesus' death, therefore, could not have gone unnoticed. Everyone knew something significant had happened.

Jesus is laid in the tomb

Afterward Joseph of Arimathea, who had been a secret disciple of Jesus (because he feared the Jewish leaders), asked Pilate for permission to take down Jesus' body. When Pilate gave permission, Joseph came and took the body away. With him came Nicodemus, the man who had come to Jesus at night. He brought about seventy-five pounds of perfumed ointment made from myrrh and aloes. Following Jewish burial custom, they wrapped Jesus' body with the spices in long sheets of linen cloth. The place of crucifixion was near a garden, where there was a new tomb, never used before. And so, because it was the day of preparation for the Jewish Passover and since the tomb was close at hand, they laid Jesus there.

JOHN 19:38-42 *(see also Matthew 27:57-61; Mark 15:42-47; Luke 23:50-56)*

CHANGED LIVES

The Gospel writers describe four particular people who were changed in the process of Jesus' death: The criminal, dying on the cross beside Jesus, asked Jesus to include him in his Kingdom (Luke 23:39-43). The Roman centurion proclaimed that surely Jesus was the Son of God (Mark 15:39). Joseph and Nicodemus, members of the council and secret followers of Jesus (John 7:50-52), came out of hiding. These men were changed more by Jesus' death than by his life. They realized who Jesus was, and that realization brought out their belief, proclamation, and action. When confronted with Jesus and his death, we should be changed—to believe, proclaim, and act.

───────────●●───────────

Joseph of Arimathea and Nicodemus were secret followers of Jesus. Joseph was a leader and an honored member of the Jewish council (the Sanhedrin). Nicodemus, also a member of the council, had come to Jesus by night (John 3:1-2) and later tried to defend him before the other religious leaders (John 7:50-52). They risked their reputations to provide for Jesus' burial.

───────────●●───────────

Guards are posted at the tomb

The next day, on the Sabbath, the leading priests and Pharisees went to see Pilate. They told him, "Sir, we remember what that deceiver once said while he was still alive: 'After three days I will rise from the dead.' So we request that you seal the tomb until the third day. This will prevent his disciples from coming and stealing his body and then telling everyone he was raised from the dead! If that happens, we'll be worse off than we were at first."

Pilate replied, "Take guards and secure it the best you can." So they sealed the tomb and posted guards to protect it. MATTHEW 27:62-66

NOTHING CAN STOP IT

The religious leaders took Jesus' resurrection claims more seriously than the disciples did. The disciples didn't remember Jesus' teaching about his resurrection (Matthew 20:17-19), but the religious leaders did. Because of his claims, they were almost as afraid of Jesus after his death as when he was alive. They tried to take every precaution that his body would remain in the tomb. The tomb was sealed by stringing a cord across the stone that had been rolled over the entrance. The cord was sealed at each end with clay. But the religious leaders took a further precaution, asking that guards be placed at the tomb's entrance. With such precautions, the only way the tomb could be empty would be for Jesus to rise from the dead. The Pharisees failed to understand that no rock, seal, guard, or army could prevent the Son of God from rising again. Because Jesus came back to life, we know that nothing that happens to us can prevent us from rising again and enjoying eternity with our Lord.

The tomb where Jesus was laid was probably a man-made cave cut out of one of the many limestone hills in the area. These caves were often large enough to walk into.

Jesus rises from the dead

Saturday evening, when the Sabbath ended, Mary Magdalene, Mary the mother of James, and Salome went out and purchased burial spices so they could anoint Jesus' body. Very early on Sunday morning, just at sunrise, they went to the tomb. On the way they were asking each other, "Who will roll away the stone for us from the entrance to the tomb?" But as they arrived, they looked up and saw that the stone, which was very large, had already been rolled aside.

When they entered the tomb, they saw a young man clothed in a white robe sitting on the right side. The women were shocked, but the angel said, "Don't be alarmed. You are looking for Jesus of Nazareth, who was crucified. He isn't here! He is risen from the dead! Look, this is where they laid his body. Now go and tell his disciples, including Peter, that Jesus is going ahead of you to Galilee. You will see him there, just as he told you before he died."

The women fled from the tomb, trembling and bewildered, and they said nothing to anyone because they were too frightened. Then they briefly reported all this to Peter and his companions. Afterward Jesus himself sent them out from east to west with the sacred and unfailing message of salvation that gives eternal life. Amen. MARK 16:1-8 *(see also Matthew 28:1-7; Luke 24:1-8; John 20:1)*

RESURRECTION REALITY

The Resurrection is vitally important for many reasons: (1) Jesus kept his promise to rise from the dead, so we can believe that he will keep all his other promises. (2) The Resurrection ensures that the ruler of God's eternal Kingdom will be the living Christ, not just an idea, a hope, or a dream. (3) Christ's resurrection gives us the assurance that we also will be resurrected (1 Corinthians 15:12-19). (4) The power of God that brought Christ's body back from the dead is available to us to bring our morally and spiritually dead selves back to life so that we can change and grow. (5) The Resurrection provides the substance of the church's witness to the world. We do not merely tell lessons from the life of a good teacher; we proclaim the reality of the resurrection of Jesus Christ.

The women purchased the spices on Saturday evening after the Sabbath had ended so they could go to the tomb early the next morning and anoint Jesus' body as a sign of love, devotion, and respect. Bringing spices to the tomb was like bringing flowers to a grave today.

Jesus rises from the dead

Early on Sunday morning, while it was still dark, Mary Magdalene came to the tomb and found that the stone had been rolled away from the entrance. She ran and found Simon Peter and the other disciple, the one whom Jesus loved. She said, "They have taken the Lord's body out of the tomb, and we don't know where they have put him!"

Peter and the other disciple started out for the tomb. They were both running, but the other disciple outran Peter and reached the tomb first. He stooped and looked in and saw the linen wrappings lying there, but he didn't go in. Then Simon Peter arrived and went inside. He also noticed the linen wrappings lying there, while the cloth that had covered Jesus' head was folded up and lying apart from the other wrappings. Then the disciple who had reached the tomb first also went in, and he saw and believed—for until then they still hadn't understood the Scriptures that said Jesus must rise from the dead. Then they went home. JOHN 20:1-10 *(see also Luke 24:9-12)*

STAGES OF BELIEF

People who hear about the Resurrection for the first time may not be able to comprehend this amazing story immediately. Like Mary and the disciples, they may pass through four stages of belief: (1) At first, they may think the story is a fabrication, impossible to believe (John 20:2). (2) Like Peter, they may check out the facts and still be puzzled about what happened (John 20:6). (3) Only when they encounter Jesus personally will they be able to accept the fact of the Resurrection (John 20:16). (4) Then, as they commit themselves to the risen Lord and devote their lives to serving him, they will begin to understand fully the reality of his presence with them (John 20:28). If people don't understand when you tell them about Jesus' resurrection, give them time. Even the disciples didn't believe it at first!

The linen cloth that had been wrapped around Jesus' body was left as if Jesus had passed right through it. The cloth that had covered Jesus' head was folded up and lying to one side. A grave robber couldn't possibly have made off with Jesus' body and left the linens as if they were still shaped around it.

Jesus appears to Mary Magdalene

Mary was standing outside the tomb crying, and as she wept, she stooped and looked in. She saw two white-robed angels, one sitting at the head and the other at the foot of the place where the body of Jesus had been lying. "Dear woman, why are you crying?" the angels asked her.

"Because they have taken away my Lord," she replied, "and I don't know where they have put him."

She turned to leave and saw someone standing there. It was Jesus, but she didn't recognize him. "Dear woman, why are you crying?" Jesus asked her. "Who are you looking for?"

She thought he was the gardener. "Sir," she said, "if you have taken him away, tell me where you have put him, and I will go and get him."

"Mary!" Jesus said.

She turned to him and cried out, "Rabboni!" (which is Hebrew for "Teacher").

"Don't cling to me," Jesus said, "for I haven't yet ascended to the Father. But go find my brothers and tell them, 'I am ascending to my Father and your Father, to my God and your God.'"

Mary Magdalene found the disciples and told them, "I have seen the Lord!" Then she gave them his message.   JOHN 20:11-18 *(see also Mark 16:9-11)*

HE IS NEAR

Mary didn't recognize Jesus at first. Her grief had blinded her; she couldn't see him because she didn't expect to see him. Then Jesus spoke her name, and immediately she recognized him. Imagine the love that flooded her heart when she heard her Savior say her name. Jesus is near you, and he is calling your name. Can you, like Mary, regard him as your Lord? Are you filled with joy by this good news, and do you share it with others?

Jesus did not want to be detained at the tomb. If he did not ascend to heaven, the Holy Spirit could not come. Both he and Mary had important work to do.

Jesus appears to the women

The women ran quickly from the tomb. They were very frightened but also filled with great joy, and they rushed to give the disciples the angel's message. And as they went, Jesus met them and greeted them. And they ran to him, grasped his feet, and worshiped him. Then Jesus said to them, "Don't be afraid! Go tell my brothers to leave for Galilee, and they will see me there." MATTHEW 28:8-10

HE WON'T GIVE UP

Jesus told the women to pass a message on to the disciples—that he would meet them in Galilee, as he had previously told them (Mark 14:28). But the disciples, afraid of the religious leaders, stayed hidden behind locked doors in Jerusalem (John 20:19). The disciples had already run away from Jesus at the time of his greatest need; one of them had betrayed Jesus to his death, and another had denied ever knowing him. Imagine the sorry group they must have been as they sat hidden and locked away. But Jesus did not give up on them. He met them first right in their secret room in Jerusalem (Luke 24:36) and then later in Galilee (John 21). Jesus gives second chances—and more! No matter how bad your sin, he is ready to forgive. He has great work for you to do!

By "my brothers," Jesus meant his disciples. This showed that he had forgiven them, even after they had deserted him. Their relationship would now be even stronger than before.

Religious leaders bribe the guards

As the women were on their way, some of the guards went into the city and told the leading priests what had happened. A meeting with the elders was called, and they decided to give the soldiers a large bribe. They told the soldiers, "You must say, 'Jesus' disciples came during the night while we were sleeping, and they stole his body.' If the governor hears about it, we'll stand up for you so you won't get in trouble." So the guards accepted the bribe and said what they were told to say. Their story spread widely among the Jews, and they still tell it today. MATTHEW 28:11-15

AMAZING NEWS

Jesus' resurrection was already causing a great stir in Jerusalem. A group of women were moving quickly through the streets, looking for the disciples to tell them the amazing news that Jesus was alive. At the same time, a group of religious leaders were plotting how to cover up the Resurrection. Today there is still a great stir over the Resurrection, and there are still only two choices: to believe that Jesus rose from the dead or to be closed to the truth—denying it, ignoring it, or trying to explain it away. Which choice have you made?

The problem with the council's story that the disciples stole the body is that these same disciples later suffered greatly; some were even martyred for their faith in the risen Christ. If they knew that they had stolen a dead body in order to perpetrate a hoax, it is highly doubtful that they would willingly die for that hoax.

Jesus appears to two believers traveling on the road

That same day two of Jesus' followers were walking to the village of Emmaus, seven miles from Jerusalem. As they walked along they were talking about everything that had happened. As they talked and discussed these things, Jesus himself suddenly came and began walking with them. But God kept them from recognizing him.

He asked them, "What are you discussing so intently as you walk along?"

They stopped short, sadness written across their faces. Then one of them, Cleopas, replied, "You must be the only person in Jerusalem who hasn't heard about all the things that have happened there the last few days."

"What things?" Jesus asked.

"The things that happened to Jesus, the man from Nazareth," they said. "He was a prophet who did powerful miracles, and he was a mighty teacher in the eyes of God and all the people. But our leading priests and other religious leaders handed him over to be condemned to death, and they crucified him. We had hoped he was the Messiah who had come to rescue Israel. This all happened three days ago.

"Then some women from our group of his followers were at his tomb early this morning, and they came back with an amazing report. They said his body was missing, and they had seen angels who told them Jesus is alive! Some of our men ran out to see, and sure enough, his body was gone, just as the women had said."

Then Jesus said to them, "You foolish people! You find it so hard to believe all that the prophets wrote in the Scriptures. Wasn't it clearly predicted that the Messiah would have to suffer all these things before entering his glory?" Then Jesus took them through the writings of Moses and all the prophets, explaining from all the Scriptures the things concerning himself.

By this time they were nearing Emmaus and the end of their journey. Jesus acted as if he were going on, but they begged him, "Stay the night with us, since it is getting late." So he went home with them. As they sat down to eat, he took the bread and blessed it. Then he broke it and gave it to them. Suddenly, their eyes were opened, and they recognized him. And at that moment he disappeared!

They said to each other, "Didn't our hearts burn within us as he talked with us on the road and explained the Scriptures to us?" And within the hour they were on their way back to Jerusalem. There they found the eleven disciples and the others who had gathered with them, who said, "The Lord has really risen! He appeared to Peter."

Then the two from Emmaus told their story of how Jesus had appeared to them as they were walking along the road, and how they had recognized him as he was breaking the bread.　LUKE 24:13-35 *(see also Mark 16:12-13)*

STEP OF FAITH

Why did Jesus call these followers foolish? Because even though they knew the biblical prophecies well, they failed to understand that Christ's suffering was his path to glory. They could not understand why God did not intervene to save Jesus from the cross. The world has not changed its values: A suffering servant is no more popular today than two thousand years ago. But we have not only the witness of the Old Testament prophets but also the witness of the New Testament apostles and the history of the Christian church, all pointing to Jesus' victory over death. Will we step outside the values of our culture and put our faith in Jesus? Or will we foolishly continue to be baffled by his good news?

Jesus' followers from Emmaus were counting on him to redeem Israel—that is, to rescue the nation from its enemies. Most Jews believed that the Old Testament prophecies pointed to a military and political Messiah; they didn't realize that the Messiah had come to redeem people from slavery to sin. When Jesus died, therefore, they lost all hope. They didn't understand that Jesus' death offered the greatest hope possible.

Jesus appears to the disciples behind locked doors

And just as they were telling about it, Jesus himself was suddenly standing there among them. "Peace be with you," he said. But the whole group was startled and frightened, thinking they were seeing a ghost!

"Why are you frightened?" he asked. "Why are your hearts filled with doubt? Look at my hands. Look at my feet. You can see that it's really me. Touch me and make sure that I am not a ghost, because ghosts don't have bodies, as you see that I do." As he spoke, he showed them his hands and his feet.

Still they stood there in disbelief, filled with joy and wonder. Then he asked them, "Do you have anything here to eat?" They gave him a piece of broiled fish, and he ate it as they watched. LUKE 24:36-43 *(see also John 20:19-23)*

HIS REPRESENTATIVES

The disciples knew that the tomb was empty but didn't understand that Jesus had risen, and they were filled with fear—even when Jesus appeared to them. Despite the witness of the women and the biblical prophecies of this very event, they still didn't believe. Today the Resurrection still catches people by surprise, and many refuse to believe. What more will it take? For these disciples it took the living, breathing Jesus in their midst. For many people today, it takes the presence of living, breathing Christians. As part of Christ's body on earth, you have the responsibility to be his representative to a lost world. What do people think of Christ when they think of you?

Jesus' body wasn't just a figment of the imagination or the appearance of a ghost—the disciples touched him, and he ate food. On the other hand, his body wasn't merely a restored human body like Lazarus's (John 11)—he was able to appear and disappear. Jesus' resurrected body was immortal. This is the kind of body we will be given at the resurrection of the dead (1 Corinthians 15:42-50).

Jesus appears to the disciples, including Thomas

One of the twelve disciples, Thomas (nicknamed the Twin), was not with the others when Jesus came. They told him, "We have seen the Lord!"

But he replied, "I won't believe it unless I see the nail wounds in his hands, put my fingers into them, and place my hand into the wound in his side."

Eight days later the disciples were together again, and this time Thomas was with them. The doors were locked; but suddenly, as before, Jesus was standing among them. "Peace be with you," he said. Then he said to Thomas, "Put your finger here, and look at my hands. Put your hand into the wound in my side. Don't be faithless any longer. Believe!"

"My Lord and my God!" Thomas exclaimed.

Then Jesus told him, "You believe because you have seen me. Blessed are those who believe without seeing me."

The disciples saw Jesus do many other miraculous signs in addition to the ones recorded in this book. But these are written so that you may continue to believe that Jesus is the Messiah, the Son of God, and that by believing in him you will have life by the power of his name.   JOHN 20:24-31 *(see also Mark 16:14)*

GOOD DOUBTS

Jesus wasn't hard on Thomas for his doubts. Despite his skepticism, Thomas was still loyal to the believers and to Jesus himself. Some people need to doubt before they believe. If doubt leads to questions, questions lead to answers, and the answers are accepted, then doubt has done good work. It is when doubt becomes stubbornness and stubbornness becomes a lifestyle that doubt harms faith. When you doubt, don't stop there. Let your doubt deepen your faith as you continue to search for the answer.

To understand the life and mission of Jesus more fully, all we need to do is study the Gospels. John tells us that his Gospel records only a few of the many events in Jesus' life on earth. But the Gospel includes everything we need to know to believe that Jesus is the Christ, the Son of God, through whom we receive eternal life.

Jesus appears to the disciples while fishing

Later, Jesus appeared again to the disciples beside the Sea of Galilee. This is how it happened. Several of the disciples were there—Simon Peter, Thomas (nicknamed the Twin), Nathanael from Cana in Galilee, the sons of Zebedee, and two other disciples.

Simon Peter said, "I'm going fishing."

"We'll come, too," they all said. So they went out in the boat, but they caught nothing all night.

At dawn Jesus was standing on the beach, but the disciples couldn't see who he was. He called out, "Fellows, have you caught any fish?"

"No," they replied.

Then he said, "Throw out your net on the right-hand side of the boat, and you'll get some!" So they did, and they couldn't haul in the net because there were so many fish in it. JOHN 21:1-6

A CALL FROM THE BEACH

Jesus had performed a similar miracle for the disciples before. Luke 5:1-11 records how the disciples had experienced an unsuccessful night of fishing, only to have a record-breaking catch when they followed Jesus' instructions. At the time, they had been amazed to see that not only did Jesus teach, heal, and cast out demons, but he also cared about the disciples' day-to-day routines. Here the disciples had gone back to what they knew best—fishing. And Jesus came to them right where they were, performing another miracle to demonstrate his great love for them. Jesus meets us where we are, gently showing us where he wants us to be. Is he standing on the beach calling to you? Pull in your boat and listen!

Jesus reminded his disciples of his power and called them once again to be his followers.

December 26 READ JOHN 21:7-14

Jesus appears to the disciples while fishing

Then the disciple Jesus loved said to Peter, "It's the Lord!" When Simon Peter heard that it was the Lord, he put on his tunic (for he had stripped for work), jumped into the water, and headed to shore. The others stayed with the boat and pulled the loaded net to the shore, for they were only about a hundred yards from shore. When they got there, they found breakfast waiting for them—fish cooking over a charcoal fire, and some bread.

"Bring some of the fish you've just caught," Jesus said. So Simon Peter went aboard and dragged the net to the shore. There were 153 large fish, and yet the net hadn't torn.

"Now come and have some breakfast!" Jesus said. None of the disciples dared to ask him, "Who are you?" They knew it was the Lord. Then Jesus served them the bread and the fish. This was the third time Jesus had appeared to his disciples since he had been raised from the dead. JOHN 21:7-14

WILLINGNESS TO SERVE

Simon Peter must have felt pretty worthless. He had run away when Jesus was arrested, and then he had denied he even knew his Lord. Only a few hours before that happened Peter had told Jesus, "Even if I have to die with you, I will never deny you!" (Matthew 26:35). But then Jesus gave himself up without a fight, and Peter's courage gave out. He had failed his Lord.

Although the Lord had already visited the gathered disciples twice before this fishing scene, Peter's guilt and failure were unrelieved. He had decided to do something he could be successful at—fishing. But he failed at that, too.

Then the Lord appeared and gave him success—so many fish that "they couldn't haul in the net"! Peter swam to the Lord as fast as he could, and then hurried to bring the catch of fish when the Lord asked. Jesus was beginning to restore Peter. He can restore each of us when we fail.

Impetuous Peter jumped out of the boat and swam to the shore when he realized that it was Jesus on the beach. Clearly he wanted to talk to Jesus and to experience Jesus' forgiveness.

Jesus talks with Peter

After breakfast Jesus asked Simon Peter, "Simon son of John, do you love me more than these?"

"Yes, Lord," Peter replied, "you know I love you."

"Then feed my lambs," Jesus told him.

Jesus repeated the question: "Simon son of John, do you love me?"

"Yes, Lord," Peter said, "you know I love you."

"Then take care of my sheep," Jesus said.

A third time he asked him, "Simon son of John, do you love me?"

Peter was hurt that Jesus asked the question a third time. He said, "Lord, you know everything. You know that I love you."

Jesus said, "Then feed my sheep.

"I tell you the truth, when you were young, you were able to do as you liked; you dressed yourself and went wherever you wanted to go. But when you are old, you will stretch out your hands, and others will dress you and take you where you don't want to go." Jesus said this to let him know by what kind of death he would glorify God. Then Jesus told him, "Follow me."   JOHN 21:15-19

DO YOU TRULY LOVE HIM?

Jesus asked Peter three times if he loved him. The first time, Jesus said, "Do you love (Greek, *agape*: "volitional, self-sacrificial love") me more than these?" The second time, Jesus focused on Peter alone and still used the Greek word *agape*. The third time, Jesus used the Greek word *phileo* ("affection, affinity, or brotherly love") and asked, in effect, "Are you even my friend?" Each time Peter responded with the Greek word *phileo*. Jesus doesn't settle for quick, superficial answers. He has a way of getting to the heart of the matter. Peter had to face his true feelings and motives when Jesus confronted him. How would you respond if Jesus asked you, "Do you love me?" Do you really love Jesus? Are you even his friend?

This was a prediction of Peter's death by crucifixion. Tradition indicates that Peter was crucified for his faith upside down because he did not feel worthy of dying as his Lord had died. Despite the future, Jesus told Peter to follow him.

Jesus talks with Peter

Peter turned around and saw behind them the disciple Jesus loved—the one who had leaned over to Jesus during supper and asked, "Lord, who will betray you?" Peter asked Jesus, "What about him, Lord?"

Jesus replied, "If I want him to remain alive until I return, what is that to you? As for you, follow me." So the rumor spread among the community of believers that this disciple wouldn't die. But that isn't what Jesus said at all. He only said, "If I want him to remain alive until I return, what is that to you?"

This disciple is the one who testifies to these events and has recorded them here. And we know that his account of these things is accurate.

Jesus also did many other things. If they were all written down, I suppose the whole world could not contain the books that would be written.   JOHN 21:20-25

DON'T COMPARE

Peter asked Jesus how John would die. Jesus replied that Peter should not concern himself with that. We tend to compare ourselves to others, whether to rationalize our own level of devotion to Christ or to question God's justice. Jesus responds to us as he did to Peter: "What is that to you? As for you, follow me." When you follow Christ and live as he wants you to, there is no need to compare yourself to others. People make comparisons for many reasons. Some point out others' flaws in order to feel better about themselves. Others simply want reassurance that they are doing well. When you are tempted to compare, look at Jesus Christ. His example will inspire you to do your very best, and his loving acceptance will comfort you when you fall short of your expectations.

Early church history reports that after John spent several years as an exile on the island of Patmos, he returned to Ephesus, where he died as an old man, near the end of the first century.

Jesus gives the great commission

Then the eleven disciples left for Galilee, going to the mountain where Jesus had told them to go. When they saw him, they worshiped him—but some of them doubted!

Jesus came and told his disciples, "I have been given all authority in heaven and on earth. Therefore, go and make disciples of all the nations, baptizing them in the name of the Father and the Son and the Holy Spirit. Teach these new disciples to obey all the commands I have given you. And be sure of this: I am with you always, even to the end of the age."

MATTHEW 28:16-20 *(see also Mark 16:15-18)*

GO AND TELL

God gave Jesus authority over heaven and earth. On the basis of that authority, Jesus told his disciples to make more disciples as they preached, baptized, and taught. With this same authority, Jesus still commands us to tell others the Good News and make them disciples for the Kingdom. We are to go—whether it is next door or to another country—and make disciples. It is not an option but a command to all who call Jesus "Lord." We are not all evangelists in the formal sense, but we have all received gifts that we can use to help fulfill the great commission. As we obey, we have comfort in the knowledge that Jesus is always with us.

Jesus' words affirm the reality of the Trinity. He did not say baptize them into the names but into the name of the Father, Son, and Holy Spirit. The word Trinity does not occur in Scripture, but it well describes the three-in-one nature of the Father, Son, and Holy Spirit.

December 30 READ LUKE 24:44-49

Jesus appears to the disciples in Jerusalem

Then he said, "When I was with you before, I told you that everything written about me in the law of Moses and the prophets and in the Psalms must be fulfilled." Then he opened their minds to understand the Scriptures. And he said, "Yes, it was written long ago that the Messiah would suffer and die and rise from the dead on the third day. It was also written that this message would be proclaimed in the authority of his name to all the nations, beginning in Jerusalem: 'There is forgiveness of sins for all who repent.' You are witnesses of all these things.

"And now I will send the Holy Spirit, just as my Father promised. But stay here in the city until the Holy Spirit comes and fills you with power from heaven." LUKE 24:44-49

STUDY GOD'S WORD

The phrase "Moses and the prophets and in the Psalms" is a way to describe the entire Old Testament. In other words, the entire Old Testament points to the Messiah. For example, Jesus' role as prophet was foretold in Deuteronomy 18:15-20; his sufferings were prophesied in Psalm 22 and Isaiah 53; his resurrection was predicted in Psalm 16:9-11 and Isaiah 53:10-11. Jesus opened the disciples' minds to understand the Scriptures. The Holy Spirit does this in our lives today when we study the Bible. Have you ever had trouble understanding a difficult Bible passage? Besides reading surrounding passages, asking other people, and consulting reference works, pray that the Holy Spirit will open your mind to understand, giving you the needed insight to put God's Word into action in your life.

Luke wrote to the Greek-speaking world. He wanted them to know that Christ's message of God's love and forgiveness should go to all the world. We must never ignore the worldwide scope of Christ's gospel. God wants all the world to hear the Good News of salvation.

Jesus ascends into heaven

Then Jesus led them to Bethany, and lifting his hands to heaven, he blessed them. While he was blessing them, he left them and was taken up to heaven. So they worshiped him and then returned to Jerusalem filled with great joy. And they spent all of their time in the Temple, praising God.

LUKE 24:50-53 *(see also Mark 16:19-20; Acts 1:6-11)*

WITH YOU ALWAYS

As the disciples stood and watched, Jesus began rising into the air, and soon he disappeared into heaven. Seeing Jesus leave must have been frightening, but the disciples knew that Jesus would keep his promise to be with them through the Holy Spirit. This same Jesus—who lived with the disciples, who died and was buried, and who rose from the dead—loves us and promises to be with us always. We can get to know him better through studying the Scriptures, praying, and allowing the Holy Spirit to make us more like Jesus.

Jesus left the disciples physically when he returned to heaven (Acts 1:9), but the Holy Spirit soon came to comfort them and empower them to spread the gospel of salvation (Acts 2:1-4).

DAILY SCRIPTURE INDEX

Seek God Daily

The Daily God Book
Through the Bible

The Daily God Book
A Year with Jesus

THE DAILY GOD BOOK
A YEAR WITH JESUS

the
daily
God book
THROUGH THE BIBLE

the Daily God Book
A YEAR OF LISTENING FOR GOD

the
DAILY
GOD BOOK
words of
wisdom

The Daily God Book:
A Year of Listening for God

The Daily God Book
Words of Wisdom